Revolt and revolution in early modern Europe

Endpapers and front cover:
engraving 'Marodeurs tués par les paysans'
courtesy archives Editions du Seuil

By the same author:

Histoire des Croquants. Etude des soulèvements populaires au XVIIe siècle dans le sud-ouest de la France (1974)

Croquants et Nu-pieds. Les soulèvements paysans en France du XVIe au XIXe siècle (1974)

Fête et révolte. Des mentalités populaires du XVIe au XVIIIe siècle (1976)

La vie quotidienne dans l'Aquitaine du XVIIe siècle (1978)

Le chaudron et la lancette. Croyances populaires et médecine préventive, 1798–1830 (1984)

Yves-Marie Bercé
Translated by Joseph Bergin

Revolt and revolution in early modern Europe

An essay on the history of political violence

Manchester University Press

Copyright © Manchester University Press 1987

Published by Manchester University Press,
Oxford Road, Manchester M13 9PL

First published in French by Presses Universitaires de France, 1980

First edition © 1980 Presses Universitaires de France
This translation © Manchester University Press 1987

British Library cataloguing in publication data
Bercé, Yves-Marie
  Revolt and revolution in early modern Europe: an essay on the history of
  political violence.
  1. Revolutionists—Europe—History 2. Europe—Politics and
  government— 1517–1648 3. Europe—Politics and government—
  1648–1789
  I. Title II. Révoltes et révolutions, *English*
  322.4'2'094   D204

ISBN 0 7190 1967 2

Photoset in Linotron Sabon by
Northern Phototypesetting Co, Bolton

Printed and bound in Great Britain by
Robert Hartnoll(1985) Ltd., Bodmin, Cornwall

Contents

Preface to the English edition

It is the custom of publishers to place on the covers of their books a brief and flattering sketch in which the author attempts to capture the distracted attention of readers who browse through the shelves of bookshops. When I was composing mine in 1980, it was with false modesty that I claimed that it was not my ambition to formulate the laws of some improbable science of the mechanisms of violence. Having rejected such a theoretical ambition, I asserted that this essay was designed to 'replenish the rather limited range of historical data, from which sociologists and political scientists usually draw their material for the construction of their models'. In other words, realizing that for all its improbability the said science continued to produce an abundance of books and articles, I attempted to put some more genuine flesh on the hypotheses of its adventurous practicioners. In the battle of ideas, I chose the role of the subordinate officer who pushes his men towards the field of combat rather than that of the strategist who determines the overall shape of the engagement. Others will judge whether it was prudent or short-sighted of me to think that it was the historian's duty to establish the facts, and then leave it to others of a more ambitious nature to identify norms and rules among them.

This rather timid approach was, however, still too presumptuous. We have to admit that the early modern centuries are disappearing more and more from teaching syllabuses, and that works on political science no longer feel the need to look beyond the two world wars of our own time. It is true that the sequence of historical events has accelerated at the same time as information about those events has mushroomed. The idea of drawing lessons from a more remote past thus appears wholly unfashionable, rather like those collections of examples that earlier humanists assembled when compiling their annals of antiquity. The discipline of comparative history is in danger of merely producing a code of timeless ethics founded on the truism and, at worst, the flashy illusion.

Nevertheless, I still believe it is possible to formulate a typology of political violence in Europe from the great discoveries of the sixteenth century to the awakening of nationalism in the nineteenth. In my opinion the apparent diversity of developments and cultures reveals on inspection a fascinating harvest where analogy, convergence and synchronism abound. That there is an essential unity to the various histories of Europe's nations is, despite the occasional political polemic, not really in doubt. Transcending the frontiers of pre-industrial Europe, climatic or geographical determinism produced a profound similarity which is to be found, despite the disguises of nomenclature and the distorsions of chronology, in institutions, behaviour and in change itself. It is this which enables us to generalize about Europe's societies and political practices. It also enables us, for example, to juxtapose riots in Mediterranean ports with those of Baltic cities, or to compare the cultural role of innkeepers in Spain or even in Poland. If we were to extend our attention to even more exotic horizons, we would perhaps discover the same possibilities of model-building. Indeed, only the considerable restraints imposed on us by historical methodology and the limited range of a single author's knowledge, would prevent us from embarking on such an adventure.

During the three or four centuries that constitute early modern Europe, change remained sufficiently slow and marginal for the geographical unity of the continent to correspond to a different, chronological, unity – that of a period of village settlement, of limited urbanization, of economies scarcely touched by commercial relations, of rural self-sufficiency and of parish-pump localism.

In this relatively homogeneous and unchanging framework, it is local solidarities that seemed to me to represent the most general trait, and the richest in explanatory force for an understanding of this 'world we have lost'. The local community was the fundamental bond, the first resort in cases of confrontation, and the most potent source of outbursts of collective violence. I was led to adopt this interpretation by the study of hundreds of French peasant revolts for my 1972 doctoral thesis on the *Croquants* of south-west France, as well as by the reading of countless urban chronicles, family memorials, legal archives and other narrative sources. From the anti-fiscal revolts of the sixteenth and seventeenth centuries to the rejections of military recruitment and conscription of the revolutionary and napoleonic period, it is the village community that remained the *raison d'être*, the generator and the focus of movements of revolt; of brief, shattering interruptions of everyday existence; and of the sudden intervention of force in social relations.

Of course, a community could be pervaded and torn apart by internal tensions, with irreconcilable hatreds tranforming families, clans and kinship networks into vengeful factions. Conflicts of interest pitted farmers against labourers, landowners against sharecroppers, or lords against their tenants. Frustration and humiliation ranged rural gentry and bourgeois against each other. It is not difficult to detect such types of hostility, connected as they are to kinship by blood, economic differences, social rivalry, and many other factors. But in the pre-industrial world, they do not seem to me to arouse the same passions as the defence of the local community, which proved more capable than anything else of unleashing and sustaining collective violence.

It can be argued that this interpretation is the victim of the language and ideologies of the historical period in question, and that the community which it invokes is no more than the product of economic circumstances, of the entrenched social and mental structures engendered by these primordial factors. Elegant and valuable as are the learned demonstrations of this view, one cannot fail to note the facility with which most historians conveniently discover at the root of every convulsion in the period that they are studying, some kind of economic crisis, whether of growth or of scarcity, or if not, a social hierarchy that is either too closed or too open. What we know about these potential and virtually constant causal factors seems to me to plead rather in favour of a wilful autonomy that inheres in all those phenomena which for the sake of convenience we label 'cultural'. Let us use the analogy of the powder-keg and the spark, in which the stock of powder acts as the 'conjuncture', and culture is no more than the tiny accidental spark. Why does the powder not always explode?

The fuse may be damp or too short, the flint produces no spark, or there is no one to strike a light. Many storm clouds pass over without breaking. We have to conclude that storms and powder-magazines have a logic of their own. Similarly, I would argue that the relations of conjunctural circumstances and political events have their own peculiar alchemy, which those pursuing the 'sense of history' are incapable of unravelling.

Montaigne devoted a chapter of his *Essays* to showing that 'the taste of good and evil depends in large part on the opinion we have of them'. He writes: 'Men, says an old Greek maxim, are tormented by the opinion they have of things, not by the things themselves'. And he continues, 'opinion is a powerful performer, bold and immoderate . . . a straight oar looks bent in the water. What matters is not merely that we see the thing, but how we see it'. [*Essays,* Bk. 1, ch 15] Montaigne's evidence is surely sound enough to enable us to demonstrate the power of opinions, representations, imaginations and passions in the history of societies. My aim was, therefore, to contribute to the history of the subjectivities, myths, fears and enthusiasms which are the most potent engines of political development. The events that are chronicled in our newspapers furnish us with too many illustrations of the empire of ideas, certitudes and illusions over millions of the living and the dying for me to want to change my view now.

If the history of men's behaviour patterns is so satisfying to the human mind, it is unfortunately the case that its horizon recedes the more one tries to advance towards it. Since a preface affords an opportunity to indulge in a measure of revery, I would venture to suggest that a history of temperaments would be of more direct relevance in explaining the chronology of violence. One could ask whether a given period or civilisation offers more or less scope to the angry or the composed, or whether it encourages the development of the lazy, the aggressive, the envious and so on. Sixteenth-century authors certainly regarded physiogonomy and astrology as genuine auxiliary sciences of history, and saw the horoscope as the foundation of good government. I like to think that they were in a sense correct, and I readily conjecture that such lore, which is to-day utterly unintelligible to us, will one day become the indispensable guides of, and sources for future historians.

Finally, I wish to say that if the English edition of my work is altogether more scholarly and complete than the original French, the credit is wholly due to the intelligence and patience of my translator.

Yves-Marie Bercé
Paris, September 1986

Translator's note

Traduttore, traditore – the English language may lack such an enviably neat way of expressing the dangers besetting those who try their hand at translation, but anyone who has done so will instinctively recognise its truth. If the present version has avoided a wholesale 'betrayal' of the original, it is due in large part to the kindness of several friends who read various parts of it along the way. I shall not name them here, if only to underline my personal responsibility for what follows. It is also a pleasure to record the willing co-operation of the author at all stages of my work; his assistance was invaluable in clarifying difficult passages and in tracking down the references scattered throughout the original edition. A supplementary bibliography has been added to make the book more useful to English readers.

Introduction

There are many ambitious works which attempt to identify the unity of revolutionary phenomena, and to establish how they correlate and diverge, with a view to constructing the laws of the statics or dynamics of institutions and social groups. Unable to present theoretical models or the laws of applied social mechanics in this book, we shall at least attempt to refurbish the body of facts which sociologists and political scientists are wont to draw upon.

The book's title, *Revolt and Revolution,* calls for definitions which clarify the respective limits of the two concepts. Such definition brings into question the seriousness of events, the intentions of the participants and the profundity of the ruptures so created by comparison with the *status quo ante.* If we bear in mind that ideas of a linear development of history and of progress only found acceptance in the eighteenth century, we are justified in ascribing an innovatory role to the French Revolution of 1789, and no previous insurrectionary episode could be regarded as a revolution. But rather than become involved in disputes over labels, we shall be content here to follow historiographical practice. In calling certain major crises, such as the War of Dutch Independence or the Great Rebellion in England, revolutions, we are merely adopting general usage, without such a choice implying reference to a tightly drawn and necessarily arbitrary definition. In order to exorcise such disputes, we shall concentrate on what revolt and revolution have in common. Both resort to collective violence in the sphere of political action, when the tranquil evolution of institutions is disturbed by the intrusion of naked force. Whatever the stakes being played for, the rank and number of participants, their aims and methods, such events have in common a dereliction of peaceful procedures, the exclusion of ordinary rules, and the choice of an outright break and of the excesses of armed conflict. It is, therefore, political violence, the common

1

denominator of revolt and revolution, which is the subject of the present study.

From the sixteenth to the eighteenth century, the early modern period affords a relatively well-delimited spectrum, with its evolving state machinery, and its very unevenly developed economies that were to a greater or lesser extent embarked on the slow transition from self-subsistence to market relations. On the eastern, southern and mountainous borderlands of Europe, pockets survived as fragments of a backwardness which continued to bear witness to earlier forms of society. Further on, the revolutions of the late eighteenth century signal a turning point for models of politics and social relations that is too decisive, and too rich in its historiography, for us to hope to contribute anything original to the study of them. This work ends, therefore, at the eve of the French Revolution. However, the major social and economic changes of the rural world which occur later on in the nineteenth century allow us to extend our search for examples that illustrate the peculiar disturbances of the rural world, down to 1848.

The limitations of the present work are those of an individual scholar, with his inadequacies of documentation and linguistic knowledge. Its value may lie in contributing new connections, suggestions and hypotheses to the central nexus of a subject that is still a long way from a final conclusion.

1 The guiding myths

The *Lectures on the Philosophy of History,* written around 1830, were the most complete expression of historical idealism. In them, Hegel attributed to the Reformation the birth of the modern state, dating it to the sixteenth century, with the triumph of freedom of thought and the final advent of reason. 'This is the sense in which we must understand the state to be based on religion. States and laws are nothing else than religion manifesting itself in the relations of the actual world'.[1] The Hegelian hypothesis that the spiritual crisis of the Reformation laid the foundations of early modern politics may serve as a *leitmotiv* for our present purposes. Do ideas, writings and words play the major role in the unfolding of revolts to the detriment of material causes, to which other authors are accustomed to ascribe the upheavals of history? Is there at the source of each great explosion a current of thought, the articulation of a demand or the outline of a programme which served as the motive force, the model or the objective of insurrection?

Against the seduction of ideas, Marx pitted the common sense of the materialist.

> Does it require deep intuition to comprehend that man's ideas, views and conceptions, in one word, man's consciousness changes with every change in the conditions of his material existence, in his social relation, and in his social life? What else does the history of ideas prove, than that intellectual production changes its character in proportion as material production is changed? The ruling ideas of each age have been the ideas of its ruling class.[2]

The purely academic debate about the determinism of facts or of ideas remains unresolved after decades of materialist research. To escape the difficulty it raises, historians are apt to invoke mechanisms of interaction and retroaction, which means that a phenomenon can be at once both cause and effect, without anyone being able to say with certainty where is the first link in the chain connecting different phenomena.

Rather than deliver judgement on the effectiveness of ideologies or on their capacity to generate events, this study will endeavour to reveal the historical conditions of their expression, and the circumstances which, in *ancien régime* societies, surrounded the articulation of discontents and complaints – in other words, the genesis of arguments that refused to accept the existing order of things.

The drafting of grievances

There has probably never been a kingdom in which there was no possibility of recourse to the sovereign by individual petition or collective address. Indeed, the institutions often provided that such discussions should occur at certain intervals and in a prescribed setting. They ranged from the duty of princes and great vassals to give counsel, remonstrances by sovereign courts or by assemblies of estates, down to the grievances, complaints and petitions of the humblest subjects. This universal right of address to the sovereign derived from his function of supreme justiciary who could not turn away any plaintiff. In time, however, circumstantial limitations on this right appeared, reserving its full use to certain dignitaries, confining it to specific occasions, and limiting it to a few points of law or administration.

In the French monarchy, all the orders and constituted bodies could address their remonstrances to the king. For example, the assembly of the clergy of a diocese or of the entire kingdom, the corps of officials of a bailiwick, or indeed the magistrates of a sovereign court, could send a deputy to the king's council on a matter concerning them, submit to him more general representations or even formulate remonstrances amounting to a critique or, in practice, to a refusal of a government decision. Until the seventeenth century, the Estates General were an effective political instrument. They were the most solemn form taken by this duty of 'aid and counsel' which all orders of the kingdom were morally obliged to render to the monarch. The fact that their meetings multiplied during regencies or civil wars shows that the king was inclined to forget their potential when he felt secure in his power. During the troubled period from 1560 to 1652 in which religious wars and royal minorities followed each other, there were no fewer than six convocations, successful or abortive, of the Estates General. Those contemplated for March 1649 and September 1651 during the Fronde foundered only because the 'companies' of office-holders feared political competition from this representative body, and the possible contradiction between the grievances of the Estates and the remonstrances of the courts. However, preparatory parochial and even provincial assemblies were held, and a number of petitions, containing the elements of a far-reaching reform of the state, were preserved.

Until the sixteenth century and frequently later, numerous provinces and lesser regions were capable of assembling provincial or local estates which, more reliably than the Estates General, owing to their regular meetings, examined the problems posed by the billeting and raising of troops, and by the amount and allocation of taxes. They could also take the initiative and present remonstrances. Burgundy, Brittany, Provence, Languedoc and Béarn, to name only the most important, retained their Estates until 1789. Far from being deprived of their powers, as is too frequently repeated, they offered the inhabitants of their provinces an enviable measure of protection, since Provence and Brittany bore no more than one per cent of the burden of direct taxes at the height of the fiscal escalation of the seventeenth century.

The humblest of the king's subjects had the right – admittedly an onerous one – to send a petition to the royal council. Indeed, requests from petitioners were the normal method of activating this organ of government. There also existed the possibility of presenting placets or of writing to ministers, whose voluminous correspondence contained complaints, denunciations, memoranda and proposals from a very wide range of correspondents.

Such usages were not confined to the French system. The assemblies of estates – Zemsky Sobor in Russia, Diets in Central Europe, Spain's Cortes or England's House of Commons – were capable, at least down down to the seventeenth century, of playing an important political role. The

Diets of certain kingdoms (Poland, Hungary, Croatia) possessed the power to elect their sovereign and, in the process of doing so, to impose on him catalogues of reforms. Most of the Diets and assemblies of estates in Germany or in Scandinavia could draft remonstrances (*gravamina*), and would not hesitate to defend them in the most heated discussions, or even by taking up arms.

These examples of procedures available for the challenging of governments seemed to enable all sorts of discontented people to have direct recourse to the monarch in cases of anxiety or of disagreement. Revolts, even those dominated by illiterate peasants, were familiar with the practice of such petitions, drafted in the form of catalogues of demands. They listed complaints, both minor and serious; they itemised in rather clumsy articles schemes which occasionally went as far as to bring into question the very foundations of the state itself.

Admittedly, the recognition of the right to petition did not mean that the presentation of a request would be easy and available to all, still less that the demands would be met, but at least the existence of the right did open the door to hopes of an irrepressible kind.

Those who drafted rebel petitions were in no way conscious of embarking on rebellion or of lacking in fidelity to the king. They set themselves to follow the model of established petitions of grievance; they protested without any duplicity their attachment to the crown; they conformed as best they could to the textual model of the traditional petition.

Depending on events and on the balance of forces, it could arise that individual petitions delivered to the king by a deputy from the rebels – by some local notable, whether under constraint or out of conviction – actually received an official reply. A minister would annotate the articles of the petition in the margin, and the principal concessions were then put together in a decree of the council or even, with greater diplomatic solemnity, in a royal declaration.

Subjects who believed that they were only opening the king's eyes to their predicament were unaware that their action was seditious. Without either realising or wishing it, they had moved from the permissible petition to a manifesto for rebellion. Thus the Croquants of Aquitaine, the Russian serfs and the Austrian peasants who sent letters or delegates to their sovereign might, depending on the circumstances, be either received and given a hearing, or else sent packing, imprisoned or pursued as being guilty of criminal insolence.

In 1726, the Jura villages subject to the prince-bishop of Basle wished to protest against the codification of hundreds of ordinances and different customs in this tiny sovereign bishopric. The inhabitants of five communities of Ajoie, an area around Porrentruy, felt that their forest rights were under threat. They produced from their archives an old register of 1517 in which these rights were defined. In September 1730, they assembled in an open field and elected agents entrusted with pleading their cause at the tribunal of the prince-bishop in Basle or, if necessary, before the emperor, their distant suzerain. For ten years, five sessions of the estates of the bishopric, and six years of pleading at Vienna, the Ajoie delegates argued their case. The antiquity of their title deeds, the limited nature of their dispute, the absence in the bishopric of any executive force apart from that of the communities themselves, and even the vacancy of the episcopal see, all appeared to be guarantees of success. But the arrival of a new prince, the persistence of his learned jurists and his alliance with France led to the intervention of troops brought in from Franche-Comté. The village deputies were arrested in April 1740 and executed that October. In this tragic outcome, the villages' titles were portrayed as subversive documents and the unfortunate deputies of the parishes were, quite in spite of themselves, transfigured into leaders of insurrection.

Convinced of the justice of their cause, the discontented would assemble in order to identify their complaints and pool their anger; they would sound the alarm and meet before the door of a church. They would be numerous, inflamed by drinking wine, and armed in their customary fashion. Instead of a petition preceding revolt, it could now happen that revolt would precede any kind of demand, and that the language of violence would take a hand before any attempt was made to express their grievances. At that point, it was after the outburst, in the flurry of events, that they tried to reflect on their undertaking, and to explain to both themselves and others the difficulties they were in. This inversion, in which arms are

7

taken up before the pen, did not change the opinion that the discontented had of themselves. They identified their assembly as a fully legitimate act of self-defence. As with the presentation of petitions, the resort to arms by communities could be regarded as a right. There was no shortage of ordinances authorising the taking up of arms against wolves, brigands or enemies. The spontaneous recourse to arms was, in this instance, no more than an over-zealous expression of fidelity, a sort of clumsy act of obedience.

We can take the case of the Norfolk peasants who rose in revolt in June 1549 against the enclosure of common lands. It began with bands of peasants joining together here and there to knock down hedges which disrupted the grazing of their flocks. They found a leader in Robert Kett, tenant of a manor. In a few days, he got together 16,000 men and marched off to demand justice under the walls of Norwich, the nearest town. It was only there, before the besieged city, that the 'communal' rebels took it into their heads to draft a catalogue of their demands. They put together twenty-nine articles in which, they claimed, they demanded nothing more than the application of the king's ordinances, because evil judges had falsified them to the detriment of farmers and tenants.

The proclamations by which rebels attempted to attract supporters, enlarge their impact, and increase their numbers, belonged to another style of politics. This was no longer the humble and supplicatory attitude of the subject, but rather a solemn declaration designed to inflame passions, to solicit adherents and a recourse to arms. It was the language of conspirators, of despoiled princes, of fallen dynasties and of sovereigns embarking on war. They affirmed rights, and threw down a challenge to authority. Such declarations bore less on socio-economic life or on the working of institutions than on the very nature of power and the manner in which it devolved. The summoning of peasant assemblies was done by word of mouth, from one commune to the next, recopied and nailed up on a market-hall pole or on church doors. Proclamations by princes, which were for the most part printed, were distributed in a rather similar, clandestine manner, although on a different scale. They were entrusted to loyal followers, were borne from castle to castle by emissaries in disguise, sent to recorders of local town councils, or placarded by night on the doors of magistrates' chambers. When they found a favourable echo and responded to an expectation, manifestos circulated in this way could have a formidable extension, which can be gauged by counting the copies that have come down to us, whether consigned in the archives of the jurisdiction entrusted with the unsuing repression, dispersed in private cartularies, or collected among the curiosities of men of learning. The most striking example of the mobilising role of a text is clearly that of the Twelve Articles of the German Peasants. We know that they were drawn up on 1 March 1525 by Sebastian Lotzer, a 'companion' furrier of Memmingen, and took up the grievances of the communes of south Germany. The text was not put together in some open-air assembly, but came from the desk of a half-educated man who was attuned to the peasants' arguments, and who was writing nearly six months after the beginning of the rural agitation. From Upper Swabia, it spread throughout the entire Germanic world, even as far as Lorraine. In the space of two months, twenty editions were printed, from Thuringia to the Tyrol and Alsace. Article Twelve stated that the original could be modified or expanded in conformity with the word of God. This free interpretation of a divine intention was the source of local variants and of versions that were either more radical or more concise.

Until the successive defeats of the various groups of rebels, the Twelve Articles assisted the propagation of the revolt. They were read out in village assemblies where everyone swore to observe them; they became the emblems of the peasantry. Even after the extermination of the peasants, they were the object of a close examination at the Diet of Speyer in 1526. Their influence has even been seen in the subsequent ordinances of the authorities which, as the Articles had demanded, tended to restore life to the communal institutions of the villages.

Finally, it could happen that the grievances were not codified until after the revolt, and that the work of collecting the petitions did not occur until the insurgents had been defeated. The government of the ruler investigated the events and pieced together the roots of the evil. To that extent, it met the expectations of the rebels. In a rudimentary state where the prince's role was more or less limited to the prerogatives of justice, this was not an impossible scenario. Thus, in June 1636, the assemblies of the Croquants of Saintonge were dispersed by the royal regiments. Two months later, the intendant identified the demands of the parishes and compiled a memorandum of them which, when forwarded to the council, turned out to be more complete than the petitions of the parishes involved in the uprising.

The manifesto in forty-nine articles of the guilds of Palermo that rose in revolt in August 1647 was not the work of popular leaders, but the result of mediation by the inquisitor who had presided over the extraordinary assemblies of the leading inhabitants, gathered in a local church. Another serious revolt in Palermo in 1773 also had its programme worked out during the event itself by a commission of leading citizens put together by the archbishop.

The language of subjects' petitions of grievance represented a very broad political tradition, and was thus in no way subversive as far as their institutional form was concerned. It was the circumstances of their expression which threatened to give them a seditious character, even if their authors tried as much as they could to avoid being compromised in this way. The content of the argument might, however, become revolutionary if a millenialist utopia came to envelop its terms, although its authors might be unaware of it.

Indeed, a narrative of the revolts enables one to distinguish periods in which events themselves run riot, from those in which ideas boil over. Arguments and writings abound, and in a matter of a few days or a few years a kind of explosion in socio-political vision occurs.

Outbursts of political expression

The tensions which had long existed in the social fabric found, in these extraordinary moments, the opportunity to express themselves. During such revealing interludes, in which the true, the false, the loathsome and the imagined suddenly announced themselves, each social group, each current of thought set about formulating its accumulated grievances.

Situations hitherto experienced in bitterness now became intolerable, and men moved from inarticulate rancour to reasoned demands. At the common source of these moments, one invariably finds some sort of evaporation of norms and an absence of power. The usual authorities – whether the legitimacy of the sovereign or the magisterium of the church – seem to have dwindled or disappeared. Royal minorities, dynastic quarrels and crises of religious outlook were capable, in one way or another, of generating this type of effervescence of argument and writing, of complaint and polemic. Where such moments were circumscribed in time and limited by the accidents of history, they would later come to appear as moments of folly, of collective madness and of public giddiness. Speaking of the Fronde, Voltaire referred explicitly to 'the spirit of giddiness which reigned during that time'.

In those times when political vision burst out, things happened as if ideas formulated for a very long time, but which had remained confined to the empyreum of untried verbiage, suddenly acquired a new urgency, and began to crystallise and proliferate. Giovanni Botero sensed that political crises could conceal this kind of dynamism, and effect a ripening of subversion. According to him, the prudence of a ruler should incite him to come to terms with the grievances of his subjects, 'because they may become increasingly embittered and alienated, and though they may at first only feel resentment, they will eventually rise in open rebellion, like the Bohemians against King Sigismund and the Flemings against the Catholic King. . . . Once blood has been drawn and lawful measures abandoned, the final break has been made and insurrection follows'.[3]

We can see the model for these enduring revolts, in which the unravelling of power and the disappearance of general controlling forces leave the way open for hitherto unseen possibilities, in the years during which the Reformation was adopted, in the crises of the French Catholic League and the Fronde, or in the revolutions of England and Naples.

The case of the Reformation convinced Gabriel Naudé that the power of ideas was more formidable than that of arms. 'If we reflect a little . . . on the astonishing progress made each day by the Lutherans and the Calvinists, I am sure that we will be obliged to marvel how the spite of two monks, whose only arms were the spoken word and the pen, was the cause of such great revolutions and of such extraordinary changes in government and religion.'[4] In the cynical and paradoxical vein which flavours his *Considérations politiques sur les coups d'Etat* with a timeless humour, Gabriel Naudé alluded to the besieged towns whose resistance was bolstered not by their captains, but by their pastors, as well as to the fanaticised crowds which sermons and religious meetings rendered stronger than armies, 'For myself, I find language so powerful that I have found nothing that is not subject to its rule.'[5]

The expansion of the Reformation staggered everyone by its speed. During the 1520s and 1530s in Germany, and the 1550s and 1560s in France, towns and élites went over to the new faith. Admittedly, such growth only seemed sudden because it was in fact the culmination of a long and continuous process. The origins of the Reformation should, according to one careful and perceptive historian, be sought in much more distant and permanent ideals, that is to say, in the desire for a radical recharging of energies and the search for a personal relationship with God.[6] But such continuity with the Middle Ages cannot be perceived without hindsight; contemporaries like Florimond de Raemond could only see the explosive force of the printing press and the effects of the break with Rome. It is no accident that the birth of new forms of belief, and the disappearance of the certainty of unity coincided with the spread of printing. At the time of his break with the papacy (1519), Luther had printed and broadcast throughout Germany, in the space of three years, no less than 300,000 copies of his tracts. The Rhine axis, that concentration of roads and towns, and thus of universities, printers and booksellers, was the first to be affected by his propaganda.

This revolt against Rome's supremacy and rejection of a religious magisterium put an end to the spiritual unity of medieval christendom. The abolition of doctrinal authority and of church control opened the door to a proliferation of ideologies, to prophesyings and to sects. This spiritual explosion was truly a revealing time. Here is Florimond de Raemond's description of it in his chapter entitled, 'How everyone wished to found his own religion': 'The liberty taken by everyone to interpret Scripture in his own manner was why the bourgeois of the towns assembled their councils, established a form of religion that suited them, and took on pastors in accordance with their own desires. In our time, we have witnessed the merchant seated behind his counter measuring Scripture with his yardstick; the builder doing so with his square; the teacher classifying it in accordance with his rules of grammar, and the doctor with those of natural philosophy; even simple womenfolk wished to judge it as if it was their needle and thread.'[7]

Printing similarly played the role of an ideological arsenal in implanting the Catholic League. The adhesion of the city of Lyon, town of fairs, full of printers and pedlars, was decisive. From 1589 to 1594, over one thousand booklets of Leaguer news, songs and prints rolled off its presses. Palma Cayet noted, 'The booksellers and printers produced so many kinds of small items that the lower orders became involved in this League almost without thinking'.

In Paris, the selling of tracts had expanded beyond the University quarter of the town and, since 1578, pedlars had been allowed to set up their stalls inside the precinct of the *Palais de Justice* in the Ile de la Cité. Subject to inspection by the city's provost, their number was in theory limited to 50 in 1610 and 100 in 1653. In reality, the production of fly-sheets and tracts, run off clandestinely in the course of a single night, could not be controlled. From 1648 to 1652, the years of the Fronde signalled a new outburst of writing and debate. It was claimed that there were at that point about one thousand pedlars of books in and around the Pont Neuf, and that the Samaritaine had become 'the common library of all Paris'. About 4,000 *Mazarinades* were printed, and runs of up to 5,000 copies were sometimes sold. From the burlesque of the early days, these tracts changed to political argument. It is beyond doubt that the dissemination of inflammatory news from Paris, Bordeaux, Toulouse, Aix or Rouen broadened the initial rebellion against Mazarin, and then, soon afterwards, broadcast the arguments of the different parties.

During the English Civil War, the collapse of royal power and the related rejection of all ecclesiastical authority brought about a similar inebriation. As early as 1641, the first session of the Long Parliament deprived the central institutions of their authority. The termination of censorship was reflected in a flood of gazettes and political tracts. The most diverse and extreme ideas, by the standards of the time, enjoyed free rein. New churches, prophetic sects, radical reformers and millenarian preachers discovered their true vocation and multiplied throughout the country until the triumph of Cromwell. A country which was merely reformist in mood in 1641 developed during the Civil War ideological possibilities of a revolutionary kind. After 1653, but long before any hope of a restoration of the monarchy had appeared, this tide began to ebb; disillusionment and rancour reversed the trend and brought the inventors of utopia into disrepute for many years.

The Naples revolt and the eclipse of Spanish power brought into the open an analogous excitement of imaginations, this time in the context of a Mediterranean society. With the viceroy's successive climb-downs in 1647, each social group became emboldened, threw itself into making its demands, and published its grievances and objectives. The suppression of the *gabelles* and the resurrection of the powers of the towns and of the crafts would have appeared wholly unlikely only two months previously. Hopes became positive demands right across the social spectrum, even including the students and the church poor. Students demanded a reduction of their fees to the old rates of the time of the Aragonese kings. The beggars demanded a distribution of alms every day, as had been the practice, in their view, under the reign of the good queen Jeanne of Anjou. The strangeness and diversity of the grievances astonished the chroniclers. But while noting this sudden revelation of hidden tensions, one should also note their rapid obliteration. The Spaniards' victory and the return of peace less than a year later, wiped out permanently that summer's blossoming of demands.

The rapid and fleeting nature of these popular enthusiasms was denounced by political thinkers. It was a commonplace to warn against the fickleness of crowds and the instability of their ideas. Gabriel Naudé wrote in 1639: 'Since the best coups d'état are effected by recourse to the populace, one should know fully what its disposition is, and with what boldness and assurance one may make use of it, and steer it round to the service of one's purposes. Those who have provided the most complete and specific description of it rightly portray it as a many-headed beast, vagabond, directionless, mad, thoughtless, and without norms, intelligence or judgement. . . . The people are a theatre where orators, preachers, false prophets, imposters, political tricksters, mutineers, the disappointed, the superstitious, the ambitious, in a word all those who have some new objective, stage their most furious and bloody tragedies.'[8] Again in 1764, Beccaria referred to the 'fanatical sermons that excite the easily roused passions of the curious multitude. For their passions gather force from the number of hearers and more from a certain obscure and mysterious enthusiasm, than from clear and quiet reasoning, which never has any influence over a large mass of men.'[9]

The over facile lure of ideologies and the futility of infatuation were not the sole brakes on these explosions of political vision. Most of the time they repeated themes which were very old, the permanence of which is revealed, under differing guises, through all the variety of historical circumstances. In any catalogue of such leitmotifs, millenarian expectation, the certainty of a forthcoming establishment of God's reign on earth, would undoubtedly take first place.

The reign of God on earth

The world is bad and must be changed; it is old and its end approaches. These ideas, perhaps as old as humanity itself, found additional illustration in Christian eschatology. The logical coupling of suffering and redemption, the necessity of Christ's sacrifice before his resurrection, joined together thereafter the notions of endurance and renewal. To the teaching of the Gospel was added the prophecy of the Apocalypse. The point at which misfortune reaches its peak is the sign of the end of time. The elect, who have been capable of recognising these signs, have the duty of purifying a dying, sinning world by fire and the sword. After the final outbu st of violence will follow God's reign on earth and the dawn of eternal happiness.

These basic themes – the expectation of the revelation of the great moment of history, the necessity and value of a final unleashing of violence, and the imminent completion of history – are to be found in all ages of history. As Tertullian wrote, 'Our desires call out for the ruin of the present age and thus the end of the world, so that the great day of the Lord may come, the day of anger and punishment.' At the end of the twelfth century in Calabria, a Franciscan hermit, Joachim of Fiore, believed he had penetrated the hidden meaning of the Scriptures. Joachim's fantasies produced other visionaries, whether engendered by his writings which were never entirely forgotten, or by analogous inspirations. In fact, the Bible provided not just models from the Hebrew past, but also the revelations of the books of the prophets and of the Apocalypse. It was there, men believed, that one should seek out divine messages about the future of the world. Thus, the Scriptures were open to innumerable partial interpretations, most of which were selective and literal, and contained extraordinary subversive potential. Such direct familiarity with the Bible was spawned with all the fundamentalism and radicalism of the popular sects. The letter of the biblical text takes precedence over church dogma, and the divine word itself yields place to the interior illumination of each individual. As a result, medieval Europe was alive with millenarian convulsions – popular crusades, messianic hopes of resurrected kings and penitential panics.

The Hussite Revolution in fifteenth-century Bohemia formed another link in this chain. The Czech millenarian Taborites believed they could eliminate suffering by eliminating power, that is by establishing equality among Christians and by abolishing all institutions, wiping out both church and state. They waged war without prisoners or bounty, because the enemies of God should be exterminated and their wealth destroyed. They were themselves crushed at the battle of Lipany in 1434. But their posterity was preserved in a marginal, limited way by the communities known as the Bohemian Brethren or the United Brethren, even though these unobtrusive groups remained isolated and without much success in recruiting adherents.

Several aspects of the late fifteenth century seemed to rekindle these ancient promises. The irresistible advance of the Turks appeared as the tragic sign of the collapse of Christendom. In the Burgundian-Lotharingian provinces, the hopes and fears raised by the grandiose plans of Charles the Bold had successively fascinated people and then made them despair. News of the discovery of the New World gave credibility to even the most astonishing portents. The scandal of the schisms and of the wealth of the orders had enabled the hope of a reform of the church to take root. Recognized preachers travelled throughout western Europe, proclaiming the need for a moral revival and a re-awakening of individual consciences. Popular preachers followed a similar path. Hans Pfeiffer, musician and shepherd, preached rebellion in Franconia in the spring of 1476. Joss Fritz in 1502, and then in 1513, in Alsace and Breisgau, called for 'the justice of God alone'.

The 1510s and 1520s were tense in expectation of the supernatural. Millenarian hopes and popular prophecy found abundant scope in this century of faith and miracles which is usually depicted as a decisive stage in the all conquering path of reason. In asserting the priesthood of all believers and the free scrutiny of the Scriptures, the Lutheran Reformation multiplied the number of individual illuminations. Students, unfrocked clergy, half-educated artisans and impoverished peasants wandered from town to town all over a busy and densely-populated Germany, in search of new wisdom and hope. Neither Anabaptist prophecy nor millenarian violence are to be identified with the Reformation or the peasant revolts, but they share with them the same environments and origins.

Among the disoriented pilgrims and wanderers hungering for truth, the learned and fiery theologian, Thomas Müntzer, went in search, like so many others, of a Chosen City capable of accepting his message and willing to turn itself into the New Jerusalem. From May 1520 to April 1521, he sojourned at Zwickau, a Saxon town that was a crossroads, the centre of a silver-mining basin and, above all, the leading textile town in Germany. Preaching there, Müntzer encountered Anabaptist prophets who in turn found potential supporters among the great mass of weavers and miners. Driven out by the town authorities, Müntzer hoped to find in Bohemia traces of earlier Taborite fervour, but in vain. Returning to Saxony, he preached at Allstedt in 1523, and then at Müllhausen from August 1523 to September 1524, being disappointed each time in his search for a perpetual convenant between God and 'elect' citizens. The Peasants' War broke out just then, and appeared to him as a providential opportunity. He launched appeals for a revolution of the greatest violence, and demanded a massacre of the 'impious', to whom he refused the slightest compassion, as God had once commanded Moses. In his *Appeal to the Citizens of Allstedt* of April 1525, he urged them to 'tear down the tower of the ungodly. For as long as they live, you will have no freedom from fear. For as long as they dominate you, you will not be able to talk of God. Arise, arise, arise while the light is with you. God goes before you, follow Him, follow Him. *History has already been written*'.[10] In defence of this massacre in which God was going to fight alongside his faithful followers, Müntzer quoted several Biblical passages, taken from the Books of Daniel, Esdras, and Revelation. Convinced of victory, he led his followers out into the countryside, where they were dispersed and massacred at the battle of Frankenhausen on 15 May 1525.

After Müntzer, Römer attempted to found Jerusalem at Erfurt in 1528, and Hoffman at Strasburg in 1533, but it was in the Netherlands that the Anabaptist movement experienced its great take-off at this time. The Danish civil war closed the passage of the Sound from October 1531 to March 1534, halting the Baltic grain trade. In the towns and ports, sailors and artisans were threatened with ruin and scarcity. It was from these maritime provinces, and from Amsterdam in particular, that the prophets who moved into the Rhineland towns to found the kingdom of God, orginated. Having gained control of Münster, the millenarian prophets established there a 'holy community', the 'good society', in which for a few months a common sharing of all things that went as far as polygamy, was practised. The excesses of the siege and, lastly, the massacre perpetrated after the capture of the city on 24 June 1535 fastened a historical fortune of a horrific kind to the legend of the Anabaptist fanatics.

We should not, however, exaggerate the importance of this episode. The penchant of the idealist school of history for the discovery of precursors, and then, from the 1960s onwards, a deliberate predilection for the marginal and the deviant, and lastly the particular attention devoted to innovation, whether real or supposed – all of these different historiographical distortions have constantly accentuated and altered the study of such personalities and events. They have overestimated their historical role, and likewise failed to recognise aspects of continuity and of mythological tradition that they exhibit.

After Münster, Anabaptism became the doctrine of the small but faithful flock, peacefully separated from the world around them. Isolated and scattered, the largest communities, in Moravia or in Swabia, never formed more than one per cent of the local population. The most extreme forms of their preaching and behaviour were confined to the early 1530s and to certain districts of the Tyrol or Thuringia. Challenges thrown down to magistrates, refusals of oaths of allegiance, opposition to pastors or priests, refusals to trade or lend at interest, attempts to have property in common or freedom of divorce, were rarely taken to their logical conclusion.

Beyond the radical sects and their dogmas it would be possible to uncover in most of the conflicts of this period the implicit idea of a purifying violence which can at once destroy, build and change everything overnight. In 1556, as the Low Countries were experiencing another year of scarcity and unemployment, the protestants returned from exile and resumed public worship, encouraged by the tolerance of Margaret of Parma. Street preaching, chanting psalms and the sale of tracts multiplied. The conjunction of protestant activities with the gathering of crowds characteristic of years of scarcity, led, in August, to an outburst of popular, iconoclastic rioting. Similar crises had shaken England and Scotland. In the space of a few days, the mobs, composed mostly of women and children, ravaged churches, without the town magistrates doing anything to prevent them. As the Calvinist chronicler, Simon Goulart, indulgently wrote: 'Indeed, it is impossible that such a change of religion could occur in a country without events like this.' Divine inspiration and the sheer innocence of the participants seemed to him justifications of iconoclasm. In this savage event, the prophetic vandalism of the crowd paradoxically fitted in well with the objectives of a religious reform of an elitist, abstract and interiorised kind. The break with the church's control was not merely intellectual defiance of an established power: it was also, in the popular mind, a concrete act of exorcism. Likewise, between 1789 and 1793 revolutionary vandalism attacked 'the monuments of feudalism and superstition'. Such destruction and burning, as in religious iconoclasm, resulted from the confluence of two cultural intentions that were widely separated from each other: the spontaneous action of the rioters and the considered policy of the legislator. The symbolic break decided upon by politicians corresponded in the primitive mind to the illusion of a genuine abolition. The semblance involved was more than mere projection, but rather a complete substitution. The smashing of the image is not just symbolic, standing for man's entry into a new age and condemning the past; it aims at being a historical leap, an irreversible movement which will make any return to the past forever impossible.

The expectation of an imminent and final intervention by God in the destiny of men could colour even the most realist of political movements and the mostly worldly of aspirations. Sudden upsurges of city or dynastic patriotism aimed at responding to a divine plan. The myth of a transfer of divine favour from one empire or city to another at different times in history was applied to events in a number of chronicles. In Florence between 1494 and 1498, Savonarola announced the revelations that he had received from heaven. The liberty of Florence and its prosperity in their most worldly sense were identical with God's will. The Scriptures had foreseen this glory; contemporary signs and the prophet's visions confirmed it.

The kingdom of Portugal, deprived of its ancient dynasty by lack of heirs, and governed from Madrid between 1579 and 1640, witnessed a similar millenarian exaltation. Portugese prophetism was in large part of Jewish origin. The Jews of Lisbon, who were very numerous and subject to expulsions (1497) and massacres (19 April 1506), took refuge in expectation of the Messiah. The visionary writings of the *conversos* had come to permeate Portugese attitudes. In tune with this outlook, the Jesuits at Evora University provided a learned gloss on these repeated prophecies. The nobility's coup d'état which, on 1 July 1640, restored a national sovereign to the throne, was preceded by a decade rich in wonders. The event was announced by the birth of monsters, mysterious inscriptions on trees and rocks, and celestial happenings. The days when the Spaniards departed and John IV Braganza was acclaimed were moments of festivity; days and nights were spent in the streets in acknowledging the realisation of the prophecies and the coming of the divine destiny of the Portugese kingdom.

The burgeoning maritime expansion of England in the sixteenth and seventeenth centuries also gave rise to a myth of divine election. The Elizabethan generations drew their certainty of the singularity of the nation's calling from the dramatic episodes of the break with Rome and their military rivalry with Spain. *The Book of the Martyrs* by John Fox enjoyed a central place in the origins of this enthusiastic conviction. Forced into wandering throughout Protestant Europe, he complied a chronicle of the persecutions suffered by the protestant preachers under the papist reign of Mary Tudor. His monumental work, written in English and illustrated with wood cuts, had an immense success from the time of its completion in 1563. It spoke directly to the heart; it was read in the churches and was widely reprinted. The dispersion of the Armada sent to subdue England; the intrigues, real or imaginary, of the henchmen of the Roman Babylon sealed this intertwining of England's destiny with God's design. It was what Thomas Brightman declared in his *Revelation of Revelation* of 1609: the destiny of humanity depended on Englishmen's fidelity to their duty. The assertion of Laud's Arminian tendencies after 1630 and the supposed sympathies of Charles I towards Catholicism, represented a direct, apocalyptic threat that was denounced in the sermons addressed to the Long Parliament during Lent 1641. Puritans and members of the sects, by contrast, awaited the coming of the true faith. The hopes or, perhaps, the misfortunes and frustrations of the civil war brought about – helped by the breakdown of censorship – a proliferation of sects for which uprooted peasants, unemployed artisans, and unpaid soldiers formed a potential audience.

Of all the biblical blooms of the English Revolution, only the Diggers and their most inventive spokesman, Gerard Winstanley (1614–76), went as far as to condemn private property. Drawing their inspiration from both Christian egalitarianism and English national mythology, whose home-grown liberty and divine calling had manifested themselves in every age, the Digger manifestos made individual property a consequence of sin. The dissolution of property would inaugurate the third and final age of humanity. But, in reality, Winstanley and his *True Levellers' Standard Advanced* are out of place in this inventory of millenarian dynamism, as it was not the tract which triggered events; on the contrary, it was the ripening process of years of civil war which produced this manifesto without a future. Winstanley's writings found scarcely any echo outside his little group of pioneers, the break-up of which went unnoticed. Winstanley died in obscurity, while the peaceful Restoration of 1660 relegated to profound and enduring discredit ideas developed during the Revolution. Their posthumous fortune is due, as with Anabaptism, to the intellectual genealogies which attempt to retrace the centuries-long, promethean itinerary followed by a transcendant revolutionary cause.

The social radicalism of the Diggers was opposed by other sects, and had in its own time less of an impact than the mystics, such as the Quakers, or the true millenarians, like the Fifth Monarchy movement. From 1653 to 1661, the hopes and disillusionment of many participants in the civil war found sustenance in an old myth from the Book of Daniel. In a nightmare, the tyrant Nabuchednezzer saw an idol with feet of clay and a golden head being overturned by a stone which grew into a mountain. The earth, the bronze, silver and gold of the statue were the successive kingdoms swept away by history. The mountain was the fifth and final monarchy. Cromwell should, therefore, give way to a kingdom of the Saints, which would be without church, priests, sacraments, government, kings or laws. But the Restoration, as we saw, extinguished millenarian expectations for a long time.

The revolt of the Camisards provides one last example of the belief in God's earthly sword. The movement was born in a prophetic outburst. Some Protestant peasants of the Cévennes had abjured their religion merely out of resignation. The *Accomplissement des prophéties* of 1686 in which the minister Jurieu announced the imminent destruction of the Beast reached them from the Huguenot 'Refuge' abroad. Minor prophets traversed first the Dauphiné, then the Vivarais. While the Peace of Ryswick (1697) removed all hope of a defeat of Louis XIV, and the persecution of the Huguenots continued, the visions and revelations – 'the gift' – continued to inspire shepherds, children and ordinary folk, summoning 'the children of God' to leave Babylon, and to take up arms in order to form the 'camp of the Lord'. In this way began the guerilla war of the Cévennes in July 1702, which lasted over two years, when up to 25,000 men of the royal army were tied up in the mountains at the time of Jean Cavalier's surrender.

The Camisard episode does not quite close this chronicle. The belief in the establishment of the reign of God, here and now, has only changed in appearance. Classical historiography considers millenarianism as primitive, transitory forms of a revolutionary doctrine as yet incapable of analysing the world and understanding history. One day, it would yield to more elaborate forms, once reason had found its place in history. On the contrary, millenarianism is, perhaps, a timeless attitude of the human spirit, a product of the magical slant of our thinking which is nowadays concealed in our unconscious. No doubt, it forms a contrast with the rational guise of Utopia, but it constantly and invisibly continues to accompany and saturate the latter. In other words, every revolution may be fundamentally millenarian from the moment it sees a sense in history, and a future that is both certain and necessary. This postulate of direction, of indispensable stages and of violent transitions – the very horror of which is justified by their integral place in the course of history – has been the foundation stone of the ideology of most contemporary states. It is implicit in all official thinking, it is taught and broadcast – it is everywhere. It believes that it is the product of reason alone, and will not admit to itself its magical origin and power. In the end, it may be that action grounded in belief and looking towards the future is an indispensable spring to history itself.

The rediscovery of Paradise restored to earth, and the image of the river at which the wolf and the lamb refresh themselves together, may be irreplaceable spurs, which it would be pointless to confine to particular eras or historical settings.

The golden age

The coming of the ideal reign which would realise the virtues of 'good government', justice and liberty that men dreamed of, was tied to their conception of time. The passage of the years was not necessarily a linear process in which a change for the better represented a step forward, a form of progress. It could be circular, where auspicious change would then constitute a return to lost perfection, the restoration of a past long since vanished. The completion of a circle of time – its 'revolution' – formed a cycle. Men could imagine cycles in which empires succeeded one another, with that of the Greeks following that of the Egyptians and preceding that of the Romans or, within an empire, of types of régime following each other. Thus Machiavelli perceived in history a succession of forms of government: monarchy, aristocracy and democracy appeared, reached their perfection, and then fell into decay and corruption, ineluctably beckoning on the next stage of the cycle.

The circular notation of time means that the past will, of necessity, become the present once more; nothing truly new can occur. '*Quid est quod fuit? Ipsum quod futurum est. Quid est quod factum est? Ipsum est faciendum.*'[11] These inevitable legacies and the imperturbable rotation of the wheel of fortune were such as to inspire modesty and resignation in the man of wisdom. The powers that be would be replaced by others, without the order of history suffering any alteration for all that. Even Montesquieu referred in his *Persian Letters* of 1721 to these inescapable vicissitudes of the ages. 'Revolutions occur every ten years, casting the rich down into misery and elevating the poor on swift wings to the pinnacle of riches.' Whatever the nature of the cycle, the form and the regularity of the revolutions, nothing was more certain than the eternal return of things and their innate immutability in the light of eternity itself.

The expectation of a fortunate return of the cycle presupposed the existence of a very remote period of history, of a moment so distant in time as to be perhaps 'original', in which men had known peace and happiness. This belief in a golden age somewhere back in time, found a kind of natural confirmation in each generation in the spontaneous and timeless feeling of greater well-being related to the early biography of every individual. In a cosmogony which was anthropomorphic, past time was viewed in terms of a world that was youthful. In order to recover that primitive innocence it was necessary to change the direction in which things were moving, to reject harmful inventions, return to good and ancient customs, and renew a world that had become too old. This backward-looking ideal did more than merely reflect the unending conflict of generations. It derived its power from the conviction that original sin had perverted the hearts of men and that evil, once brought into the world, corrupted more and more each day the morals of individuals and the history of the entire human race. Men's fragile earthly happiness was threatened by sin. Nostalgia for the golden age and a lost paradise would lead the discontented to oppose change, and to demand, not innovation, which was detested, but re-novation, which would prove miraculous.

The prestige attached to the world's 'youth' fitted remarkably well into popular attitudes. The accumulation of natural and human calamities, especially in the century from 1560 to 1660, made suspicion of the future a part of popular wisdom. The permanent threat of biological misfortune engendered a reassuring adherence to values and institutions which possessed guarantees of immemorial antiquity and local custom. For as long as the demographic régime of low life-expectancy obtained, any experience that was long was a rare and precious thing, tradition retained its strength, and change led to rejection and revolt. And this is one of the paradoxes of the theme of the golden age: far from ensuring an imperturbably pacific conservatism, it could become a source of violence; revolt became a legitimate option against any novelty which looked like an act of aggression. In the view of the reactionary insurgents, it was a question of getting rid of disorder, of returning to a state of affairs prior to that of the unsettling innovation. The popular hatred of novelty became uneasy at the sight of inventions and creations emanating from the towns, from a world that was educated, urbanised and property-owning. In making their way into the countryside, they took on the appearance or reality of so many acts of provocation and expropriation.

The history of every nation might contain a treasured moment or an episode that had passed into legend and that was then 'elected' in the collective memory as the fixed anchor of its own specific golden age, the idealised setting for the glory and happiness of the nation in question. Such myths were often supported by a learned gloss, when the states of the fourteenth and fifteenth centuries stumbled on propaganda techniques, and deliberately set out to magnify their past and to rewrite the chronicle of their origins. Thus, England produced the mythical Arthurian cycle, while France poured its dreams into the Great Chronicles of its kings. Among them, the reign of St Louis provided a model government sufficiently far removed to be tinged with legend, to appear as overflowing with justice, devoid of taxes, and pre-dating wars and misfortunes. Louis XII and Henry IV both provided later epochs with updated images of good kings. Manifestos of rebellion envisaged reductions in the amount of taxation, in the number of offices and the powers of the state to what they had been during these blessed reigns. A common feature of such reigns was that they occurred in years that were spared calamities, and were situated upstream from the great military confrontations, on peaceful shores that would retrospectively come to figure as utopian havens. A seditious text of the Norman Nupieds revolt of 1639 declared. 'I shall soon return the first privilege of the noble, the peasant and the holy church, by which I mean, to the state in which we were when Louis XII brought us a golden age.'

During the years before the English Revolution, the parliamentary orators who opposed the absolutist innovations of the Stuart kings, claimed to do so out of fidelity to the national past. Their arguments were based on the research of common law jurists, such as Edward Coke's compilations of jurisprudence which every English man of law had in his library. According to this tradition, Magna Carta contained the principles of an ancient constitution, inherited from the Saxon kings, older indeed than even the royal prerogatives. The English example shows clearly the political ambiguity and the subversive potential of the utopia of a restored past.

Among the Scandinavian and Slav peoples, we also encounter the provocative memory of primitive liberties going back to the early Middle Ages, to the heart of the darkest ages.

In the Italian states, the theme of the *buon tempo antico* was taken from Latin authors. In the second book of the Georgics, Virgil condemned the decadence of his time, and located Rome's forgotten happiness in the time when it was a village with only a modest wall around it for protection. Dante, writing at the beginning of the fourteenth century, could perceive only vice and envy among his contemporaries. He believed that Florence had known virtue before 1250, prior to the conquest of the surrounding area (*contado*) and the corruption of morals wrought by power and by the strife between Guelphs and Ghibellines.

In Naples, nostalgia for times of peace and the demands made during moments of disturbance, both harked back to the good old times of the Aragonese kings. '*Saie quanno fuste, Napole, curona? Qanno rignava Casa d'Aragona.*' After the revolt of 1647, the Spaniards were clever enough to send as viceroy to Naples Pietro Antonio d'Argona. His name and his noble manners recalled in the collective memory ancient splendours and moments of glory common to both his family and this ancient southern kingdom. His name contributed to the illusion of resuming for a time the dynastic and political independence of the distant reign of Ferrante I.

Despite the absurd character that these conceptions may hold for today's reader, one cannot be satisfied with the ready-made explanation for them on offer – that popular credulity corresponds to the imposition by the ruling classes of their ideological constructs. The golden age was not an idle notion for the peasantries of the sixteenth and seventeenth centuries. The changes occurring during these centuries more often than not represented defeats for them, both in terms of political role and their share in economic benefits. The age of liberty and abundance were in reality behind them. But above all, the golden age, like all historical myths, corresponds to a timeless tendency in mankind. It is a fundamental nostalgia, inherent in our passage through life. The transfiguration of the past spares no generation. In our own time, the golden age has assumed the characteristics of primitivism and a return to nature. Finally, the ironies of historical events invert the meaning of myths, transforming repetition into invention, and discovery

27

into routine. The need for roots throws up false genealogies and anachronisms that are themselves innovative, many examples of which are provided by the study of nationalist ideologies and of attempts at provincial revival. As W. E. Mühlmann amusingly wrote, 'The history of humanity is just a series of creative misunderstandings, of imagined connections; derivation is merely a kind of "cunning of history" in its work of innovation.'[12]

The just king and the king deceived

The king is unaware of his subjects' misfortunes; he is misled by his evil ministers who hide from him the tribulations and grievances of his people. But as soon as their complaints reach him, he will acknowledge their value and, in the fullness of his justice, will grant satisfaction to the poor and the oppressed. This myth contains several distinct elements: the king's justice, the usurpation of power by evil ministers and, lastly, the utopia of a direct relationship between a charismatic monarch and each of his subjects.

In both popular imagery and learned doctrine, justice was the fundamental function of kings, the first duty of the 'christian prince', the essential principle of 'good government'. Antoine Loisel wrote that 'it is the unanimous conclusion of all philosophers that justice belongs directly and inherently to the state or to the sovereign prince. . . . is the most beautiful and principal ornament of his crown, the highest and most divine part of his power . . . the primary end for which kings are established.'[13] All monarchs sought the ideal sobriquet of 'just'; all monarchies passed down anecdotes in which the justice of a good king was at work, and in which he was seen to undo the schemes of the evildoers, punish the excesses of the powerful and render right justice to the destitute.

The guilt of the minister and the darkness of his soul were contrasted with the guilessness of the king. The royal favour which singled him out made him an object of jealousy, a parvenu whose exceptional political fortune and social advancement appeared replete with unjust gain and exaction. Many favourites and ministers of French kings finished on the scaffold, and the political trials from Charles VII to Francis I illustrated the fragility of their power in the early phase of a centralising monarchy. The companions of Henry III and Henry IV likewise attracted popular hatred. The continuity during the seventeenth century of the position of principal minister focussed resentments even more. Cecil, Buckingham or Stafford in England, Granvelle, Antonio Pérez or Olivares in Spain likewise fulfilled the role of scapegoats. Such accidents were inevitable in a position that was without institutional saction, deprived of those guarantees which birth and rank might have provided, and subjected to the caprice of events; its sole, precarious protection the friendship or confidence of the sovereign.

The idea of an administration without 'intermediaries', of a government that was simple and direct, took shape in the debates of open-air assemblies that met at church doors or on fair days. Examples of it were to be found in the king's reserved justice, which allowed him at all times to reserve a lawsuit to himself, in the custom of presenting petitions to his council, or also in the management of taxes by the assemblies of the provinces which possessed estates (*pays d'états*) – a management that seemed a relic of ancient practices which the installation of royal officials had uprooted in the provinces called *pays d'élections*. As late as the seventeenth century, the image of the king living off the revenues of his domain and distributing justice like St Louis under the shade of an oak tree was still a widely accepted model.

The theme of the king who had been deceived was above all reassuring, since it postulated the permanence of a supreme justice. It preserved the integrity of the sovereign principle, and safeguarded the legitimacy and continuity of the state. The theme was, at the same time, violently subversive, since it justified in advance any rush to arms aimed at unseating bad ministers and removing all obstacles between the justiciar-king and those subject to his justice. Sure enough, we find the argument of the king deceived at the very centre of a great many instances of collective violence. Even in the total frenzy of the bloodiest outbursts, rioters shouted 'Long live the king'. They attached to their manifestos and grievances, protestations of fidelity and of their belief in the king's capacity to listen to them and to give them justice that was right and prompt. They argued that their uprising had no other objective than to attract the king's attention towards this unknown corner of his empire. The Palermo rebels who put the viceroy to flight, ravaged the houses of the tax-farmers and opened the prisons, waved about in each of these actions portraits of their sovereign, the king of Naples (September 1773).

In each of the Russian revolts, the person of the tsar was invariably associated with the rebels' march on Moscow. Just before capturing Tsaritsyn in 1670, Stepan Razin harangued his Cossacks and urged them to march from the Volga into Russia against traitors and the enemies of the tsar, in order to drive from the Muscovite state the treasonable boyars and Duma deputies and, in the towns, the voïevods and officials. In Razin's view, the exactions of these dignitaries and of government agents were carried out without the approval or knowledge of the tsar.

As the most perfect expression of this myth, we may take the address of the estates of Béarn meeting in Orthez in December 1685 to complain of an increase in domain fees. 'Should this complaint be brought before His Majesty, it is impossible that he should not be indignant, for his justice does not permit his subjects to be distressed. . . . If this province itself produced gold and silver, or its mountains were converted into some other metal, the end product would not satisfy the excessive claims of the farmer of the domain; it is clear that such methods are opposed to the benign and humane intentions of the king who, far from desiring the destruction and affliction of his subjects, only desires, on the contrary, their relief and preservation.' This document, which has nothing to do with the popular spontaneity of moments of insurrection, shows the late extension of the myth among the literate and political classes. Indeed, it is to be found, in less condensed versions, in political literature, especially of the sixteenth century. The Jesuit Father Ribadeneyra does not avoid it in his *Christian Prince,* intended as a manual of christian politics in its repudiation of the cynical maxims of Machiavelli. He writes: 'Let the king's money be used faithfully and without deceit; let the ducat be worth a ducat and the <u>real</u> a <u>real</u> to the king; to this end, let not his money pass through many hands. . . . Experience shows that a goodly part of the king's money goes in salaries to his ministers and, instead of the ten which the people owe their king, the ministers burden them with twenty-five to thirty, and that with such violence and rigour that they are destroyed and ruined, feeling more the loss incurred at the hands of the receivers than they do in paying the principal to the king.'[14] He recounts how Bodin, attending the estates of Languedoc in 1556, witnessed their petition to suppress the receivers and to pay their taxes directly to the king. Similarly, the Croquants of 1637 offered to bring their *taille* payments directly to the king at the Louvre itself.

The theme of the king deceived had another variant in certain national chronicles that was just as provocative – that of the hidden king, who could no longer defend his faithful subjects, and who were left to the spitefulness of a tyrant or usurper. The Emperor Frederick had not died, king Sebastian of Portugal had not fallen in Morocco, and the tsarevitch was still alive; they would return in order to deliver their subjects, relieve them from oppression, and restore the grandeur of their kingdom. At the high point of their suffering, the pretender is recognised, the crowds gather behind him, and his supporters rush to arms. There were as many as five so-called Dmitris during the Time of the Troubles. Razin brought a tsarevitch with him, and Pugatchev asserted he was Peter III. They wished to incarnate a fundamental legitimacy that would convince the discontented and rally the rebels in the hope of achieving all their dreams and expectations.

The most prominent of the revolts carrying the image of the king deceived were the French and the Russian. Even if Italy and Spain always show examples of an enduring fidelity to it, it is difficult not to postulate a localisation of the phenomenon that corresponds to the most complete sacralisation of monarchical power. Historical tradition had generated in such places a religious expression of royal power, with its rites and beliefs. The theme fell apart when the sacralisation itself lost its credit and power of suggestion. In 1789, the peasants of many provinces still believed that it was the king's will to punish the bad aristocrats and that the convocation of the Estates General represented this long-awaited audience with a just king. The longest survival was in Russia where peasant revolts, sequels to the abolition of serfdom in 1861 and 1876, exhibited this religious confidence in the tsar, whom the wickedness of the boyars alone separated from his people.

Contemporary historical criticism persistently fails to recognise the power of this theme. It surrenders the history of ideas and, what is more, the processes of the unconscious, to other disciplines. It is felt that to acknowledge the influence of myth in order to explain older social movements would mean adhering to the past's representation of itself, and to be taken in by them. In consigning them swiftly to the dustbin of anecdotal illusions and in preferring to them the most mediocre of socio-economic analysis, historians fancy that they are performing a work of demystification, and that they have exhausted the subject by writing of naive monarchism and of conservatism bred by ignorance.

It is true that a myth is a myth and that, in strict fact, the king was, of course, by no means deceived. Louis XIII called the Croquants 'villains', without any semblance of compassion. The Tsarina Catherine sent before the judges peasant serfs who had been imprudent and bold enough to bring their complaints against their seigneurs before her personally (1767). On the other hand, it is no less true that in the period of the greatest sacralisation of power, the exercise of justice – the first royal prerogative – was a duty of conscience imposed on the king. Institutions profoundly influenced by christianity all contributed towards establishing a paternal image of the king.

Furthermore, and independently of its monarchical interpretation, the theme of a supreme tribunal as a benevolent and permanent court of appeal, proves to be an element of stability and peaceful continuity in society. Today, innocence is no longer the mark of consecrated monarchs, but of sovereign institutions and ideologies, whose prestige is not undermined even by their acts of genocide. We must therefore repeat that myth cannot be reduced to a kind of pedagogy or to a model imposed from above; it must originate from a spontaneous desire to recover certitude, and to refresh the human spirit by some kind of coherence of the universe. In this way it escapes from the ups and downs of a particualr era, and represents an instinctive, timeless human need.

To return to early modern centuries, the myth of the innocent king did more than merely ensure the permanence of regimes. It generated hostility, defiance and resistance to the authorities most immediately above the people, whose legitimacy could be constantly questioned and doubted. It provided rebels with a simple justification, a search for impunity, and a transfer of guilt which might not itself be devoid of calculation. Just as re-novation and the return to the golden age did not exclude actual in-novation, so the theme of the king deceived was an effective political engine, a leaven of violence for at least two centuries, and one which led to more changes than one. Thus resistance to fiscal aggression could lead to economic development, the rejection or refusal of religious oppression could remove the obstacles to intellectual adventure, and so on.

2 The political objectives of early modern Europe

Our survey of the myths which disturbed society demonstrated that, in the final analysis and beyond their numerous historical guises, their themes answered to needs that were timeless. It remains now to consider ideas which were more susceptible to limitation in time, political objectives which during early modern centuries presented real threats and direct alternatives to the established order.

We shall concentrate successively on the right of resistance to tyrants, attachment to the town that was one's native land, the vocation of the nobility as a trustee of national liberties and, finally, the central theme of political equality that was very widely propagated from the eighteenth century onwards. There is nothing exhaustive about this: it simply suggests which were the main policies, among which idealised aims were less important than methods that were more closely adapted to the circumstances of the time, and that were closer to models already realised or capable of realisation.

Resistance to the tyrant

A great many works on the history of ideas or on politics concentrate their attention on the modern world, and begin their discussions with the nineteenth century. Such a short perspective leads to earlier centuries being considered as a kind of long and obscure wait, during which, we are led to believe, the order of things willed by God was not disputed. Power and hierarchy were frozen in a theoretical immutability which would have disarmed any revolt in advance, and even made any challenge to it unthinkable. Only with the crises of belief of the early modern era could a slow emancipation of minds and political criticism begin gradually to appear.

In fact, there never existed such an imaginary time in history during which the given order of things found its own immanent justification. There has never been such an age of immobility.

Besides, all the ideas current on the organisation and functioning of society may be reduced to a few propositions which had long been enunciated. Their successive formulations remained confined to the restricted domain of intellectual jousting, until the day when events came together in such a way as to confer on them a new potential.

Thus the hypothesis of a contract between sovereign and subjects was present in the medieval conception of the state, as was the idea of possible contradictions between divine and civil laws. These two notions were capable of legitimising rejections and insurrections long before the age of the Enlightenment. Of course, religion made it the normal duty of the subject to obey and, therefore, not to seek redress against the abuses of a bad monarch other than by patience and prayer. But it could happen – and the Bible and ancient history offered many instances of it – that the excesses of a monarch might exceed all bounds, going as far as to transgress openly the will of God or to ignore the obligations contained in the original contract, mythical or real. At this point, he became a tyrant. Thinkers distinguished between tyranny by oppression and tyranny by usurpation, depending on whether its perpetrator secured power by legitimate or by violent means. The theory held that the period of tolerance extended to the first should be longer. Whatever the position of the tyrant, it was taught in the Schools that tyrannicide could at times become a virtue, as the heroic examples of Judith and Brutus had shown. The right of resistance could be illustrated with quotations from Cicero and Seneca, Dante and Gerson. But the depostion or murder of a tyrant did not fail to provoke a dilemma, because of an inability to find a court to which the matter could be referred, particularly in the age of humanism, when the rediscovery of Roman law reinforced the rights of the prince.

The investigations and intellectual disputes generated by the great rift of the Reformation placed on the agenda the tragic problems of the limits of obedience and the bases of revolt. The debates moved out of the timeless orbit of the Schools and, for the generation of the 1560s and after, took on a novelty that was both terrible and direct. The old, abstract notion of tyrannicide became one of current interest, present in the mind of anyone who was interested in the course of history.

The Saint Batholomew's Massacre spurred a larged number of Protestant publicists into developing a theory of revolt. Among their works, often anonymous and disseminated throughout Protestant Europe, the *Vindiciae contra tyrannos,* published in 1579, was the most widely distributed. In it, the prince as an individual is distinguished from the crown. The crown is the sovereign authority of which the prince is only the embodiment. Once the office and the person were distinguished from each other, it was possible to argue that a monarch like Charles IX, who infringed both human and divine law, had made himself unworthy of the crown. He had publicly brought about the dissociation of the criminal individual from his sacred function. Revolt against such a tyrant was thus based on religious duty as much as on political logic.

This conclusion was not to be forgotten. Its power lay in its malleability. The arguments of the *Vindiciae* were taken up by Jean Boucher, the Leaguer parish priest of St Benoît in Paris. The tyrant now was Henry III, whose murder was justified, as he was a traitor in respect of both the church and the state. *Ipso facto,* this double, fundamental treason entailed his downfall.

Another equally widely circulated, subversive treatise was the *De jure regni apud Scotos* of George Buchanan (1506–82), Calvinist tutor to James VI. He borrowed from Scotland's eventful history anecdotes about kings who were either shackled or overthrown by the assemblies of the nobility. He related how James I was assassinated in 1437, James III in 1488, that the minority of James V was a succession of rebellions and, finally, how Mary Stuart was driven from Edinburgh in 1567. The peculiar political traditions of Scotland ensured that legitimacy oscillated between royal devolution and the privileges of noble-dominated estates.

Scottish experiences were an illustration of the idea of a contract to be found at origins of the state. The institutions of Aragon provided a similar contractual competition, thereby justifying potential revolt. It was seen clearly in 1591 when the inhabitants of Saragossa and the greater part of the Aragonese nobility rose up in defence of the disgraced minister, Antonio Pérez. A French contemporary took the trouble to explain the institutional basis of the event. Palma Cayet wrote: 'The Aragonese liberated themselves from the Moors who had occupied Spain for seven centuries. After remaining for some time in this state of liberty, they desired to have a king and sought the opinion of the pope, who advised them to impose laws on him, so that they would not fall into any sort of tyranny. They made two laws, one to the effect that if the king wished to break their laws, they were to be freed from their oath to him, the other that the lords of the kingdom could form an alliance or confederation against their king in the event of oppression or of an infringement of their rights. On the king's accession to the throne, the Aragonese take an oath to him, saying, "We, who are as good as you and you as us, make you our king on condition that you preserve our privileges and liberties; if you do not, we shall be freed of our oath" – which is why it is said that the kings of Aragon are at the same time masters and servants."[1]

Old ideas of resistance to the tyrant who breaks divine laws or the contract signed with his subjects, experienced a vigorous revival during the troubles of the second half of the sixteenth century. The different conflicts arising out of the Reformation and the formation of early modern states were what occasioned this rediscovery. In the various clashes between the power of the ruler who was taken for a tyrant and the rights of his subjects, the latter were represented in the most visible political structures of the age, namely the assemblies of estates. These might be either meetings of nobles forming the noble corporate estate or alternatively conferences of magistrates in control of town councils. Corresponding to these types of assembly – which were often found together in most kingdoms – were two socio-institutional objectives which between them dominated the political vision of early modern Europe – the noble and the city-state. Both provided subversive possibilities which could be pitted against the existing sovereign authority.

The city-state

A man's native land was nothing other than the area inhabited by his ancestors, the age-old framework in which generation had succeeded generation. It stopped at the boundaries of one's familiar environment, whether it was the village and its hamlets, or the town with its extra-mural jurisdiction. At the most, a wealthy or cultivated individual might extend such an attachment to the juridical entity or the physical unit that was the seneschalsy, the county or the province. One's native place engendered feelings of belonging and aroused forms of devotion which the still rather academic idea of the nation could not. The latter was only powerful in those states where a monarchy firmly established from time immemorial identified itself with a form of legitimacy that appeared fundamental and was derived from divine right or, to put it another way, from nature itself. In Western Europe, a small number of monarchies, such as France, England and Castile, were successful in inspiring in their subjects feelings of belonging. Everywhere else, and even within these states themselves, parish-pump patriotism had much greater vigour.

The old self-sufficient agrarian economy, the daily requirements of self-defence against external aggression, whether human or natural, the isolation which resulted from the slowness of communications and the feeble mastery of space – all conspired together to impose local solidarity. Inhabitants, even of the smallest communities or of those least disposed to mutual assistance, had necessarily to meet together in order to take decisions of common interest. They had to provide for repairs to the church or the roads, to act together in respect of dates for transhumance and grape-picking, to arrange crop-rotation and the grazing of stock, to examine possible law-breaking, to take litigation before a judge or, in case of need, to arm themselves against danger. This power enjoyed by the basic institutions of communities of inhabitants was universal, whether sanctioned by state laws or not, from Slav to Latin countries. In France, wherever a commune or municipal institution was not to be found, the humblest villagers would have their parochial assemblies and, should the need arise, elect their syndics and procurators.

When political power at the centre of the state passed into foreign hands, either through the accidents of devolution or the superior might of an invader, communal institutions were strengthened, since they appeared to be the only available recourse, and the guardians of a lost legitimacy. It was so among the Balkan communities during centuries of Turkish occupation. Throughout the Mediterranean basin, the mountainous zones with their pastoral farming villages offered places of refuge, preserving religions, languages and traditions. A customary law developed there, in which communual bonds were stronger than elsewhere. The control of the valleys, and the military and political domination of the foreign invader enabled the village cell to extend its authority to encompass functions which elsewhere were to be assumed by the central power. Such parochial autonomy, more accentuated and more enduring, was also to be found in Corsica, Sardinia and Sicily. For a long time, these regions exhibited the outdated image of modes of sociability and of belonging which had flourished at the end of the Middle Ages.

The medieval merchant cities were perfect examples of forms of communal patriotism. In a world that was very fragmented and dangerous, these havens of human intercourse, peaceful activities and relative abundance seemed models of 'good government'. They inspired the enthusiastic adherence of their citizens and inhabitants. The towns of central Italy, whose former condition has been preserved by the relative stagnation of recent centuries, display this patriotism by a kind of architectural perfection. Around the great square which opens out at the centre of the defensive site and which is the heart of the warren of neighbourhood-streets, rise the façades and porches of the church, the town hall and residences of the leading families who carved up the city's offices among themselves. Soaring towers, arcaded galleries, and balconies dominate the paved, open space of the square where crowds will gather on important days. The relatively broad and numerous oligarchies who governed them could take their seats in the enormous assembly rooms designed by architects for the splendid upper floors of the civic palaces. The heraldic emblems which signified the glory and autonomy of the city adorned the walls and many of the archways; they graced the banners which fluttered on the top of the towers. They were the guarantees and the proofs of urban liberties. The growth of the early modern centralised states produced a challenge to them that is reflected in the civil wars of the Renaissance.

Florence, the most powerful of the Italian cities, witnessed the growth of an idea of urban destiny that was unequalled – the image of a chosen city. Its most obvious manifestation was that of millenarian expectation, known as Piagnonism, preached by Savonarola. His doctrine derived its name from the Piagnona, the great bell of St Mark's which summoned the audiences of the inspired Dominican who heralded the new age. Florence, the new Jerusalem, combined virtue and fortune; it was not just the mother of cities, but the centre of the world, designated for the establishment of Christ's reign. From 1496 to 1530, this myth thrilled the inhabitants of the great Tuscan city, and only disappeared with the final and all too worldly triumph of the Medicis.

Because the 'good government' of each town became ineluctably mixed up with the causes espoused by the patrican dynasties which provided its despots and captains, city problems became soaked in the blood of factional strife. Sooner or later, the distant tutelage of Venice, Rome or Florence seemed preferable to tumult on the public square of one's native city. Subjection to one or other of these rising powers paradoxically became the real guarantee of the city's salvation. During the sixteenth century in Italy, a balance emerged between liberty and the authority of the prince.

The flight of bourgeois allegiances and of political thinking outside the circle in which they had been born, and the desire for a more distant and abstract authority were not experienced without uncertainty, hiccups and differences.

The transition from urban patriotism to loyalty to the state implied the unification of local customs and usages, which would be subsumed by centralised laws. The merchant bourgeoisies needed a juridical framework that answered to the expansion of trade routes, allowing them to know under what conditions they operated, and to make financial calculations with some security. Such unification could only occur under a sovereign authority, which would effect it by gradually replacing local customs with royal jurisprudence, by substituting Roman law for them, or even by ordering the reduction of customs to a written code. However, this vast

legal undertaking supported local particularism and the historical identity of town and region in appearance only. In reality,
it fixed once for all empircal practice, and produced both
imitation and uniformity; it confirmed the grip of the sovereign who took the initiative of ordering the codification of the
customs, sending out commissioners for the purpose, to
adjudicate on contradictory issues and to redraft the texts
themselves. Legal learning, even of a very local kind, belonged
to magistrates who, having escaped from their place of origin
by their studies, felt the pull of a career, the prestige of a court,
and understood and welcomed political power that was extensive and comprehensive. In short, the European bourgeoisies,
whether commercial or legal in origin, abandoned the service
of the city for that of the state.

The most serious outbursts of urban patriotism baulking
against the grip of the new national states were the revolts of
the communes of Castille (1520) and of Ghent (1540). The
armed revolts of the Dutch provinces or of numerous French
towns, whether Protestant or Leaguer, also belong to some
degree to this pattern.

On the death of Queen Isabella in 1504, the old and wealthy
kingdom of Castile lost its political stability. Four precarious
governments followed each other before the arrival of the
young Charles I in November 1517 from Flanders, where he
had grown up. His election as Emperor, and then his departure
for Germany in May 1520 shattered the uncertain loyalty of
the Castilians. As a consequence, the kingdom's Cortes was
obliged to vote new taxes, which were all the more scandalous
in that they were to serve to secure this alienation of the
government. The Castilian towns now took up arms against
the deputies to the Cortes who were accused of betrayal,
against the Flemish advisers of the young king, and against the
royal commissioners, who were forced to leave. The municipal
magistracies were enlarged, and their debates during the revolt
revived the style of the general assemblies of all citizens such as
had been practised during the medieval centuries. The delegates of the rebel cities formed new Estates of the Kingdom,
called the Holy Junta, or better, the Cortes and General Junta
of the Kingdom. The regularity of these assemblies, the voting
and administration of taxation by the towns, and their upkeep

of a militia – such were the means employed to bring about a return to self-government by the towns. In the name of the king, power would remain with the three traditional orders and especially with the urban patriciate composed of magistrates and notaries, merchants and master craftsmen.

But in the end, the army of the Communeros, though by no means negligible, was defeated at Villalar, on 23 April 1521, by a royal army led by grandees who had remained loyal to the emperor. It is noteworthy that the neighbouring kingdom of Aragon remained faithful to Charles; nor did the kingdom of Valencia, which was also rocked by popular disturbances, unite with the Castillian communes.

In this way, the revolt of the Communeros, in its geographical confinement and its institutional ambitions, came across clearly as the proclamation of a kingdom which wished to limit sovereignty to a federation of free cities. An exhaustive account of it would need to include the discontent of the weavers of Segovia or Toledo, whose workshops were starved of the raw wool exported to the Netherlands, and the obsession with a lost legitimacy personified by Queen Joanna the Mad, who had been dethroned and confined. However, the central consideration of the revolt of the *Communidades* was its rejection of this new state which aimed to free itself of its municipal and provincial origins, and which suddenly turned itself into a distant and foreign jurisdiction which had taken on continental dimensions.

By a remarkable symmetry, another obstacle to the establishment of Charles V's empire came from the town in which he was born, and from the province whose advancement had appeared hateful to the Castilians. Along with Italy, Flanders had been the leading medieval centre of urbanisation and economic development. Ghent, a textile metropolis housing 60,000 inhabitants inside the great 12·7 kilometre reach of its walls had, more than any other Flemish city, a troubled history that was due to the political power of the crafts which had seats on the city council [*Collace*]. For many years, the Estates of Holland and Brabant had shouldered the expense of the emperor's armies against the king of France and his allies, the duke of Guelderland and the German princes of the Schmalkaldic League. A new tax on retail wine sales brought about another revolt of the people of Ghent in 1539. 'Seeing they were masters of the city, the rebels urged other, neighbouring cities to take up arms in defence of their liberties and privileges.' But neither the governor of the Netherlands, Charles V's sister, nor his enemy, Francis I, nor the other cities of Flanders were willing to embrace their cause. The people of Ghent had thus to endure punishment for their crime of lèse-majésté. Charles V entered the town on 24 February 1540. The city as a whole was placed on trial, in accordance with Ghent law. Its privileges were revoked, its ancient charters confiscated, the town's artillery taken away, its bell brought down from its tower, the gates knocked down and the moat filled in. The power of the guilds was destroyed, and the jurisdiction of the city over its hinterland terminated. Repression of this kind affected a whole city, striking both its institutions and the movements which symbolised them. Similar examples can be found by the dozen throughout early modern Europe. They are evidence of the communal character of the crime of revolt; of the urban patrimony shared by both rebels and their judge as a point of reference; and of a legal inheritance acquired at birth and which was identified with the spires and towers that crowned the skyline of one's native city. Repression of this type marked the dismantling of the city-states, and the transition to modern centralised states founded, for the most part, on national identity.

Once again in 1577, when the Calvinists seized control of Ghent, the old municipal magistracies recovered their prerogatives, the confiscated charters re-appeared, and the guilds resumed their place on the *Collace*. Observers said that 'the people of Ghent wished to create cantons for themselves, as in Switzerland'. In truth, however, this latest municipal transformation only resurrected the appearance of the medieval city's institutions. It represented more the success of a Calvinist revolutionary party which imposed itself by open force, monopolising offices, and purging and exiling people. This was no longer just the power of the corporations and communities of the city, but that of a party whose organisation extended far beyond it.

The evolution of the northern Netherlands towards independence in the 1570s followed the same ideal of municipal patriotism. Its ultimate success represents a kind of exception to the decline of city-states when faced with centralising forces which, from Machiavelli to Bodin, were at work throughout Europe.

From 1572 to 1579, the Calvinists became masters of dozens of towns all over the Netherlands. Protestant theologians had demonstrated the validity of a right of resistance in opposition to a legitimate but oppressive government. Political theorists had begun to develop the idea of a law that arose from nature itself, that was fundamental and not contingent. However, neither religious justifications nor the belated explanations of the politicians could have secured the final adherent or the smallest triumph. Fiscal threats and military repression had sparked off the struggle; subsequently, the most common link was the programme of the prince of Orange, namely the restoration of their liberties and of the powers of the Estates General.

The Estates of Holland were dominated by municipal oligarchies; in the other, more rural provinces, the nobility enjoyed a less insignificant place. But whatever the relative political weight of the different orders, the seven provinces which formed the Union of Utrecht in January 1579 and which broke away for good from Spain, appealed to an ancient constitution, in which sovereignty was derived from municipalities elected by leading citizens, and was blended into one in a federation of towns, regions and provinces. The sessions of the Dutch Estates-General always resembled confrontations between ambassadors more than deliberations of elected deputies. It was in the name of this patrimony of local privileges that the United Provinces revolted, obtained and then preserved their independence.

During the crises of legitimacy of the wars of religion, most French towns similarly demonstrated the power of such attachments, of the entrenched character of communal institutions, and of their ability to protect, organise and administer themselves. Whether they opted for one side or the other, their behaviour evinced a genuine political, military and religious autonomy which began at the bench-marks indicating the extent of their jurisdiction. When they turned themselves into Protestant fortresses, they were doing no more than demanding in the religious sphere a communal liberty that was not disputed in law. It was a liberty which corresponded to the division of the kingdom into orders and corporate bodies, one in which local communities were held to be corporations. Royal edicts confirmed Calvinist expansion by establishing the notion of *places de sûreté*, transforming certain towns into religious islands and Protestant homelands. Such military bases illustrated the enormous possibilities for power which the concept of communal privileges and liberties still possessed at this time. Calvinism, erected as an order in the kingdom by the Edict of Nantes, was, in the temporal sphere, a federation of towns. The history of these Protestant towns during the most complete application of the Edict, between 1598 and 1629, reveals the intensity of municipal life, the sharpness of the intrigues and tension affecting local offices in which quite formidable powers were vested.

French towns were thus masters of their own destiny. For instance, in 1574, Angoulême rejected a royal order disposing of the town in order to make it a Protestant *place de sûreté*. Its inhabitants and governor closed their gates to Condé, even if they would later have to defend their behaviour when presenting apologies and when pleading their case before the parlement. More clearly than the Reformation, the Catholic League represents an alliance of towns conscious of their institutional powers and taking decisions themselves about their future. From 1585 to 1594, Leaguer Paris kept up an extensive correspondence with the towns of the Union. The authority of Paris was not confused with royal, judicial or fiscal centralism; it ensured no more than fidelity on essentials, religious identity and military solidarity. This programme was present explicitly in the official manifesto of the League, the petition of grievance of the city of Paris for the 1588 Estates General. The two key elements of municipal autonomy were underlined in it – freedom to administer communal revenues [Finances, art. 321], and free elections to communal offices [Police, art. 1]. According to the petition, they were privileges held 'from antiquity by the towns and communities of this kingdom'.

Finally, the Fronde revealed comparable relations between Paris and the cities engaged in opposition to Mazarin. Each city, protected by its ramparts and confident in its bourgeois militia and its artillery, decided to hold for one or other party in the conflict, or else to remain as far as possible free from danger and involvement. Struggles for control of the offices of the town councils reached a final fever pitch at this time, as in Angers and Paris, and in the towns of Provence or Guyenne. The Ormée party dominated Bordeaux for two years and kept it within the Condé faction, issuing its decisions in the city's name, and seeking its legitimacy in the antiquity and breadth of its legal patrimony.

In the United Provinces, that latter-day refuge of the old city-states, urban disorders could alter the Provinces' common policies, as in 1672 and 1748. In the Swiss cantons, it was the isolation of the mountains which preserved, down to our own time, the federal political structure of the cantons, in which one's native land and sovereignty itself ended at the limits of the town or region. The era of urban patriotism came to an end with the triumph of monarchical centralisation under Louis XIV. From 1660 to about 1690, their remaining political, military and fiscal prerogatives were destroyed. This institutional development was to prevent henceforth – until the short-lived Federalist movement of 1793 – any genuine localisation of political loyalties.

The noble state

Another political model – that of the state personified in the families of the nobility, and limited to their order – experienced its greatest theoretical diffusion and its greatest hopes of practical realisation during the sixteenth and seventeenth centuries. By their essential dignity and their innate capacity, nobles alone had the vocation to govern and serve the state. They were to discharge this duty in accordance with a code of honour that was the product of Christian morality and the noble way of life.

The idea of a noble state was buttressed in the second half of the sixteenth century by the development of the myth of a noble race, and of the political theory which flowed from it. The order of the world could be nothing but a reflection of heaven, admittedly marred, but which nevertheless mirrored the heavenly hierarchy. Some were therefore born to command, and others to obey. These natural qualities were hereditary, reproducing themselves from one generation to the next. A right of conquest derived from either the Trojans or the Germans was found to lie at the origin of the lineages that composed the noble race. The nobility were their decendants, free men who subjugated and protected the conquered peoples, from whom the other orders of society were descended. This idea of a noble race as the upper layer in a ranking of mankind ordained by nature, found its most coherent expression at the precise moment when, around 1560, in several European countries, though in different time-scales and contexts, changes within society slowed down, and social groups tended to take shape and harden.

Even in this period of reduced mobility, accidents of war and the other misfortunes of the times ensured that destinies would vary. Noble lineages died out or disappeared owing to the destruction of their property, the absence of sons or death in combat. At the same time, parvenus and favourites got hold of their fortune and entered their ranks. Such set-backs and usurpations proved to be all the more scandalous in that they were relatively infrequent. They seemed to disturb the natural hierarchy; it thus became a duty to rise in revolt against them in order to defend the rights of a violated justice and of an outraged nobility, in order to restore subverted honour and the necessary harmony of the world. As Laurens de Laville wrote in 1633, 'there is nothing else that is capable of tolerating the intermingling of men than the degree of honour that is greater in some than in others, with each in his estate according to what he is; if this is removed, society is rendered impossible'. Assemblies of nobles, conspiracies, plots and alliances set themselves as their objective the preservation and restoration of an order unceasingly threatened by the misfortunes of history and the evil of men. The *Conspiracy of Fiesque*, written by Retz in 1639 and published in 1655, was the account of an unsuccessful revolution in Genoa in 1547, and relates the efforts of its hero to recover for himself and his family the rank in their city of which they had been unjustly deprived. The literary reputation enjoyed by this story of political frustration testifies to the audience there was for such an ideological theme. The manifestos drafted during every subversive resort to arms expressed the resentment of those who, suppossedly born to lead and conquer, found themselves reduced to obscurity, poverty and humiliation.

The development during the seventeenth century of another social model in which individuals were no longer ranked according to their innate virtues, but according to the services, functions, responsibilities and offices they filled, exacerbated this central anxiety inherent in the western noble ideal. On top of that, dynastic accidents led to royal minorities. Long interludes of this kind opened the door to the dissatisfactions of those nobles who on every such occasion believed they had the opportunity to resume their ancestral role of the king's born counsellors and of protectors of his subjects in the provinces and the countryside. With or without orders from the provincial government, the nobility mounted their horses and rode off to meet in assemblies. Meetings were arranged in forest-clearings or in some out of the way castle in order to discuss the means of saving the state and restoring the nobility.

The most famous families of the great provincial barons, dukes and peers, or princes of the blood, possessed above all others, the right and calling to direct these noble assemblies. This was why the prestige of the *grand* Condé won hands down against the dismal reputation of Mazarin, a foreign-born minister who claimed to exercise supreme authority in the name of the child-king, Louis XIV.

During 1650 and 1651, a large section of the French nobility joined the army of the rebel princes. The provinces whose nobility remained loyal to the court party were those whose governors had been clients of Richelieu and, later, of Mazarin. A governor could bring into play his personal authority, which was in turn based on traditional prestige, and on his network of kinship and family clientship. Weariness brought on by the ravages of war and the proclamation of Louis XIV's majority finally triumphed over the Fronde of the nobility.

But in 1715 again, the devolution of the throne appeared unsure. Had the young and sickly Louis XV died, the crown would have fallen to a discredited Regent, to the king of Spain or to a legitimised royal bastard. One current of noble opinion, of which Saint Simon has been the witness for posterity, once again believed that it could identify itself with the nation and lay claim to the mythical role of the magnates who, once upon a time, elected the king or came to offer him their counsel in the assemblies of March and May.

These specifically political and military vicissitudes were peculiar to France, where the rule of *dérogeance* excluded working for profit, and more or less limited the financial base of the nobility to rents from land alone. In states where there was no such statutory limitation to prevent direct involvement by the nobility in production and trade, an added economic factor played a part in the historical rivalry between the noble state and the centralised state. This was the position in many of the lands of the Vienna and Madrid Habsburgs, whose dependencies were to be found all over the continent. Moreover, in them noble power was strengthened by national identity, while centralisation was personified by foreign dynasties. The power for subversion of the nobility there was all the greater in that the centralising alternative appeared as an intrusion from outside.

The total involvement of the nobility in an act of rebellion led to secession. In between such an upheaval and support for demands that were more or less strongly felt, there was room for changing sides, negotiation and compromises. Some nobles might hesitate between indignation at royal abuses and, on the other hand, the fear of civil war and suspicion of the excesses of mobs. Thus, the barons of the Netherlands sounded the alarm of discontent, while being ready to rally to Margaret of Parma when faced with the excesses of uncontrolled iconoclasm in 1566. It then took five years of repression under the duke of Alba in order to bind the nobility finally to the party of the prince of Orange in 1572. The transition to popular violence, far from strengthening a cause, threatened to discredit it, while only mobilisation under arms of the nobility proved to be the decisive factor in the outcome of events.

The Habsburgs had to purchase the loyalty of their marginal nobilities by endlessly granting them more and more powers. Royal prerogatives were broken up, offices and dignities were distributed to them, while the theatres of operations of the Spanish and imperial armies provided them with careers as commanders throughout the whole of Europe. Thus, in the kingdom of Naples, the anti-fiscal urban revolt of 1647 admittedly revealed some anti-Spanish feelings among the nobility. But the viceroys had been successful in distributing favours, titles and power to them; their policy had fixed the nobility's grip on the provinces beyond the point of no return. Consequently, the barons of the kingdom of Naples had for the most part nothing to gain from open revolt; continuing loyalty ensured, in the final analysis, the triumph of Spanish arms.

By way of a general résumé of the dilemmas faced by nobilities that were divided between attachment to a foreign dynasty of the centralising kind and, on the other hand, the defence of national legal traditions which guaranteed noble power, we may take the case of Sardinia, the poorest and most marginal of Spain's dominions. For four centuries, this small and impoverished kingdom remained subject to its Aragonese viceroys. The feudal powers that existed in an island which was mountainous, difficult to reach and cross, with no towns or ports, and confined to pastoral farming, left very little scope for Madrid's representatives, the viceroy and the royal tribunal, the *audiencia*. Subjection to Spain was demonstrated by the Sardinian parliament's vote of an annual 'gift', the *donativo,* and of taxes devoted to the upkeep of the coastal watch-towers and a flotilla of galleys. This limited fiscality was based on the revenues derived from the export of sheep belonging to the barons. The island was also a reservoir of men, whose recruitment was organised by the younger sons of seigneurial families.

From Philip II onwards, the absolutist model provided a rather timid alternative to baronial power. Slowly, the viceroys succeeded in extending their fiscal, jurisdictional and military powers. They curbed the powers of the Parliament which the barons controlled, and authorised vassal communities to present their grievances directly to them. The revolts which shook Spain's peripheral domains in the 1640s did not affect Sardinia.

Only in 1663 did the Parliament try to take advantage of the War of Devolution with Louis XIV, revealing clearly Madrid's weakness, first by lowering and then by refusing the annual *donativo.* The viceroy, the marquis of Camarassa, felt he could dismiss the deputies on 28 May 1668 by shutting himself up in the citadel, but he was assassinated on 21 July. The Sardinian barons believed that the Spaniards, bogged down in the Flanders and Franche-Comté campaigns, would be in no position to react. But in fact, at the end of the year, a new viceroy arrived, backed by armed force; he exiled certain people and won over others, and seized by guile nobles who had been compromised in the conspiracy. Their leader, the marquis of Ceda, was beheaded at Cagliari on 15 June 1571.

This isolated and unsuccessful attempt by the Sardinian nobility to influence the destiny of their island kingdom contains two lessons, one military, the other economic. As in most revolts, the stakes were part of the European diplomatic chessboard. In its cause (fiscal), its timing (coinciding with a major conflict), and its outcome (dependence on foreign assistance or abstention), the revolt was tied to a set of factors that were continental in scale, and of which the rebels were not masters. All of those nobilities engaged in conspiracies or insurrections had to seek external support, on which their success or failure depended. Examples of this, drawn from British, Dutch, French or Spanish history, could be easily multiplied.

Above all, the exclusion of the Sardinian nobility from the major political decisions had as its explanation – or rather as its *quid pro quo* – the complete economic hegemony of the barons, who were masters of the island's assets, lands and herds.

The monarchies of eastern Europe illustrate these same conclusions. There the crown had generally remained elective, without the establishment of a law of succession or the historical affirmation of a national dynasty ever allowing for a personification of central power and its regular transmission over generations. In the Diets, the nobilities acquired very extensive political, military and fiscal privileges, and in order to secure military support in the unending struggle with the Turks, or their backing in an assembly or in a succession crisis, monarchs distributed pensions and dignities, villages and lands. The growth of the powers of noble Diets enabled them to impose on sovereigns at their coronation, sworn capitulations which worsened the surrender and disemberment of an already precarious central authority. They were in a position to make considerable demands of sovereigns who might be distant strangers, like the Viennese Habsburgs, kings of Bohemia, Hungary and Croatia, or of monarchs who owed their crown to noble factions, like the kings of Poland or the rulers of the Roumanian principalities. The Diets also imposed the measures necessary to ensure the seigneurs' control of peasant labour. The nobles' jurisdictional and administrative privileges made them truly sovereign within the confines of their estates. At the beginning of the sixteenth century, the Polish crown was excluded from jurisdiction over disputes between lords and tenants. At the same time, appeals from seigneurial to crown courts were discontinued in Bohemia and Hungary. The seigneur kept to himself all the functions of authority: he was judge, military leader, collector of taxes, jailer and even patron of the parish.

This transfer of sovereignty went to great lengths in eastern Europe. It was the product of a legal system unfamiliar with Roman law. It was speeded up by the economic and military imbalance that arose from the Ottoman grip on south-eastern Europe, which blocked the ancient trade-routes towards the Black Sea, and imposed continuous warfare over several centuries. Every effort made by the sovereign state to reduce the freedom of action of the Diets or to encroach on local liberties, whether by imposing religious unity or a centralised fiscal system, came up against conspiracy and armed revolt. The national revolts of Bohemia (1618) and of Hungary (1702) had their base in the nobility. The governments they would have established, had they been successful, would have been noble oligarchies, since they embodied resistance to the progressive absolutism of Vienna.

The model of the noble state fell apart earlier in western Europe, where the oblivion that fell on it corresponded to the coming of modern states based on other values and other social groups. The French and Spanish monarchies relied on families from the educated bourgeoisie, which soon became an office-holding nobility. These families identified themselves with the service of the state; they built up their fortunes for, and through such service. Subsequently, the nobility, dispossessed of its political role, was itself profoundly altered in character. It was no longer exclusively a landed and military nobility, among whom recognition was customarily founded on common assent. Henceforth, it was to include a nobility that owed its political strength, its upward ascent and its growth to its responsibilities, functions and offices. The French monarchy asserted that nobility was nothing without the king, and that it could not oppose him, since it did not exist independently of him. That being so, it was identical with service to the monarchy, and could no longer constitute an alternative to centralised government.

It should be added that from the early, uncertain steps of the centralised state, the social group that its servants, its legists and legal practitioners constituted – however limited in size – was a necessary antagonist of noble power. Such conflicts were particularly sharp in the Empire between the political servants at Vienna, and the nobilities of the states subject to Habsburg family authority or, as in the kingdom of Naples, between the jurists of the capital and the barons of the provinces. In France, this opposition between the office-holders and the old nobles was clearly expressed at the Estates-General of 1614 and during certain episodes of the Fronde. A long political tradition handed down by the orators and historians of republican Rome was kept alive at a later date by the power struggles of the Italian communes which pitted town families against local nobles. Machiavelli was its most celebrated spokesman: 'Those republics which have preserved their political existence uncorrupted do not permit any of their citizens to be or to live in the manner of gentlemen . . . if by chance any of them fall into their hands, they kill them, as being the chief promoters of all corruption and troubles. And to explain more clearly what is meant by the term gentlemen, I say that those are called gentlemen who live idly by the proceeds of their extensive possessions.'[2] For Machiavelli, this reference to a city republic was not to be identified with the political agitations of his time; in fact, it implied that true nobility resided in the dignity of the urban patriciate. Of course, this anti-noble polemic would not fail to awaken echoes across a wide range of both social and political formations; by the eighteenth-century, it would lead to an unambiguous detestation of 'feudalism'.

Political equality

During the early modern period, ancient and medieval cosmogony slowly lost its powers of conviction. History was no longer the uninterrupted and necessary unfolding of a divine plan – or, at least, accidents, setbacks and upheavals could, in the minds of men, completely erase it. Bodin in 1566 and Louis Le Roy in 1575 asserted that it was the role of the historian to record such transformations. The chronicle of events became rather bumpy, and the range of possibilities broadened enormously. These fluctuations in the destinies of states were accompanied by, and found room for social upheavals. In turn, the notion of intangible social hierarchies began to waver. Men had believed that the arrangement of the stars in the sky and of everything on earth expressed the design of the Creator; even the apparent disorder of human activities was found to correspond to such a disposition. Thus, some men were made to command and others to obey, joining hands in the Great Chain of Being. Any desire to invert their order would have been tantamount to overturning nature's own edifice. To pour abuse on the popular Catholic uprising of the Pilgrimage of Grace [1536], one of Thomas Cromwell's pamphleteers wrote ironically of the absurdity of the rebellion: 'Would it not be foolish and unheard of for a foot to say it wanted to wear a hat just as the head does or for a knee to say it wanted to have eyes, or some such caprice'. Taking up this metaphor of the body, the lieutenant general of the Cahors *présidial* court condemned the Croquants in 1594 and imagined what would happen if the members of the human body were to rebel against the stomach and refuse to feed it. Similarly, revolt by peasants was in contradiction with social harmony, inevitably provoking general and suicidal disaster. One could no more alter this hierarchy than one could the harmony of the stars in the sky, since it was all the work of God. 'It is therefore meet that everyone should remain content with his destiny and condition.'

Such imperturbable hierarchies were no longer possible as a frame of reference. As new and more powerful telescopes revealed unknown arrangements in the heavens and superseded the older hierarchies of the universe which were now reduced to the level of mythology, so the human stage could escape from ancient constraints. The abandonment of such cosmic conventions entailed, via belief in the unity of the universe, reasoning by analogy and an enduring anthropomorphism, a re-examination of human affairs. It was no longer thought that ranks or merit were eternal and transmitted by blood; it was realised that social status was not exclusively derived from birth, but also from the standards set by ancestors, and even from education and the instruction given to young people. At the same time, accounts of travel and the record of discoveries made throughout the world were popularised and multiplied. They showed that principles and ethics varied around the world; as yet the social and political models of Europe had not become those of minority or charged with guilt, but their relative position in the world was better understood.

If theories of the untouchable character of the social order were waning, the situations which they had sustained did not disappear so easily. It was first necessary to replace ancient knowledge by another, coherent system capable of satisfying the need for a universal logic and of mastering the flowering of disparate kinds of knowledge as well as the free and extravagant curiosity that were so characteristic of the late sixteenth century.

A Bacon or a Descartes would establish the autonomy of scientific thought, and about fifty years later Newton would develop a cosmogony based on reason and observation. The swift and extensive appeal of their propositions was evidence of their representativeness and their historical timeliness. Their successors and disciples henceforth possessed the conceptual tools that enabled them to claim a knowledge and, later, the mastery of nature. They were convinced that the universe had laws which could be discovered. They believed that science could open the way for technology; therefore, that man had a purchase on things, and could direct his own destiny. Progress became possible, even certain. As previously, these conclusions moved without difficulty from the physical to the political world, which in turn took on board this same arrogant optimism. If one had faith in progress, one could no longer doubt that human institutions could always strive towards perfection, and that this perfection would be capable of changing humanity. Invention became both possible and necessary. As a political driving force, it replaced the old objectives of restoration and substitution. Violence was no longer to be conceived in terms of renovation and revolt, but of innovation and revolution.

Happiness now entered the realm of the possible, and was synonymous with the ideal order of society. Utopian works could flourish, reflecting the idea of progress and the metaphor of enlightenment scattering the gloom of ignorance and fear that had hitherto prevented man from becoming master of his fate. Utopia was no longer situated on a miraculous island or in some forgotten past, but was here and now. Utopia (nowhere) became Uchronia (no time); it was no longer an improbable universe, but a kind of speculation on history to come, and a reasonable projection of it. Its practical realisation only depended on the coming of a philosopher-king and the maturing of the minds of his enlightened subjects.

From Hobbes to Montesquieu, the political philosophers who found themselves part of this change revived the old notion of a law of nature above all positive laws in force in different places. This idea of natural law was completed in the seventeenth century by the hypothesis of a social contract to be found at the beginnings of history, by virtue of which individuals in unison symbolically renounced their rights as contained in nature or reason, the better to establish a government, be it princely or popular in character. To say that all society was the consequence of this original contract amounted to declaring that no institution was willed by God or by the order of nature, but was merely human and contingent. The revolutions of the Enlightenment were by the same token justified. The principles of natural law did not have to be established: they had merely to be acknowledged and *declared* as so many self-evident, timeless truths. It was in this spirit that the Declarations of Rights were drafted, first by the colonists of Virginia in revolt against England in 1776, and then by the French Constituent Assembly in 1789.

Happiness was within reach, and it implied a particular political model. A nation or a people was possessed of a fundamental sovereignty. All power flowed from their act of delegation, otherwise it was pure usurpation; all power necessarily required a form of supervision exercised through representatives. The working out of these postulates was spread over several decades and expressed by several treatises, among which the *Spirit of the Laws,* published in 1749, constituted the *chef d'oeuvre.* They were reinforced by other contemporary factors – a religious crisis and demographic change.

Events in France, the most populated and powerful state in Europe, were decisive, or at least exemplary, in this intellectual conjuncture. The Revocation of the Edict of Nantes in 1685 was followed by the dispersion of thousands of Protestant exiles throughout northern and eastern Europe. The reverberations of this exile and the polemical activities of some of the *émigrés* became the ferment of propaganda that was hostile to the systems of thought and government that obtained in Louis XIV's France. The scandal of this persecution was to be orchestrated for a long time by the Protestant powers, until it became a commonplace that unsettled even the most loyal supporters of the power of divine right.

In 1713, the publication of the bull *Unigenitus* condemning Jansenism sealed the alliance between gallican magistrates and Jansenist clergy in France. Their dominance in the parishes and the courts of justice, in the seminaries and the parlements, represented a rejection of absolute authority, whether it was the doctrinal authority of the pope in opposition to the body of the faithful, or that of the sovereign in opposition to the community of the nation. The unwritten constitution of the French monarchy, which made the latter mystical and personal, was now a subject of controversy in the opinions and minds of contemporaries. Throughout the eighteenth century, the writings of clergy and jurists evolved in this sense. At one extreme of this trend, we find a barrister called Gabriel-Nicolas Maultrot who published his *Origine et étendue de la puissance royale suivant les Livres saints et la tradition* on the eve of the decisive break that was 1789. Behind this ambiguous title, he presented an explicit refutation of the bases of absolutism in the name of a specifically religious analysis that was clearly Jansenist in its argument. Thus, through a line of writing that spanned the centuries, the doctrines of the *philosopes* were connected to the religious disputes and events of the reign of Louis XIV.

The revolutions were also the product of demographic trends. Eighteenth-century Europe experienced population growth, owing to both increased life-expectancy, with the disappearance of the great death-dealing epidemics – the last outburst of plague in the west was in Marseilles, in 1720 – and the reduction over several decades of the climatic and harvest catastrophes which, as in 1693 and 1709, ravaged entire regions. In every era, the coming of age of a great mass of young people signifies a divorce from the inheritance of their parents, which undoubtedly occurred around 1750–1760.

These more populous generations were also more educated, although that may be coincidence rather than consequence. The different rates of growth in the human numbers and of improvements in their education varied considerably, and only detailed research would enable us to compare their successive stages. Literacy and schooling followed a gradual development that began in the sixteenth century. Such advances corresponded to the need to read the Bible in Protestant countries, and that of familiarity with the catechism in Catholic ones and, secondarily, to the needs of trade and of urban life. When education spread, ideas that benefited from the passionate enthusiasm of newcomers assumed a wholly new power.

The decisive generation was the one which inherited both responsibility and the realm of thought just after the Seven Years' War. This major conflict broke up both European and world equilibriums, and questioned existing political and diplomatic hierarchies. Above all, it permanently shattered state budgets and confronted them with the necessity of structural reforms.

The new generation of public men liked to meet together in the *sociétés de pensée* (assemblies of intellectuals where current ideas were discussed) which spread across Europe at this time. Initially, their form and their models were none other than the venerable learned academies which, since the time of humanism, made up the 'republic of letters', consisting of a network of correspondence and friendship among international scholars. In a matter of a few years, these cultivated

clubs, which were popularised and multiplied to an extraordinary extent, became social circles of which men wished to
be members in order to be seen, to succeed and get on, but also
to debate, fight, learn and belong. These societies grouped
their members around 'philosophy', bringing them together
not out of simple social affinity, but out of ideological community. The societies established themselves as instruments in
shaping public opinion; in certain critical situations, they even
became effective pressure groups, the vigour of which would
be seen in 1788 and 1789.

The societies studied laws and agriculture; they cultivated
liberty and patriotism. The crises of price-inflation that occurred in the 1760s and 1770s increased the interest of the notables in these societies dedicated to improvement and to a
common good, the terms of which and the models for which
were contested by scarcely anyone. Later counter-revolutionary writers most of the time offered only refutations of
them, not competing proposals of their own. The new ideas
propagated by the societies were accepted even in the offices of
ministers and the antechambers of courts.

In Italy, for example, the *sociétés de pensée* movement
reached its apogee in the club and journal founded in Milan in
1764 under the name of *Il Caffè,* from the name of the bitter
but stimulating drink then in fashion at meeting-places. This
tribune brought together young men whose history is significant. What they had in common was their precocious age and
membership of the leading families of the Milanese oligarchy.
They had begun to breathe the air of their time as they
marched across Europe under arms in the recent war, or
during educational journeys – which were traditionally
reserved for sons of good families – to the universities or other
countries of Europe, which they discovered around the age of
twenty. They were united by their individual revolts against
paternal tyranny, their intellectual dissatisfaction, and their
avid welcome of political novelties emanating from France or
England. Such was the early career of Cesare Beccaria and
Pietro Verri. The latter, whose father had argued in defence of
Milan's liberties against the reforming centralism of Vienna,
would, on the contrary, become the encomiast and protago-
nist of the philsopher-emperor's interventionism. In fact, these

terrible young men of the 1760s were anything but over-looked. No sooner were they listened to and admired, than they were propelled into becoming agents or originators of currents of reform which were to begin to work in most states.

In this same critical period following the end of the Seven Years' War, we find a growing restlessness in the English colonies of North America. The idea of autonomy developed there within an educated commercial bourgeoise which, as in Europe, had its universities, newspapers, clubs and *sociétés de pensée*. The same ideas of natural law, innate liberty and the necessary consent of subjects, were discussed. The colonists had learned English common law, which postulated the supremacy of law and the submission of all authorities, even the king's, to its rules. Disseminated and celebrated by Edward Coke at the beginning of the seventeenth century, the common law was something which every Englishman possessed from birth. By its antiquity and rational nature, it was identified with natural law itself. Under the Stuarts, it was seen as the rampart of English liberties against absolutism. In the New World, it was strengthened by the scriptural inspiration of the Puritan pioneers, as well as by an empiricism dictated by conditions in the colonies. The political concept of a contract was religious in origin; it was the covenant between God and his creature before becoming the contract between the sover-eign and his people. During the eighteenth century, the colo-nists, who were by now town-dwelling bourgeois, no longer saw themselves as chosen saints of God, but simply the citizens of a free country, and free of fiscal demands that were held to be unwarranted. Thus, the idea of a fundamental contract or covenant which stipulated protection from the king and obedience from the people, became subversive, as it had been among the rebels of the sixteenth century. Since the protector had turned into a tyrant, the subject was entitled to be unfaithful.

The American model of ideological fermentation, as of its powerful and rapid diffusion, was an inspiration to revolu-tionary France. The years of Louis XVI's reign and of the revolutionary assemblies witnessed the multiplication of newspapers and, especially, of the numbers of their subs-cribers, which rose from hundreds to thousands. Some newsheets had as many as ten or twenty thousand subscribers, where English papers did not have more than 3,000 readers. A French publicist of 1790 took his cue from Frankein's *Poor Richard's Almanach*: 'For twenty years before he founded the liberty Americans enjoy, Franklin nourished their reason. He was a printer who wished to become a journalist; and who, like us, but no doubt better than us, published village newsheets'. Such was the first number of the *Feuille villageoise* which, from September 1790 to August 1795, attempted to be the schoolmaster of revolution to rural France.

From the outset, the revolutionary period demonstrated the power of factors like opinion and communication. The evidence of the petitions of grievance drafted in the spring of 1789 provides the most splendid image of an explosion in political communication. The drafting of the petitions was, of course, directed by the notables who, down to village level in the countryside, had been able to steep themselves in the dominant vocabulary and ideas. Many of them were subscribers to newspapers, or at least to the *Mercure de France*. In the towns, they were members of the *sociétés de pensée*, or even of the Masonic lodges. These 'enlightened' bourgeois were led, by their business activities, their acquaintances and their family connections, to correspond with each other. The offshoots of philosophical societies wove together forms of solidarity that extended beyond their districts or provinces. Municipalities had the very old custom of exchanging information, recommendations and directives. It is therefore easy to account for the uniformity of demands, repetitions of language and identities of expression in the petitions. The received ideology of the middling bourgeoisie, whether urban or rural, flowed without hindrance through the mass of petitions. A coherent theory and language emerges from even the clumsiness of the most rural of such documents – namely the vocation of the deputies elected to personify the nation as a whole and, consequently, the elimination of a social and political order arranged in orders and corporations, and the establishment of an egalitarianism among citizens who are the source of power and conscious of it. The current weakness of the state and the successive climb-downs by Louis XVI from the summer of 1788 onwards gave these numerous and convergent authors both the hope and the illusion of a new beginning. They had the impression of being present at a new dawn, and the will to cast into the oblivion of night what had gone before. To make a revolution, in the sense that political scientists understand it, was to believe one was breaking completely with the past and putting one's faith in a new era. It is, in any event, tautology to accept that events correspond to our definitions of them, since the definition itself derives from the event.

In other European countries, the same ideological ferments brought about political unrest of a localised kind in Geneva in 1782, in the Netherlands in 1786, and at Liège in 1789. They were prolonged by the favourable reception given to French innovations in most educated circles. These initial successes, limited by the uneven development of the different bourgeoisies and then compromised by the military imperialism of the French revolutionaries, were evidence of the subversive dynamic of the Enlightenment when extended to the whole western world. Moreover, the importance of ideological factors in the great crises of the late eighteeth century, and the role of the societies, lodges and journals in their expansion, have long been recognised. Historians of the French Revolution have emphasised them either in order to praise the generosity and enthusiasm of these cultivated groups, or to denounce the spectre of conspiracy in the activities of a small, minority elite well versed in the arts of dissimulation and propaganda. Both views carried the same grain of truth, in that they recognised the orginality of their action, and identified new forms of political sociability.

3 Leaders

The history of political violence enables one to distinguish the role of agitator – what sociologists call action leadership – from that of the instigator of change – opinion leadership. The former are the acknowledged ring-leaders on riot days, leaders of rebellion, agitators who capture the attention and the devotion of the crowd, those who can sway an audience, command a group of soldiers, or lead an assault. Since they are made famous by their victory or their punishment, such leaders may well appear as exceptional individuals to us, but it would be risky to identify any particular social group because of that. It is tempting to say that their personal characteristics – aggressiveness or eloquence, extroversion or paranoia – determine their role. It would be of greater value to historians if they could uncover these personality traits and speculate on how they took shape. Unfortunately, the historian does not have available to him the sources needed to get to the core of psychologies and destinies. We must therefore be content, rather more prosaically and superficially, to describe those social groups which, owing to their position and functions, seem for the most part to have produced such personalities. After those made famous by their leadership and involvement in the short-lived moment of action, the category of instigators of change would comprise those who invent or, more modestly, those who introduce innovations, who educate and inform, who arouse and transform. Since change and variation are part of the very nature of history, all exercise of power implies a small measure of innovation and adventure. It would thus be necessary to list at the top of this category, governing groups, sovereigns, their ministers and councillors. Having stated this initial truth, we must then approach social entities that are more obscure, but no less effective, whose actors are cultural mediators. Their influence, necessarily slow and lacking in glamour, may nevertheless be viewed as more fertile in results than the convulsions we encounter in mere political events.

Troublemakers

The traditional cadres of early modern society – the lord, the parish priest or the mayor – are often to be found at the head of revolts.

The lord

For several centuries throughout western Europe, lords were accompanied on all occasions by dozens, even hundreds of men under arms, whether it be for war, the hunt, or a dispute over an inheritance. These bands were composed of subjects, like servants or tenants, and followers, like relatives, men bound to them or friends. Raising men in this way might be obligatory and closely tied in with service to the sovereign, or it might be illegal when, for example, it involved private wars or revolts in open defiance of royal orders. The way in which subjects were attached to an immediate lord, and followed him out of personal enthusiasm, or through compulsion if necessary, is common knowledge. In the religious divisions of the sixteenth century, whole regions went over to the Reformation because their lord had opted for the new religion. A more extreme example is that of the Catholic peasantry of the Turenne lands who served in the Calvinist regiments raised by their viscount. Shouting the feudal family's name, tenants banded together and rushed to take up arms. This traditional war-cry could on occasion bring fighting men together in spite of their lords' true wishes, for the loyalty of subjects was emblematic and not necessarily to the person holding the title. On 26th June 1703, in the streets of Naples, the valets of the duke of Monteleone freed a debtor-prisoner. In support of them, a crowd of 4,000 persons pushed back the *sbires* with shouts of 'Viva Monteleone', although the duke himself, in order to halt this untimely triumph, was obliged to turn himself over as a prisoner.

With the development of the idea of reason of state, the bond of military loyalty binding subjects to their lord, would come to appear ambiguous. Giovanni Botero wrote in 1589: 'There is both good and bad in the feudal lords of a kingdom. The bad thing is their authority and power, which are suspect to the supreme ruler as presenting possible sources of aid or

refuge to any rebels against his authority. . . . The good con-
sists in this, that these lords are, as it were, the bones and the
strength of the state. . . . Kingdoms that have a numerous
nobility seem to be almost immortal . . . for France had passed
almost entirely under the rule of the kings of England, yet she
recovered through the infinite strength of her nobles.'[1] To
illustrate this danger, Botero quoted the example of the great
Neapolitan feudataries of the sixteenth century, some of
whom brought their domains over the side of France, and
others to Spain, and also of the French dukes and princes who,
having held a provincial governorship for generations, could
count on so many supporters there that locally they rivalled
obedience to the king.

Military service owed to the lord was of unequal duration,
and two factors, which often went together, helped to eliminate it – the strengthening of royal authority and the disappearance of age-old and ever-present forms of insecurity. In
Elizabethan England, the military value of fiefs was already
quite clearly fading. When the Percys of Northumberland rose
in 1569 in defence of Catholicism, they could only raise a
hundred men from their estates, while the musters of the 1530s
show a figure of 2,000. Most of the soldiers of the 1569 revolt
received a promise of wages. Likewise in the English civil war
after 1642, if the regiments recruited by the different parties
were often actually supporting the cause of a leading figure,
this fidelity, which might account for their recruitment, did not
suffice to keep them in the field; all were duly paid wages.
Loyalty to a lord might not survive a prolongation of hostilities or an excessive clash with peasant interests. Thus in the
kingdom of Naples, during its revolt against Spain in 1647, the
troops brought from Calabria by the barons who had
remained loyal, lost many of their number through desertion
as soon as they arrived in Campania and came into contact
with the rebels. During the Fronde in France, the bonds of
fidelity were still fully operative, and the subjects of this or that
lord might be supporters of Condé or Mazarin, depending
where there lord's allegiance lay.

The termination of the civil wars in France under Louis XIV
and the establishment of standing armies throughout Europe,
spelled the end, not of the political power of the nobility, but at

least of their military independence. The French nobility was now restricted to military service to the king, in an army which was heavily dependent for its organisation and strategy on the services of the War Ministry. The close watch kept on them by Louis XIV and his ministers was, moreover, only part of their huge political effort to destroy once for all the traditional local loyalties that had centred around the nobility. The most extreme case of the weeding out of such loyalties, and of hostility to the centrifugal power of the territorial nobility is provided by the Russian autocracy. The system of 'reserved' lands (*oprichnina*) established by Ivan the Terrible after 1565 consisted of settling 'creatures' of the tsar, the opritchniks, on the hereditary estates of the landowners of Muscovy, and either massacring the landowners themselves or settling them on distant estates in frontier regions. Periodic changes in the roll of magnates taking part in politics as well as confiscations of estates were used as stratagems of government until the statute of 1762 brought the Russian nobility into line with western models.

The military calling was common to all Europe's nobility; it was their most visible and enduring characteristic. It was a function which ensured the continuation of the loyalty of their subjects and tenants, through the methods by which regiments were recruited. The young noble who had received a commission as an officer found more easily on his lands the volunteers who would compose his company. In this way, seigneurial bonds still survived into the armies of the eighteenth century.

One might imagine that the political prestige of the nobility impressed only the peasantry, who were their subjects in law. In medieval Italy, which was heavily urbanised from an early date, the bonds of lineage and clientship which formed around powerful families fuelled the factional strife and civil wars of the fifteenth and sixteenth centuries. These groupings were etched on to the urban map, which bristled with towers and palaces, veritable neighbourhood fortresses. They extended beyond the walls into the *contado* and the walled burghs (*castelli*) of the mountains. The growth of the Papal States during the sixteenth century at the expense of the urban despots of central Italy, illustrates the antagonism between the aristocracies and the rising centralised states that were encroaching on them. The involvement of nobles in the brigand bands of the sixteenth and seventeenth centuries, which was by no means uncommon, has its roots in these circumstances.

The parish priest

The ascendancy of the parish priest over his parishioners often had the effect of placing him at the head of a revolt, either as its instigator or even as its leader. No doubt, the most memorable instance of this is the Vendée wars, where differing historiographical traditions have taken pleasure either in denouncing the fanaticism of the clergy or in exalting their heroism. If the religious persecution of the Revolution effectively helped to rally the peasants of lower Poitou behind the 'masters' of their villages, the peculiar social functions of the hedgerow priest account more satisfactorily for the exceptional prestige of the clergy in the western provinces.[2] Where people lived in isolation behind hedgerows, a priest travelling from farm to farm was not merely a spiritual adviser, but also a tutor and a counsellor, the most educated and experienced man of the area, the best informed and most capable of speaking on behalf of his community. On Sundays, people came from all corners of the parish to attend mass, to meet, to see and to learn. In other regions of isolated settlement, in forest and mountain areas, we find the priest enjoying the same prestige. Throughout the valleys of the Pyrenees, the villages took up arms at the sound of the alarm, with the priest as their leader. For example, the parishes of the Val d'Aran fell in behind their parish priest in 1642 in their refusal to pay taxes to the king of France. The mountain folk of Soule rose up in 1661 at the summons of Goyhénèche, parish priest of Moncayolle. In the great revolts of Catalonia and Aragon the clergy frequently played a leading role. Thus, in Aragon in 1706, the riots which spread from towns to villages, acclaimed the Habsburg claimant, Charles III, and drove out both the French and the Castilians. The archbishop of Saragossa, who remained loyal to Philip V, denounced his clergy whom he saw as responsible for the rebellion. 'The origin and cause of the sedition in this kingdom', he wrote, 'stem from the monks and clergy, and especially the village priests who are the sole guides of their flocks.'

The Counter-Reformation seminaries, by turning out men who were more educated and worthy, generally reinforced the traditional role of the priest in the community. For many kinds of peasant, the entry of a son into the clergy represented a highly desirable social advancement. The clergy of the parish, being themselves of local origin, took part in local life and could easily come to hold a decisive position in their village. They were tailor-made spokesmen for their parishioners who could articulate their grievances. Royal ordinances acknowledged this dependability of the priest, entrusted to him the dissemination via the pulpit on Sundays of official decrees, and regarded him as the most credible and best informed witness when conducting local enquiries. When the king summoned the Estates General, the drafting of grievances at parish level was often the work of the priest. Similarly, in 1636, the Croquants of the Angoumois asked the clergy to prepare petitions detailing grievances voiced by the localities involved in the revolt. Familiar with the good and bad fortune of his flock, and by his profession the observer of their tribulations, the priest could either be their law-abiding spokesman or, by the same token, a preacher of subversion. Knowing the misery and the hopes of his parishioners better than anyone else, he could establish himself as the defender – both tactical and passionate – of the interests of his community.

The simple but fiery eloquence of monks, especially those of the mendicant orders, carried the crowds with them more than once. The Dominican, Savonarola, preaching in the cloister of St Mark's in Florence, was closely attuned to the urban imperialism of his compatriots. His prophecy of a new Jerusalem to be realised here and now, was identified for a number of years (1495–1498) with the civic myths of the great Tuscan city. During the great peasants' revolt of 1514 in Hungary, three of the eight leading commanders were clerics. We know that this movement had its origin in the arming of the peasant militias for a crusade against the Turks. When the crusade collapsed, the Franciscans who had been entrusted with preaching it, remained at the head of the peasantry. The original centres of revolt were in the same places as the Observants' leading houses. Despite disavowal by their superiors, young

Franciscans, driven by a millenarian spirituality, threw themselves into the revolt. Similarly, in the Neapolitan revolution of 1647, Dominicans and Franciscans distinguished themselves by their enthusiasm in open-air sermons and in processions in which relics of the patron saints of the city were produced to give their blessing to the revolt. The Andalusian grain riots of 1652 saw preaching by poor clergy. The mayor of Tarifa resolutely accused the clergy, 'for it is they who guide the minds and souls of lay people'.

The prestige enjoyed by populist preachers was all the greater in that socio-political themes harmonised with explicitly religious ones. In the outbursts of violence which shook the Catholic towns of France during the wars of religion, leadership of the enraged crowds often fell to mendicant preachers, Carmelites or Minims, whose virulent sermons at Advent or at Lent unleashed the unrest. Similarly, the resistance of the Cévennes Protestants during the Camisard uprisings of 1702–04 was encouraged by pastors who had either remained in hiding in the area, or had returned clandestinely to their persecuted communities.

Even in Orthodox Christianity, the priest seemed to embody the personality of the parish and to be, in some way, its protector. During the great Cossack rebellions, when the rebel troops approached a village, and the inhabitants opened their gates to them, the villagers would be led by their priest bearing the sacred icons, as well as bread and salt as a sign of welcome. In the Balkan mountains, it was the Serb and Bulgar clergy who led the exodus of their flocks fleeing from the Turkish advance.

There were two limiting factors to a priest's prestige – the wealth of the clergy, which was unpopular, and his alienation from popular religion. The slow and sure accumulation of an ecclesiastical patrimony had always been a trigger for anticlericalism. Contempt or hatred of it among the lower classes and envy of it among the powerful were among the causes of the Reformation and its effortless expansion throughout Germany. Nearly three centuries later, the success of the dechristianisation policy of the revolutionary assemblies in different regions can be traced to similar causes.

There was another way in which a priest might become an

embarrassment to his community and an outcast, and this was through demands, which we see for the first time in the six-teenth century, for a more intellectual and interiorised religion. One result of this was that the clergy came to mistrust traditional manifestations of popular religion. These currents of clerical reform, of which eighteenth-century Jansenism and the purism of our own time are the most aggressive varieties, gave rise to popular disaffection; as a result the priest loses his influence, and the people their faith.

The mayor

After the seigneur and the parish priest, there remains one traditional cadre which is frequently encountered as a troublemaker – the community's magistrate, the elected or nominated mayor in the towns, the 'syndic' or oldest inhabitant in the countryside. Because of their duties and the narrow social basis of their recruitment, these magistrates were frequently also possessed of judicial power in the locality. They were regarded by governments as the official representatives of their fellow citizens and responsible for everything that might happen in their midst. In the event of disturbances, their duty ought to have been to ensure obedience to central government, but to do so might run counter to their attachment to local concerns. Because their roots were in their communities, where they held property, their feelings and their interests could lead them to sympathise with revolt, should it occur. The German peasant rebels of 1525 were often led, advised and armed by the mayors [*Schultheissen*] of the villages and small towns. This attachment of the community magistrates to their localities is evidence of a unity throughout the country-side, one that embraced the poorest as well as the richest inhabitants. The mayors, themselves encouraged by the many parish priests who joined the revolt and the Reformation, won over the undecided by their example and the prestige of their offices.

Early modern states were suspicious of this ambivalence in local magistrates; they preferred to entrust responsibility for order in the provinces to commissioners drawn from the governing classes and new to the regions in which they would have to exercise their powers. Thus, in France, the *gens du roi* of the 'sovereign' courts often came from other provinces, and the intendants, installed everywhere after the 1630s, were chosen from among the councillors of state in Paris.

The viceroys and governors of Spain's dominions were generally recruited from outside their area of jurisdication. The governors and voïevoids in the Russian provinces were, from Peter the Great onwards, dispatched from Moscow to provinces where they had no landed roots. Vis-à-vis these commissioners, local magistrates could then act as defenders of their particular region. We can take an example from the great Aquitaine revolt against the establishment of the *gabelle* (salt tax) under Henry II. When the communes of the Angoumois took up arms in July 1548, the notables of Angoulême sent a provincial magistrate, Laurent Journault, an official of the rivers and forests administration and a former mayor of the town, to meet them, and to act as intermediary between the rebels and the king's council. The Journault case exemplifies the role of 'conductor' or mediator that in certain circumstances devolved on magistrates. He was, it was said, 'a man of virtue, fair-minded, and concerned for the common good. In defending by every means at his disposal the freedoms and privileges of Angoulême, he opposed the tributes and taxes imposed on the salt barges entering the town. For this he deserved to be remembered among the ranks of men of virtue, and to have rightfully conferred on him the title of father of his country'.[3]

A magistrate might also find himself forced willy-nilly into leading a revolt, the antiquity of his family rendering it synonymous with the glories and privileges of the place, or the mere prestige of his office in the commune transformating him in the eyes of rioters into a flag-bearer and symbol of local institutions. Rebels tended to parade at the head of their throng a magistrate clothed in his emblematic livery, as a kind of visible guarantee and sign of their collective resolution. At Fermo in the Marches in May 1648 the parading of communal liveries, the taking of the town hall and the deployment of a standard bearing the town's colours, all revealed a desire to tie the insurrection to the commune's history and to give it the approval of the local magistrates.

Finally, the participation of magistrates in disturbances

could take the more limited form of concealed instigation. Their complicity and their clandestine manoeuvres were frequently reported by central commissioners, who believed they detected in insurrectional violence the product of their money, their commands and their servants. At the very least, they denounced their complacent weakness and their inaction against the rebels. We have the view of the commissioner of the king of Prussia, who was also prince of Neuchâtel in Switzerland, after an anti-fiscal disturbance: 'No doubt the majority of the bourgeois would have trembled at the idea of staining their hands with blood, but being full of hatred, they contributed to this tumult; they encouraged it, some by their expressions, their airs and their remarks, others by their example, and others again by their presence. But all, or nearly all of them let things happen around them, and were not much troubled when appalling and barbarous individuals emerged who completed the crime.'[4]

The communal magistrate was certainly the least reliable of the traditional cadres of revolt. In fact, often when there were insurrections in defence of a commune's liberties, the ordinary inhabitants were pitted during the disturbances against the interests of the oligarchy. On other occasions one communal faction was set against another. When this happened, the town-hall livery was no longer a pledge of communal cohesion but, on the contrary, it came to represent the stake in a bloody civil dispute.

Veteran soldiers

Above and beyond the traditional cadres, we can distinguish in the chronicles of rebellion some more specific categories. In terms of the frequency with which they are mentioned, the most important of these comprised military veterans. Military necessity dictated their presence. Even the most miserable and ramshackle of peasant armies could muster a few lines of harquebusiers, musketeers or pikemen. From this core of rebels versed in the handling of arms, captains and tyro generals would be chosen. Often these military leaders did not belong to the social milieu from which the revolt sprang, but geographical proximity might link them to the centre of the insurrection, even when they were very remote from the issues at stake in it. It was their previous experience and their specific abilities which secured their election as leaders, and they were brought into the undertaking less by personal interests than by a vague sympathy with the rebels. Occasionally, their neighbours had to employ threats or force in order to induce them to assume leadership over them.

Of course, in these centuries of insecurity, almost everyone was armed and could turn himself into a soldier when danger threatened. Above all, many peasants had served in the wars, and had held on to their weapons. The former soldier who returned to his village was a classic social type. Talking loudly, wearing a feather in his hat or a sword by his side, he might, if he was lucky, marry a wealthy widow or run the village tavern. On the other hand, if he was poor, a braggart and violent with it, he would afford an inexhaustible literary model to picaresque novelists. Those who survived illness and wounds, and the accidents of campaigns and of discharge, found in the profession of arms, the hard road of peasant social advancement. From the wars of Italy and Flanders, the wars of religion, the German wars, and the campaigns against the Turks there was a constant stream of veterans, thousands of whom made their way into every country in Europe. To them we must added the impoverished, landless minor nobility. In debt, fallen on hard times and disgruntled, they formed a sort of noble proletariat that was more or less numerous depending on which state they belonged to, and on their own individual social status.

The Croquant generals in Perigord in 1637, La Mothe La Forêt and Madaillan, belonged to this marginal nobility that was available for every kind of military adventure. Their captains had also displayed their military ability against the Spaniards or the Huguenots. The Neapolitan rebels of 1647 entrusted the leadership of their army to former soldiers who had served in Flanders. Their generalissimo, Marco Antonio Brancaccio (1570–1650), was a knight of Malta whose hatred of Spain, or so it was said, stemmed from being his being prematurely discharged. Many other captains and sergeant-majors were noblemen. If we are to believe Capecelatro, the main chronicler of the Naples revolt, crimes against honour, disputes over inheritance, a dissolute lifestyle and a baseness of character pushed many of them into revolt.

From such moralising explanations, we should retain the image of men gone astray and who, while typical of the history of revolt everywhere, were marginal to the social groups from which they sprung.

It was the pirates of the North Sea, the Sea-Beggars, who were the spearhead of the Dutch Revolt. Disturbances in Italian cities brought into the limelight soldiers and captains of companies of *sbires,* that is the police forces employed either by the towns or the landowners. In eastern Europe, most of the insurrections were led by veterans of the unending conflict with the Turks. To name but the most famous of these leaders, Gyorgy Dosza – called the 'king of the peasants', and general of the Hungarian rebels of 1514 – had been a valiant captain in a frontier garrison. Matthew Gubec, general of the Croatian peasants in 1573, had also fought along the frontier between the Imperialists and the Ottomans. All the major Ukranian and Russian revolts were led by Cossack leaders who had once been in the pay of the tsar, the sultan or the kings of Poland or Sweden. Khmelnitski, Razin, Bulavin and Pugatchev were all Cossack leaders who had been hardened over the years by the experience of war. Only the rebel Bolotnikov (1606) was a serf, but his captivity on a Turkish galley, and his return home via Venice, the Empire and Poland taught him the ways of the world and skill with arms.

Linking together the choice of leaders in this way to their military abilities amounts, perhaps, to no more than accepting a functional truism which reveals nothing of the essence of insurrection itself. But in fact, the choice of such men is also a consequence of the immense influence which military models exercised in the political sphere; that influence would subsequently mould the structure and course of revolt.

The role of former soldiers was even more important, if we take into account the fact that many of the prominent villagers were elected captains by rebel troops because they had a military reputation or a proven aptitude for command.

In many revolts, the ringleaders are known to us solely from lists of names, which afford no indication of their profession. However, records of the Lower Austrian peasants' revolt of 1599 provide details about a hundred or so known leaders, of whom ninety-three were condemned to death. Twenty-two per cent of them were former soldiers; sixty-one per cent were peasants, albeit peasants who held eminent positions in their localities. They were passably wealthy and, rather curiously, relatively old. Their two colonels were fifty-eight and seventy-five years old respectively. The twelve captains and other officers were aged fifty-two on average. Here was a rebellion that was fundamentally peasant in both origin and action, and whose leaders were in effect representative of rural society; the criteria employed in electing them were their military reputation and ability.

There is another planned movement whose leaders have been identified – the Catalan uprising of November 1689. Its 'army of the land' attracted scarcely any town-dwellers or 'persons of quality'. Its colonel, Antoni Soler, was the richest landowner of his district, but the other captains were village notables, owners of grazing lands and livestock, festooned with elective local offices or else proprietors of notariates or village administrative functions. Many of them were simultaneously invested with traditional military powers, such as captains of forts stationed on mountain passes or provosts in the valleys. That it was they who commanded was not the consequence of any division in the local community but, on the contrary, reflected the ancient hierarchy in the exact form in which, from time immemorial, the geography of these upland valleys – vital routes for both men and their flocks – had fashioned it.

Artisans and craftsmen

From the apprentices and companions to the masters with their own shops, artisans and craftsmen represented another category of ringleader frequently noted in rebellions. Such men, naturally, played a part in outbreaks of urban violence, but village artisans also occasionally dominated peasant gatherings. The blacksmith or the shoesmith with whom every farmer or horseman dealt, or the tailor who travelled from house to house to carry out his trade, were located by the nature of their work at the very centre of rural society.

In the towns, the artisans often made up the greater part of the population. Certain crafts, which involved large numbers of people, were confined, either for social reasons or for professional convenience, to neighbourhoods and streets which thus took on a peculiar character of their own. Such topographical isolation accentuated the group's cohesion. The crafts, organised in *jurandes* or guilds, possessed a recognised juridical character almost everywhere and had done so for centuries. The economic life of a town depended on their activities. Well-off masters and companions, who were far from impoverished, possessed arms and implements that were dangerous. Groups like this were a power within the towns, and were capable of making their grievances known, by force if necessary. City chronicles allot a specific role to every craft; civic festivities saw them parade as a body in full dress and often under arms. During religious festivals, and especially on the anniversaries of their respective patron saints, the professional confraternities, which were the religious expression of a particular craft, marched in procession behind their banners. Craftsmen figure consistently in the records of even the most sordid petty crimes. When the judicial archives speak of habitual delinquents or of organised gangs of thieves, they usually refer to craftsmen. It was not merely the marginalised and the impoverished who came before the criminal courts, but rather young artisans such as weavers, tailors, shoemakers and so on, as is clear from the a study of the records of Spanish galleys in 1572. The presence of such individuals in the world of crime confirms the traditional potential for violence that existed among their ranks.

Some crafts enjoyed a more fearsome reputation than others, particularly butchers, tanners and shoemakers. The repulsive character of their work, their familiarity with blood and their skill in handling sharp instruments led to them being despised and relegated to the bottom of the social scale. Despite their relative prosperity, their confraternities usually marched towards the back of town parades. People avoided other than purely commercial dealings with them; intermarriage with them was also avoided, and the daughters of butchers and cobblers themselves married butchers and cobblers. Nevertheless, the tanners, in some cities, and the butchers in all, played a major role in disturbances. Among the leaders of the Peasants' War of 1525, Erasmus Gerber, captain general of the Alsace rebels, was a tanner from Molsheim, and

Sebastian Lotzer, leader of the Baltringer army, was a companion-furrier. And while many towns hesitated to join the revolt, certain crafts like the market-gardeners and butchers at Strasbourg, did so en bloc. When towns either went over to the Reformation, or refused to do so, the local butchers were at the heart of the conflict. In 1562, the butchers of Alençon expelled the Huguenots. The great abattoir of Paris, which could muster 1,500 men armed with cutlasses, shared in the successes of the Catholic League in 1588–89.

More than any other craft, the textile workers had, during the Middle Ages, been in the forefront of events. In the party struggles for town magistracies, the weavers were undisputed masters. Their agitation made the history of Ghent and other Flemish towns a bloody one. The wool-carders rocked Florence, and played a leading part in the disturbances of the German cities in the fourteenth and fifteenth centuries. They are to be found on every occasion when there was trouble in these same textile cities. Demographic growth and inflation during the sixteenth century increased the incidence of crime against property, particularly among artisans. Prices rose, competition became stiffer, wages fell and, consequently, the day-labourers in the textile sector became exasperated. However, their political and economic power had declined markedly. Commercial patterns shifted, and many crafts had ceased to operate at all in Flanders and central Italy. In Ghent, at the time of Artevelde (1345), the weavers could demand for themselves one-third of the representatives of the common people on the city council. During the riots of the sixteenth century in the Belgian towns, the crafts that had been excluded from political power and that had declined from their former prosperity, attempted to regain the position of superiority they had enjoyed in the government of the communes during the Middle Ages. During the great revolt of 1539 and, later, during the Calvinist dictatorship of 1577, the Ghent weavers demanded and obtained restoration of their place on the municipal council, though this gain was to prove short-lived. In reality, however, Ghent's prosperity was no longer based on textiles, but on its grain staple. The textile market-hall had remained unfinished since 1441, while a vast bargeman's building was erected in 1530. The weavers who numbered

4,200 men in 1349, taking into account the allied crafts that depended on them, could muster no more than a hundred or two in 1584, while other crafts such as the bargemen, the butchers and the fishmongers wanted peace.

In the Naples rising of 1647, the silk weavers formed a corporation and presented to the viceroy their own specific demands concerning customs duties. On their own, they mustered a thousand men under arms. With the wool weavers and the other textile artisans, they formed over ten per cent of the population of this great Mediterranean city.

According to the record of marriages registered for 1642–44, the profession with the greatest numbers after the textile-workers was that of domestic servant, followed by simple day-labourers, tailors and shoemakers. Masaniello was a fishmonger and Annese a gunsmith.

The Andalusian riots of 1652 brought to the fore the silk weavers of Granada and Seville, who lived in a neighbourhood to themselves in the north of the city, near the market. The attitude of craftsmen varied from town to town: the fishermen led the rioting at Ayamonte, the weavers at Bujalance did nothing, while those at Cordoba were very active.

The involvement of artisans in a revolt could be all the more marked in that a legitimate institutional role had been granted them in many cities. The annals of urban disturbance in Sicily provide the most perfect example of this. At Catania and Palermo, the guilds (*Maestranze*) were given responsibility for keeping order. Each craft guild was allotted particular gates and bastions in the fortifications, and each had to watch part of the walls. In Palermo, shaken by riot in 1647, the streets were patrolled night and day by the fishermen or the coppersmiths. There were seventy-two recognised masterships in the city (Ghent had fifty-two), and their members had the right to bear arms and to hunt in the country areas subject to its control. They made up, it was said, a quarter of the inhabitants of this populous city. The tanners (*consarioti*), whose exports of leather goods (*coriami*) were flourishing, occupied a cramped district, now demolished, in the town centre; their hovels, connected by foul-smelling paths and underground passages, constituted an inaccessible redoubt. The riots of May and August 1647 spread from this district. The fishermen's guild was no less powerful and organised, and was capable of arming over 700 men. In May 1647, the tuna-fishing season prevented them from taking part in the riots, but on 22nd August, they marched out of the alleys of La Cala, massacred the leader of the rebellion, and restored order in the town on their terms. In 1708, it was once again the guild of fishermen which expelled the Franco-Spanish garrison, seized the arsenal, and brought the whole of Palermo to heel. During the city's last great revolt in 1773, the guilds raised 40,000 men and once more confirmed their centuries-old domination of the city.

In truth, this official role of the crafts in the government of major cities was quite common. We know that the Six Corporations of Paris elected the Provost of Merchants and that the London guilds elected the Lord Mayor. Such institutional recognition fostered among the aldermen a form of political prudence which distanced them from all factional involvement. The 'sworn' guilds (*jurandes*) of the French cities kept resolutely clear of the dangers of civil violence, even if, on an individual basis, many artisans threw themselves into one cause or another. Thus in Paris during the League, artisans joined the demonstrations of revolt en masse. Among the 30,000 or so determined Leaguers were to be found formidable groupings of butchers, horse-dealers (about 700) and boatmen from the right bank of the Seine (500).

On the other hand, leadership of the movement belonged to the lower ranks of the legal profession. Of the 120 leaders of the League in 1589, merchants were not numerous (19%) and artisans were insignificant (1·6%). During the Fronde, the shopkeepers and artisans of Paris followed the ups and downs in opinion – that is, they detested Mazarin, only to subsequently applaud the return of the king in October 1652. If craftsmen participated en masse in the Barricades of August 1648 and some of them in the capture of the city hall by Condé's supporters in July 1652, the craft corporations always avoided anything that might compromise them as an institution. In the provinces, there were instances of military leaders gaining control of towns by extracting oaths from the constituted bodies, and among them the syndics of the crafts (as at Agen and Angers), but such examples are isolated.

During early modern times, the craft guilds were everywhere characterised by a clear political stance of 'wait and see'.

The English guilds present the same image during the civil war. London's privileges had been confirmed in 1638. The guilds possessed extensive powers there – including jurisdiction, fiscal privileges, an autonomous city militia and the right to elect the mayor and aldermen. Even though their education, their opinions and their interests inclined them towards the side of Parliament, guild members refused to declare openly for any one party. Such circumspection was not confined to the merchants of the City, but was characteristic also of craft communities throughout the provinces.

There was another brake which could prevent artisans and shopkeepers from becoming agitators, and that was the particularism of each guild. Crafts guilds acted on behalf of their own members, had their own specific demands, defended or avenged their own members exclusively. If the need arose, they would not hesitate to turn their weapons against a rival craft, as we have seen happening at Ghent and at Palermo. The unity of a craft was only broken by horizontal disturbances within it – by coalitions of companions or strikes by apprentices whose demands could from time to time set them against their masters.

With the growth of cities in the eighteenth century and the emergence of the major capital cities, the craftsmen's role took on a new twist. Relatively comfortable and precociously educated compared to the rest of the population, they offered a particular welcome to new currents of thought. Just as the Reformation often had a ready impact among them, so ideas of egalitarianism and popular sovereignty would establish themselves more rapidly among these groups than elsewhere. The leaders of the Paris *sans culottes* – that is the members of the revolutionary committees of 1793 – were for the most part (72·7%) artisans and shopkeepers. Perhaps Paris had already evolved in a way that anticipated nineteenth-century developments, since the ringleaders of the contemporary disturbances in London did not exhibit the same social composition, and among whom apprentices, day-labourers and stevedores were to the fore.

This list, admittedly, is not exhaustive, but rather singles out the most numerically significant categories. Neither is the distinction between troublemarkers and instigators of change above criticism, but it does facilitate exposition, as well as enabling us to combine in our analysis the social categories better placed to handle arms with those best able to shape opinion.

Instigators of change

There can be no question here of our attempting a sociology of cultural change. We shall merely try to show how a few portraits of key individuals may elucidate the history of political violence. Ideas are explicable in several frameworks that complement each other – a sociology of ideologists and popularisers, a history of the spread of ideas and, also, a sociology of the ideas themselves. Indeed, the spread of an idea does not necessarily correspond to its implications or significance: arguments are often the offspring of intellectual patterns of which their proponents may be unaware, and which may be quite alien to their milieu and run counter to their interests. We must, therefore, be wary of all social determinism and steer clear of any total identification of a social group with an ideology.

Let us look at the social development of the Reformation, the most extraordinary cultural change of the period. We possess several statistical samples of its social spectrum. Their apparent discrepancies derive no doubt from the different historical 'moments' that they reflect. At first, an analysis was envisaged of the heresy trials in the Toulouse archives of the parlement and the ecclesiastical courts between 1500 and 1560. This was the 'evangelical phase' – decades of novelty, of intellectual illumination, and of an explosion in communications. The literate elite figure overwhelmingly in the trial records (68·5%), with as many ecclesiastics (33%) as educated, professional men. Among the latter, men of law are the most numerous, followed by schoolmasters and professors, doctors, printers and book-sellers, each of which are well represented. Artisans make up only 17% (leather and textile workers, followed by those involved in metal work and building). Merchants and nobles are relatively few, and peasants entirely absent.

When the Reformation had succeeded in establishing itself overwhelmingly in the towns, the social image of the Protestant churches there came to resemble the social spectrum. Thus, in Languedoc, the number of artisans in the reformed church at Montpellier in 1560 grew to 69 per cent. Defrocked clergy no longer figured as such in this breakdown, even though their influence may well have been decisive. The involvement of the literate remains considerable (15·5%), evidence of their social status. These results for Languedoc are confirmed by the Register of the inhabitants of Geneva from 1549 to 1560.[5] In this city, rooted in Protestantism after 1536, and to which Calvinists from all over France came in search of exile, the same percentages are repeated. Artisans made up 68·5% of the known professions, with a clear domination by textiles (29·9%), and other crafts such as leather-working, building and metal-working at around 10–11%.

In every case – at Toulouse, Montpellier and Geneva – the role of those involved in the book trade, of lawyers and of doctors is noteworthy. In Geneva, the former account for 5% of the known professionals involved and doctors for 3·2%. In the Toulouse trials, men of law accounted for 17·7%, schoolmasters 11·5%, doctors 3·7%, and those in the book-trade 2·6%. It comes as no surprise to discover that the biggest category comprises those whose profession is unrecorded. In fact, given the state of early modern society, an individual was defined by his social rank and rarely by his profession, since it was land which represented the sole occupation of the great majority of people. Where we have a professional breakdown of known Protestants, the proportion of tradesmen – that is, men with a specific professional occupation – was far greater than it was in society at large. Contemporaries did not fail to notice that Protestant doctrine was disseminated through the elites, the literate and those in authority, and that innovation came from above. As a phenomenon that was urban, intellectual, clerical and magisterial, the Reformation could become a popular affair (that is to say, more broadly disseminated throughout society as a whole) only as a result of a long process of evolution. At Geneva in 1533, the Lutherans were still in a minority, but they comprised some of the best and wealthiest families. During disturbances there, the Catholic crowds that gathered on the Molard, the principal square, numbered between 10,000 and 15,000 while the professing Lutherans were fewer than a hundred. However, the Catholics were almost all of them humble folk, women and children, while the Lutherans were bourgeois, orderly, and well armed, and protected by the magistrates. This at least is what merchants from Fribourg who tried to separate the two groups claimed, pointing out to the Catholics: 'they are different people from you, and better prepared for a fight'. In the provinces of Aquitaine, the expansion of Calvinism confirmed this elite recruitment. 'I heard it said', wrote Monluc in 1560, 'that most of those involved in financial matters were Protestant, for it is human nature to love novelty, but the worst aspect of it all, the mainspring of this catastrophe, is that the lawyers of the *parlements* and *sénéchaussées,* and the other magistrates deserted the old religion'.[6] Dominating the town councils and with a foothold in the courts, the Protestants then organised their own religious institutions. There was constant movement of the political magistrates to take up disciplinary functions within the churches, for the sources of recruitment to both elites were the same. Members were co-opted within a narrow ruling group, as in Nîmes where, out of 41 members of the Consistory between 1596 and 1602, 18 were legal officials and 14 were bourgeois and merchants.

This example of the Reformation, which established a change in attitudes, thus reveals the social categories of change – the 'opinion leaders'. As with the classification of the agitators, we must begin by noting the traditional cadres – the clergy and the magistrates. The priest was responsible for harnessing the world of ideas and of learning, and for bringing their benefits to bear on his community. Grosjean was in no position whatever to give advice to his parish priest; if there was innovation, it had to come from the priest, not from Grosjean. The great instrument of change in every age has been the school, an area of spiritual responsibility which was the undisputed preserve of the clergy. From Protestant academies to Jesuit or Oratorian colleges, from the primary school to the university, the education of young people and the dissemination of knowledge were activities which could not be divorced from a knowledge of God. One learned to read in order to understand the Scriptures or the catechism. The history of education, which we cannot summarise here, is indispensable to any explanation of the progress of ideas and the changing world-picture.

In societies where the ranking of groups and individuals was, whatever the nuances involved, held to be immutable, men of law, personifying the primacy of authority, were pre-eminent in their communities. Innovations created by rulers were channelled through them, and they were the protagonists in the decisions that set in motion the principal utopia of early modern times – the centralisation of the state. Thus, the history of institutions and the sociology of public roles should, like the history of education, have their place in the present analysis. Men of law were at once the official interpreters of political change and its leading beneficiaries, the harbingers of new modes of thought and of living, the spokesmen for, as well as the models of change.

During these centuries of very slow technological development, and in which individual talent counted for little in social esteem, an over-simple image of an unchanging world ought not to hide from us the potential of such cultural mediators, positioned as they were at the same level as the populace itself. Examples of this are local notables such as notaries, doctors, tavern-owners, travellers, and so on.

Local notables

Each little region, its isolation protected by geography and by custom, was an island possessed of its own modest originality and its own 'micro-history'. Rupturing this isolation and wrenching areas free of the dead-weight of custom would be the work of local notables captivated by the prestige of written law and new forms of science. To illustrate this process of learned acculturation, we have the example, taken from Montaigne, of Lahontan at the foot of the Pyrenees. Around 1560, within the space of a few years, its inhabitants saw their traditions transformed by the opening at nearby Orthez, in Calvinist Béarn, of a school of law and medicine. 'They lived a life apart, with their own fashions, dress and habits, ruled and governed by certain particular systems and customs, handed

down from father to son, to which they bound themselves with
no other constraint than that of reverence for their practice.
This little state had continued from all antiquity in so happy a
condition that no neighbouring judge had been put to the
trouble of inquiring into their doings, no lawyer retained to
give them counsel, no foreigner ever called in to settle their
quarrels; and no one of this district had ever been seen beg-
ging. They avoided marriages and dealings with the outer
world, so as not to corrupt the purity of their government
until, so they tell, one of them, within the memory of their
fathers, whose soul was spurred by noble ambition, took it
into his head, in order to bring his name into credit and
reputation, to make one of his sons *maître* Jean or *maître*
Pierre, having sent him to some neighbouring town to learn
how to write, finally made him into a fine village notary. This
son, having become important, began to disdain their ancient
customs and to put into their heads the notion of the pomp of
the regions on this side of the mountains. The first of his
cronies whose goat had a horn broken off he advised to
demand justice from the royal judges nearby; and he went
from this one to another until he had debased the whole place.
On the heels of this corruption, they say another of worse
consequence followed immediately, the work of a doctor who
had the notion of marrying one of their daughters and of
settling among them.'[7] The doctor introduced an understanding of illnesses; 'scientific' remedies replaced garlic, and the
good old days were over. In this pleasant fable from the
Essays, some have seen the myth of a primitive innocence
driven out by the false glitter of modernity. It is true that the
mountain communities were, throughout Europe, museums of
past institutions and *mentalités*. Medieval liberties survived
there and became political archaisms, like the estates of the
Pyrenean valleys or the village republics of Serbia (Knez). The
authors of novelty, the notary and the doctor, are both
identified in Montaigne, but above all, this account in the guise
of a fable, reveals the main reasons for their acculturation.
They were avid for social advancement, and the means to
satisfying their ambition was access to education. Montaigne's
Béarnais story may well summarise centuries of cultural
change in the rural West.

The tavern as popular stage

The spread of the tavern and its gradual rise to the status of a social stage and a necessary meeting-place, a forum for conversation, are features of the early modern era. Demographic growth – that of the sixteenth and of the eighteenth century – as well as the constant growth of towns, are the key to this proliferation of drinking places. In between the two periods of growth, the extension of transatlantic voyages had accustomed maritime nations to alcoholic beverages and, through them, had popularised the consumption of beer, wine and rum. The building of taverns and refreshment places along the main roads and in the suburbs of large cities, and the appearance of the scourge of drunkenness, began to be denounced by the moral authorities in society. Legislators set about regulating opening hours, the behaviour of drinkers, the quality of the products sold, and the accommodation of travellers. It is known that in the 1710s, Paris had about 5,000 such taverns, or one per hundred inhabitants. Bordeaux, the point of departure for the wine fleets heading for the ports of northern Europe, had several hundred. A middling-size town, seat of a royal court, might have around fifty, and a simple walled town about ten. Such liberal estimates should not surprise us if we realise that in a country of vineyards, all the producers, even the humblest, ran a tavern for the degustation of their new vintage. In England, the consumption of beer and gin saw the same growth. At the beginning of the eighteenth century, London sales of alcohol increased by about 35% every ten years – there were over 10,000 taverns there in 1735, 7,000 of them in Middlesex alone, without counting the City and Surrey. Tavern-keepers openly advertised that their clients could be 'drunk for a penny, dead drunk for tuppence', and 'have a straw-bed for nothing'. Fiscal measures such as the *aides* in France or the Gin Acts in England did nothing to hamper this growth, but merely served to give the state a stake in it. The tavern was fast becoming the preferred centre of popular sociability, competing with the local church, as the place where news and rumour were dissemminated, emotions and frustrations expressed.

The shoe-smith's forge and the shoemaker's shop were also

common meeting-places. A small, irreverent tract, chosen from the mass of popular works of the Troyes printers, provides information about the role of the restless individuals that were to be found in every disturbance. Apart from mending shoes, the *Devoir des savetiers* [Duty of Cobblers] also included that of 'finding out diligently what is happening among one's neighbours, a function that is useful to both individuals and the state . . .' 'It is we', these would-be cobblers continued, 'who are the first at the fires of celebration, it is we who hurry to ring the bells, who oblige the bourgeois, whether they like or not, to provide wood and close their shops, it is we who pull the artillery, who prepare the fireworks, and who proudly preside at every public ceremony. In a word, the sadness and joy of the people depends primarily on us'.[8]

This vignette of the village master-of-ceremonies enables us to guess at his potential for invention and popularization. Knowledge of the world also increased with travel, even on a modest scale. If great voyages were rare, a less ambitious itinerary was followed by many wandering professionals – merchants attending fairs, traders with their clients, agents and porters, the growing number of messengers between one town and the next, soldiers travelling through provinces between campaigns, and travellers who were either completing their leisurely youth or leaving to serve their apprenticeship. Many more specialised craftsmen were obliged to wander in order to satisfy distant employers; artists and engineers, organ-builders, clockmakers, fountain-makers, surveyors, gunners, mill and crane-mechanics, and many more. Because of their trade and their travels, these technicians and men of talent were embodiments of change. This role was reinforced by the fact that science and techology were not seen as separate; men of learning merely enjoyed the title of 'artist' or 'craftsman', and learned academies themselves were equally concerned with questions of technology.

In any case, ordinary human feeling taught men to see in certain difficulties of existence a spur to invention. The position of the bastard son or, more straightforwardly, that of younger sons is a case in point. The transmission of the family estates to the eldest son, the consequently diminished social status of younger ones, the contrasts of fortune within a single family and the uncertain nature of an individual destiny, all these factors conspired to create dissatisfied personalities who found themselves compelled to face up to the challenges of study, exile, service or emigration. This steady stream of restless adventurers was explained by an English younger son around 1600: 'My elder brother', wrote Thomas Wilson bitterly, 'must have all, and all the rest that which the cat left on the maltheap, perhaps some small annuity during his life or what pleases our elder brothers worship to bestow upon us if we please him, and my mistress his wife. This I must confess doth us good someways, for it makes us industrious to apply ourselves to letters or to arms, whereby many times we become my master elder brother's masters, or at least their betters in honour and reputation, while he lives at home like a mome (fool), and knows the sound of no bell but his own.'[9]

This tableau of the forms which opinion leadership could assume in older societies does not prejudge the role played by such leaders during the crises of violence that shook their world. The beginning of the early modern era was marked by repeated catastrophe; biological disaster hampered the continuous change which is the very stuff of human history. As always, ideology sanctioned situations imposed by force of circumstances; in doing so, it conferred some validity on the immobility of tradition. The memory, all too fresh, of epidemics, war and scarcity taught men to be suspicious of anything not tested by prolonged use. Hatred of novelty and of strangers became the most reliable and prudent weapons against threats from the unknown. Hence the misadventures of travellers or other lovers of novelty, the assassination of suspect strangers, and the hue and cry against men who reclaimed marshes, measured forests or took elevations. Pugatchev put to death an astronomer who had got lost among his Cossacks, assuring him that he would see the stars from much closer range! Numerous parish priests who tried to reform their parishioners were detested and persecuted, crushed with lawsuits and even driven from their parishes altogether. It is true that novelty might not be innocent, that reclamation-men or foresters deprived local communities of their use-rights, that geographical surveys tended to go hand in hand with fiscal reassessment, that the astronomer was often taken for a spy, and that the reforming priest was shattering some element of ancient village solidarity.

The isolation of these innovators was never more marked than in late eighteenth-century Italy. *Philosophe* ministers and magistrates from the 'enlightened' aristocracy or bourgeoisie placed the ideological arrogance and haughty optimism that their belief in progress gave them at the service of enlightened despots or of governments established by the French. They had no idea that the populace might regret the old grain laws which free trade in grain had suppressed, that the peasantry might prefer the unobtrusive inertia of the old regime to some new fiscal system, or that the faithful might take up arms to defend their patrimony of religious practices against Jansenist reformers or revolutionaries. Francesco Maria Gianni (1729–1821), *philosophe* minister of Tuscany, who served first the grand duke Peter Leopold and then the republican government of Florence, was driven out on each occasion as a result of popular unrest, first in May 1790 and then in May 1799. The young Sismondi, aged only 26, was a horrified spectator at the second revolt which put Gianni and the French to flight. The learned Genevan saw in it only the consequence of dark plottings. 'History', he wrote, 'has difficulty in explaining this simultaneous explosion of hidden resentment by a fanatical population throughout Tuscany and practically everywhere in Italy. How did the secret agents of such an extensive network find men's minds so well prepared for the implementation of their conspiracies, how did a single spark suffice everywhere to light such a fire?'[10] But such incomprehension itself illustrates the extent to which the reformers of the Enlightenment were, in socio-political terms, out of step, and may serve as a model of the cultural conflicts which extended through early modern times.

Instigators of change usually avoid the noisy and meaningless rhythm of political history. But they deserve a place in an essay on revolt if only because the crises affecting their communities occasionally bring them into the limelight. At such moments, they can be reassuring intermediaries, guides and counsellors, but they can also serve as victims and scapegoats; it all depends on whether the reason for the revolt did or did not fit in with their model of innovation, and whether the violence it unleashed served to accelerate or rather hinder their long-term mission.

4 Mechanisms of subversion

'They all raised a hoarse cheer. "Hoo-roah!" they cried, carefully keeping time with the hat as it bobbed up and down. "Hoo-roah! Noo! Consti! Tooshun! Less! Bread! More! Taxes!" ' Lewis Carroll, *Sylvie and Bruno*.

Revolutionary parties

In the course of the early modern period, few subversive movements were successful in seizing the totality of power in a sovereign state, in altering government personnel, or in remaking its laws to a greater or lesser extent. The English and Dutch Revolutions were about the only cases of victory achieved by insurrection. H. G. Koenigsberger noted that these movements had in common the organisation of a kind of revolutionary 'party'.[1] Of course, it would be completely anachronistic to conceive it as a political association; in line with the practice of the time, it was more a matter of corporations and fraternities. Adherents of these causes banded together not in terms of an idea of the city, or of political or social models, but around the religious faith of a minority. Its novelty in relation to other corporate groups or 'companies' derived from the autonomous structure of the party, which was not subject in any way to common law or integrated into the general framework of society. Supporters were admitted into it simply in virtue of their faith, without distinctions of social rank or economic status. The party constituted a web of co-operation and mutual fidelity throughout towns and provinces, and even across state frontiers, involving regular correspondence, intelligence and mutual assistance. Above all, the party was equipped with a military organisation, and with arms of its own choosing. Its objective was to ensure not merely the liberty of their faith by a capacity for self-defence, but beyond that, given that toleration was inconceivable, to attract all men to the practice of the only true religion – theirs, that is – and to secure the supremacy in the state that was indispensable for its achievement. Thus, although this was not its original purpose, the party became an instrument for the conquest of power. There was room in its ranks for political tendencies that differed considerably, and which did not necessarily correspond to social divisions. For example, pastors, magistrates and merchants might be more open to compromises and settlements which would avert civil war or a total break. On the other hand, the advocates of force might be either radical preachers, craftsmen ready for violent insurrection, or aristocrats whose political prestige and military competence pushed them in the direct of secession.

Dutch independence

In the case of the Netherlands, we have a revolt that, in the beginning, was no more than a form of provincial unrest like those to which the growth of the modern state gave rise. Granvelle's administration and his fiscal demands clashed with the particularism of regions whose sensitivity had been heightened by their rapid maritime expansion between 1540 and 1565. The authoritarian beliefs and supra-national humanism of this prelate from the Franche-Comté upset the nobil·ty, who secured his removal in 1564. The noble opposition, which lacked neither tradition, power nor eminent spokesmen, dominated political life during the Regency of Margaret of Parma. These magnates used arguments from common or feudal law against the fiscal innovations introduced by Madrid. In 1566, a year of distress, the demands of the discontented nobility were accompanied by the popular disorders characteristic of times of scarcity. On 5th April 1566, in Brussels, 200 nobles presented a declaration of the liberties of the Netherlands to the Regent, who made some show of confirming them. The public acclaimed these nobles, who, in an act of defiance, had taken the sobriquet of 'beggars' and used as their insignia a cap and a bowl. The compromise led the Calvinists to believe that the moment was right for a public demonstration of their faith. As elsewhere in Europe, Calvinism had trained disciples and founded churches among the urban elite. Their activities procured them, if not universal adherence, at least the sympathy and support of the middle classes, who were heirs of the medieval tradition of struggle against ecclesiastical jurisdiction and lordship. At that point, the Protestants seized control of a number of towns in southern Flanders, but their successes were compromised by outbursts of popular iconoclasm. In 1567, the troops of the duke of Alba were able to regain control of the seventeen provinces with relative ease.

However, Spanish authority was soon to be undermined again by the ferocity of the ensuing repression – 8,000 people were condemned to death in three years – and by the decision to levy a new tax designed to pay for the army. Set at ten per cent of retail sales, the tax was never collected, but the threat of it alienated once for all the commercial middle classes from the authority of the king of Spain. During this period, exile and persecution produced a rapprochement between the beggars 'of state' and the beggars 'of religion'. Elizabethan England and the German Lutheran cities provided them with places of refuge. There they found support and a military model in the piracy that had developed along with the commercial growth of the North Sea. The *Zeegeuzen* or *Zeeganzen* (Sea-beggars or geese), both Frisian and English, assumed from that time the label of 'Beggars'. From 1568 onwards, the rebel nobility issued patents to these maritime adventurers, some of the most famous of whom were related to them by blood or by clientship. They flew flags bearing the sack and bowl or ten coins, recalling the hated tax. Their capture, in April 1572, of the port of Brill, on the island of Voorn in the mouth of the Meuse, provided a bridgehead for the revolt and represented a decisive stage in the conquest of a territorial base.

From 1572, the combined activities of the privateers by sea and of the Calvinist factions inside the towns, delivered the towns of Holland and Zeeland one after another into the hands of the rebels. Their ever more numerous military successes doubtless owed much to the political and strategic skill of the prince of Orange, but the effectiveness of the Calvinist party was a decisive factor in cities being captured or won over, and particularly in their subsequent support of the rebel cause. Everywhere coups in the cities were the work of the local Protestant communities. On the one hand, they supplied the manpower, recruited among the artisans and sailors, for riots, and, on the other, the political leaders belonging to the merchant bourgeoisie. Often it was the town militia, under the command of the wealthiest merchants and master craftsmen, which ensured the success of the rebels. Priests and Catholic notables and loyalists were subjected to execution or expelled. The town magistracies were henceforth shared by those families who had embraced the Reformation; in this way the irreversible mastery of the Protestant party was secured, even in those towns where Catholics remained a numerical majority. Furthermore, the practice of the estates of the rural provinces of meeting and legislating without the consent of central authority led to *de facto* secession. This was a breakaway which did not follow from a doctrinal movement, but from the momentum of events; for the driving force of the rebellion, which had brought about this situation, was above all the cohesion and determination of the Protestant groups.

In the contemporary civil wars which racked France for nearly forty years, the long duration of the hostilities and the deep-rootedness of their various causes were possible only because the religious confessions had become parties. Both Calvinists and Leaguers had their own comparable hierarchies – religious, civil and, later, military – their municipal oligarchies, their networks of intelligence and of loyalty.

The League, whose Parisian leaders, the Sixteen, have recently been the subject of social and political analysis, formed a revolutionary party.[2] It was an error on Henry III's part to think that in having the duke of Guise assassinated, he would destroy the Holy Union; he mistook what was a party structure extending throughout the kingdom for a simple conspiracy. The Union was a political federation of towns, each of which had its local leaders who controlled demonstrations, currents of opinion and the resort to arms by their fellow citizens.

Finally, the royalists or Navarrists were to represent a third cause. It, too, was capable of sustaining intelligence and contacts in every town among groups of supporters who, with or without the approval of magistrates and governors, were likely to know each other, to take up arms together and, at an opportune moment, to emerge from their clandestinity.

The English revolution

During these extraordinary decades, the subversive capability
of party structures can also be guessed. We must first note the
weakness of royal power in the face of a public opinion that
can, without anachronism, already be described as national in
character. When the more general causes of the English Revolution are sought, one cannot but emphasise the contradiction
between the absolutist ambitions of the Stuart kings and the
limited means at their disposal. Lacking the divine charisma of
French or Spanish kings, the king had to reckon with a
powerful tradition of representative assemblies, whose consent was needed to taxation and the enactment of laws. He did
not have in his realm networks of commissioners or officers;
provincial government was based on magistracies exercised by
unpaid local notables. The gentry was not dependent on royal
service; nor did it depend on the aristocracy, which was rather
limited and incapable of forming powerful clientèles, as on the
continent. The provincial gentry, educated in the law schools,
even at university, and capable of making money from the
profits of trade, knew how to control their social environment.
It was they who filled the positions of justices of the peace and
the seats in the House of Commons (seventy-five per cent of
the members were from the gentry). In short, in order to
govern the country, the king needed the support of the gentry,
while their only bond with him was that of a loyalty that was
conditional. Nor did royal power have any more of a financial
or military basis. The Treasury received nothing from direct
taxation, but had to depend on meagre revenues from royal
domains, and a few irregular customs duties. There was no
standing army apart from the king's guard and a few castle
garrisons.

Puritanism was the principal ideological trigger. It can be
summarised as the religious belief of every Englishman
brought up on Bible-reading and concerned to prepare for the
kingdom of God, convinced of his country's peculiar vocation
and worried about papist machinations. This frame of mind
did not predispose men to subversion, and even less to regi-
cide. It required deliberate support from Charles I for Arminian tendencies in the Church of England in order to bring the

Puritans into violent opposition to the king, and to make them forget their loyalism of Elizabethan times. Public opinion became accustomed to opposing the decisions of the king and his ministers during the prolonged attempt at government without Parliament from November 1629 to March 1640. It was only under the pressure from defeats sustained at the hands of the Scots malcontents that Charles I resigned himself to seeking parliamentary support again. Twice, in March and November 1640, the elections returned majorities in the Commons that were determined to oppose the king's objectives. The Long Parliament, elected in November 1640, destroyed the king's prerogatives and dispatched his most energetic adviser, Strafford, to the scaffold in May 1641. The rebellion of the Irish Catholics in November 1641 forced into a corner the declared advocates of parliamentary power as well as the king and those who, throughout the country, had begun to rally to his side. The news from Ireland gave each side a pretext for taking up arms. In January 1642, Parliament ordered the towns to mobilise their militia, while the king summoned his subjects in March and raised the standard of war at Nottingham on 22nd August 1642. However, when the king's authority was swept aside in 1640, when the constitutional crisis proved insoluble in 1641, and recourse to arms was envisaged in 1642, no one imagined anything like a final break, the king's execution and the abolition of the monarchy. As in so many other situations, the momentum of events proved stronger during the English Revolution than the intentions of those involved in it. The extreme outcome of the years 1649 to 1653 was not the result of a deliberate plan, but the product of unforeseeable sequences of events in an unending civil war. The two decisive stages were, then, the emergence of a Commons with a Puritan majority, and, later, the creation of armies. It is these two points in its history and their specific developments that we need to analyse.

From the 1620s, elections to the Commons had some semblance of party campaigns. The idea of resistance to the alleged oppression of the court was among tne arguments most widely used. Patronage by the leading nobles extended to several constituencies and gave rise to groups of MPs who would in due course adopt opinions similar to theirs. The earl of Pembroke, one of the discontented peers, carried a dozen seats in this way in 1626. The two elections of 1640 were better prepared and fought than ever before. Admittedly, there were only forty days of campaigning and voting remained generally dependent on conflicts among local notables. Nevertheless, the notion of a national issue at stake did emerge. Peers hostile to the king, such as Bedford or Essex, opened their houses, dispensing beer and tobacco to all comers. Experienced political figures like John Hampden and the celebrated John Pym, travelled through the counties, organising committees and launching petitions in towns of Puritan persuasion. Party activity and the ferment of ideas continued beyond the elections, to reach their climax in the last years of the civil war. An effective instrument of national propaganda was instituted in January 1642 – a day of national fasting on the final Wednesday of every month for as long as the Irish rebellion lasted. These days were devoted to listening to sermons preached by ministers chosen by the Commons. Thus, Puritanism disposed of a regular tribune until 1649, and its arguments were duly taken up in printed works. By 1647, the conflict of ideas had come to permeate society sufficiently for MPs to be regarded less as representatives of the inhabitants of a place than the spokesmen of a party, of a body of opinions that were national in scope.

It was armed force which had the last word in the Revolution. From March to August 1642, Charles I toured the provinces in search of troops; he was greeted with acclaim more or less everywhere, but few people followed him. In September 1642, he had only 2,000 horse and 1,200 infantry. Subsequently, a number of leading royalist nobles like the earls of Worcester and Derby managed to bring their tenants to his side in relatively large numbers. Nevertheless, the core of the royalist armies continued to be composed overwhelmingly of Welsh and Irish contingents led by Catholic officers (39·6 per cent). This feature was enough to fuel the image propagated by the Puritans of a papist army set to destroy English liberties.

Initially, the parliamentary armies were based on the town militias, and especially on that of London. They were organised and financed by discontented peers, who had succeeded in placing their clients in key positions in London.

They did not hesitate at the most critical moments to summon the lower classes to arms. On the night of Thursday, 27th October 1642, as royal troops were attacking Turnham Green, Lord Saye harangued the crown at the Guildhall, the earl of Warwick recruited sailors, Lord Wharton chaired a committee to raise funds, and Lord Brooke organised military recruitment. Anxious to imitate the Romans on the Campus Martius, he had tents erected in order to collect enrolments and subscriptions. In August 1643, he established a Committee for a General Rising, to which each guild sent eight deputies. It examined the recruits in order to satisfy itself of their Puritan convictions. In fact, the recruits did not come from the City itself, which remained very reserved towards the parliamentary cause, but from the suburbs and villages subject to its jurisdiction. This method of intensive recruiting and of selecting volunteers was extended to the provinces; in this way the New Model Army was created.

These well-knit and well-armed troops proved their worth at Marston Moor on 2nd July 1644. Victory was secured by the heavy cavalry under the command of Cromwell. It was the first major success of the parliamentary armies. Strategy had recently been entrusted to a War Council of twenty-five members, the Committee of the Two Kingdoms, which included the principal officers, among them Cromwell, a number of MPs and of Scots nobles (June 1644). Finally, in June 1645, Cromwell was appointed lieutenant-general.

Henceforth, the army, with three years of campaigning behind it, was master of the political scene. Until 1653, and indeed until 1660, it would constitute the only real power in the land. War weariness, uncertainty and the agonising vacuum of legitimacy gave rise to numerous and dispersed instances of recovery and adhesion to the royalist cause; on each occasion, the cohesion and tactical ability of the army got the better of such efforts. When the Scots came to the assistance of Charles I, it was Cromwell's cavalry charges which halted them at Preston, on 17th August 1648.

The repository of the nation's destiny, the army had become, after so many years of civil war, a social milieu and even a form of legitimacy in its own right. The soldiers identified their rights and their demands for unpaid wages with the liberties of England. Conflicts between the different political tendencies and the most varied politico-religious options of the day found an echo in its ranks. Debates of national importance were organised among the officers, and propaganda proliferated within the regiments. The radicalism of the Levellers originally took shape in the army, and benefited in its growth from the rancour of unpaid soldiers. Petitions were addressed to the Commons and meetings between several regiments arranged. The famous debates held in the church at Putney in October and November 1647 were devoted to examining the Leveller declaration and to outlining the political future. Nevertheless, the country was not in a state of military anarchy; all, or nearly all of the soldiers and officers, whatever their politics, observed the discipline, hierarchy and language of arms. They conformed to the laws and customs of war, and courts martial had little difficulty in putting down the few mutinies that arose.

It has been claimed that, from 1653 onwards, the restoration of the monarchy came to seem inevitable. The protectorate established a *de facto* monarchy, and employed the same organs and methods of government. Only the unusual reform of installing the major-generals in 1655 to control the provinces, followed absolutist models. The Parliament elected in July 1656 did not rest until it finally obtained their removal. In sum, the English Revolution possessed two peculiar driving forces – firstly, political parliamentarianism capable of organising parties and creating currents of opinion and, secondly, a kind of military theocracy capable of winning decisive victories. The return of peace threw the contradictions between them into sharp relief. It was parliamentarianism which triumphed, thanks to a centuries-old national political tradition.

In the two prime cases of England and Holland, what was at stake was the total conquest of power, even if the full extent of the objective only surfaced little by little, by force of circumstances. In the majority of revolts, rebels did not have such a broad objective; they envisaged the restoration of specific rights and the rectification of certain injustices. If the weakness or lack of foresight of the authorities put power into their hands, the rebels seemed at times astonished at their easy victory. During the few hours or days in which they were masters of the stage, they put their rudimentary programme into operation. Such fleeting success was summed up in a number of unconsciously repeated scenes, which we shall describe here, while seeking to explain the reasons that lie behind them.

Patterns of behaviour in rebellion

The institutional diversity in which outbursts of rebellion occurred, determined the specific roles played by this or that member of the society in question. The point at which events began was not without significance, as it corresponded to specific forms of provocation. Subsequently, the course of the revolt revealed the social functions taken on by the insurrection and by each of the almost ritual gestures that it performed. Then there was its outcome, either in the form of an extension of the insurrection's objectives or, more usually, of its termination in repression. We shall consider in turn the situations and roles, the provocative circumstances, the functions of revolt and, finally, the common fate of these episodes.

Occasions of violence

If we had to simplify the diversity of institutions and summarise the complexity of outbreaks of violence, we could distinguish between struggles for survival and struggles for power. Anxiety arising from the inflation of food-prices and, secondly, the quest for power within the city – here we touch on the most obvious and widespread causes of urban unrest in pre-industrial societies.

Riots triggered by rises in grain prices were frequent, commonplace and quite banal. Municipal magistrates had responsibility for their town's supply of food, power to oversee markets and, in times of bad harvests, the duty to ensure that their granaries were well stocked and to set a price for basic foodstuffs. The urban lower classes, which lived from hand to mouth, were entirely dependent, in years of scarcity, on the foresight and ability of the magistrates. The crowds wanted the magistrates to force the bakers to sell bread at prices they could afford. In no time at all, they expressed their anger by gathering before the town hall, by disturbances in the markets and by pillaging merchants' stores or bakers' shops. This concern over food also led to barricades being erected to prevent the departure of wagons of grain which merchants wished to move to sell elsewhere. None of this was the work of destitute people actually suffering from hunger – they would have been quite incapable of insurrection – but of poor people obsessed by either the image or the memory of hunger. Everyone was familiar with tales of appalling famine, in which unfortunate people were reduced to eating grass or to devouring their own children; such stories revealed the basic anxiety of subsistence economies.

Bread riots could force their attention on the authorities, leading them to stop the export of grain, and to regulate its sale. If harvests really were inadequate, riots served merely to protect the towns, which were major purchasers of grain, or the grain-producing areas which refused to suffer deprivation in order to assist others. In such instances, riots served, in the last analysis, to exacerbate the isolation of each agricultural area.

Popular violence of this kind increased in the second half of the eighteenth century. The idea of the free movement of grain and a refusal to interfere with commercial initiative were gaining ground among the ruling classes. In Spain, freedom of the grain trade was proclaimed in July 1765; unfortunately, it coincided with a meagre harvest. The following spring, in the critical months before the next harvest, the rise in prices unleashed popular fury in Madrid, on 24th March 1766. To shouts of 'Long live Spain' and 'Down with traitors', the crowd denounced the policy of the reforming minister, the marquis of Esquilache, who was of Italian origin. For two months, the major cities, and especially those of the north, were infected by the fever of insurrection. There were in all sixty different riots. Esquilache was forced into exile, but freedom of trade was not revoked. In France, also, Turgot suppressed the remaining obstacles to the free movement of grain in September 1774. But he was obliged to use the army to put down the riots known as the Flour War in April and May 1775. In Tuscany, the popular riots were more successful; in June 1790, the bread rioters obtained the dismissal of the reforming minister, Gianni.

A psychosis of scarcity was part of the subsistence economy. It would endure for as long as self-sufficiency in food production, to which every region was condemned because of difficulties of transport, with the sole exceptions of areas around ports which could be rapidly supplied with food. This kind of riot really only disappeared when the railways put an end to such isolation.

Power struggles could arise in the cities, of course, when the composition of the town council was about to change, but all the anti-fiscal violence and all the outbursts triggered off by demands for taxes or for billets for troops, also aimed at controlling the city and seizing municipal offices. When they obtained such mastery, rioters would change the town magistrates or oblige them to suppress taxes or refuse garrisons. The power of towns in relation to taxation and defence remained very considerable until at least the 1660s to the 1680s, when Louis XIV's reforms set about dismantling the different forms of local autonomy. The distribution of fiscal burdens within the community and of soldiers' billets among its houses had for long belonged exclusively to the aldermen or consuls. Holding the keys of the town hall, keeping the registers of tax assessments and of population surveys, and controlling both walls and gates were powers were keenly fought over, and objects of conflicts of interest and of prestige capable of tearing apart every community of inhabitants.

The divisions outlined by such parish-pump struggles frequently reflected the influence and socio-economic power of the various 'companies' of magistrates or of the leading craft guilds. Since these types of social equilibrium corresponded roughly to patterns of habitation, and were grounded in the medieval topography of cities, such conflicts often appeared as wars between districts. Thus, in Lyon, urban violence pitted the 'old bourg' against 'the city', one on each side of the Saône. Disturbances began in the more populated parishes of St Nizier or of the *Cordeliers* and crossed the bridge in the direction of the city, seat of power and of the city's lawcourts. In Bordeaux, the parishes of St Michel and Sainte Eulalie, both medieval extensions of the city ramparts, were inhabited by sailors and shipwrights. The rioters originated in these streets, and would make their way towards the town hall and the older districts of the north-west, where the courts sat and the middle classes lived. Patriarchal organisation and solidarity based on neighbourhood, clientship and economic dependence brought together the master craftsmen and, with them, crowds of apprentices and servants. No power was capable of resisting coalitions which were that numerically powerful and which were capable of transforming a district into an impregnable fortress in a matter of minutes. This was clearly seen in the streets of Paris during the League (1588) and during the Fronde (1648–52).

Roles

No sooner had violence become the order of the day than, alongside the inhabitants whose insurrection was geared towards a specific objective, there also appeared other undesirable participants, attracted by prospects of pillage. The latter included day-labourers from the suburban parishes or from the immediate countryside, servants, sailors in port-towns, and beggars in the very large cities. The Parisian Leaguers, in organising their insurrection, distrusted these marginal groups. 'It was pointed out that there were in the city a great number of thieves and mechanical persons, who exceeded six or even seven thousand in number, who were not apprised of what was afoot, and whom it would be difficult to restrain once they had begun to pillage; and that their number would be a snowball that would grow in size with each day. On this report, the invention of barricades was suggested, that is, that barrels full of earth would be placed where each chain linked with another in order to prevent any passage-way, and that as soon as the order was given, no one could move through the streets without a pass-word and patent to do so.' In this account, we see the creation of small fortresses within towns, as well as the grip that merchants and artisans could exert on their districts. Outsiders remained clearly foreign to the cause of the revolt; pillage and naked violence were never confused with the objectives of insurrection. The involvement of these dispossessed people might make for bloodier conflicts or for a brief worsening of them, but such a change was not to be confused with a possible ideological transformation of them. Far from representing a latent revolutionary force, the poor and the excluded who choked the major cities whose inhabitants were so suspicious of them, would always be the first to support a party of surrender. The extremists of the panic-inspired insurrections encountered them in the front rank of their enemies. In every besieged city, they were the real party of treason. They clamoured loudly for bread and peace; they barracked the advocates of revolt, demanded that the gates be opened, and applauded the execution of rebel leaders. Thus in the Sicilian towns in the autumn of 1647, or in Naples from the end of that October, the poorest classes demonstrated for the return of the Spanish viceroys. In Bordeaux, the final months in power of the Frondeur faction of the army, from May to July 1653, saw royalist processions by the lower classes. Fleurance de Rivault, a political writer during the wars of religion, noted in 1595 that no cause should put its faith in the adherence of the people; when conquered, the populace always abandons, he said, the notables who took the same side. 'We see instances of this in every age . . . for the intentions of the people are obscure, ill-considered and uncertain. They are not led by honour, but by comfort and a pleasant existence. The nobility ought therefore never to involve itself in the uprisings of the people.'[3] Such disabused moralising reflected the difference, very obvious to contemporary writers, between the dangers of political subversion and, on the other hand, the threat from popular violence, two types of event whose social mechanisms and historical possibilities were clearly distinct.

In the eighteenth century, capital cities of exceptional importance, like Paris or London, already formed huge agglomerations which were swollen by the unending influx of uprooted peasants, rising around 1800 to 700,000 inhabitants for Paris and 900,000 for London. The lower classes of London were composed of shopkeepers and artisans of the City and of the suburbs (butchers, candle-merchants, tailors, shoemakers, dyers etc), and also of some more fearsome groups like the sailors, tavern-boys, textile workers and coalmen. The first group had provided the main participants in the violent clashes at the beginning of the century between Tory and Whig groups. The violence of London riots seems to have increased over the decades. In May 1768 and later in June 1780, the capital was submerged by it: the streets of the capital were in the hands of rioters for a few days or a few hours, and their victims were numerous. The constant influx of people without firm roots (sailors, apprentices) was doubtless the cause of this. Agitators such as John Wilkes, advocate of a radical anti-fiscalism, and Lord Gordon, champion of anti-papist xenophobia, appeared, who were capable of formulating an ideology, but the enthusiasm which they generated was fleeting, as were the plebeian causes that had been so frequently denounced since the sixteenth century.

Paris exhibited a more precocious tendency towards a broader politicisation of violence. The incorporation of the power of the crowd into the political issues of the moment would appear clearly during the revolutionary 'days' and throughout the disturbances of the nineteenth century. Paris had a name for being the best policed city of the age; industrialisation there still possessed paternalist dimensions (16·5 workers per employer in 1791). In fact, the violent episodes of the Revolution there were not the work of uncontrolled 'outsiders', but of organised, educated and armed craftsmen. Similarly, the Revolutions of 1830 and 1848 brought on stage, not the 'dangerous classes', but integrated social groups, middle classes and workers in the main cities. Urban disturbances no longer constituted an independent chapter, with a history specific to themselves: in the industrial societies of the nineteenth century, they tended to merge into, or, at least to frequently cross the path of general political history.

Whatever the objects of riots might be – grain, hostility to taxation and so on – roles and attitudes in them would belong to one or other group within a community. A particular craft might thus be more sensitive to a certain kind of pressure – for example, the inn-keepers to taxes on wine – or else better able to respond to it owing to tools they used in their trades – for example, the meat and leather trades. We saw, in an earlier chapter, how such functions took effect in the roles of agitators. These allocations of behaviour and of actor's roles did not escape the abbé Galiani, that suble observer of French and Italian society in the eighteenth century. 'The magnates conspire and rebel; the bourgeois complain, but do not sacrifice their virtue; the peasantry and artisans despair and pack their belongings, while the porters riot. It never changes, and none of these classes ever adopts the habits and instincts of another. With the exception of religious persecution, in which alone all classes are willing to rebel, the magnates and the powerful the most readily, because they are always the most convinced, the bourgeois and the populace with greater difficulty, since they always have a lesser fund of religion in them.'[4] We might even add more central determinisms, which assigned roles and actions during riots to children, youths or women.

It is something of a biological truism to remark on the role played by young men in outbreaks of violence, and one might hesitate to emphasise it were ideological arguments not so ready to hide such obvious facts. Demographic factors peculiar to earlier societies strengthened the role of youth in society. The earliness of puberty and of the age at which people were set to work were accompanied by a pronounced delay in the age at which they married. Consequently, there was room for a numerous age group in the years separating an early maturity from the late formation of a person's own household. Its importance in the age pyramid was all the greater, given the short average life-expectancy. Subject to youthful enthusiasms and fit to handle arms, youth could be all the more dangerous in that it escaped for a longer period of time from paternal control on one end and its own family obligations on the other. In the case of the Florentine contado in 1427, David Herlihy's statistical study shows a medium age of twenty-six for men. Half the population was under twenty-two years of age. Fathers of families were old. They were forty years old on average at the birth of their first child and, consequently, they were often dead before their children's education was finished and before their entry into adulthood.[5] The figures for Florence could be repeated more or less for the greater part of Europe until some time in the eighteenth century, when the rise in life-expectancy altered this balance. The enduring recourse to violence thus corresponded to demographic determinism. Violence does not mean revolt and, even less, subversion – the noisy youth of the period knew the power of tradition and respected the value of experience which was all too rare. The youth groups which, under a plethora of forms and names, brought together young men, from their adolescence to marriage, were institutions for social control and militant defences of the rights and customs of their communities. And we encounter these groups in the most ordinary of disturbances. On the other hand, during the critical moments of a revolt, the institution, with its festive purpose, no longer appears as such; crowds of young men were, nevertheless, involved in the action, evidence of the superabundance of youth in older societies.

We must add to these statistics the psychological prestige of the innocence and purity ascribed to the early years of human existence. The future of the city was personified in the guileless enthusiasm of small children and in the first experience of arms by its young men. There was not an urban celebration which did not see them marching through the streets. On 10th January 1589, the League, then in control of Paris, organised a procession of all the city's children who, we are told, numbered 100,000, and carried their candles from the cemetery of the Innocents to the church of Ste Geneviève. The places which they thus connected to each other were symbolic of the evangelic purity of their intentions and of the maternal protection and political resolve of Sainte Geneviève, patron saint of Paris. Likewise, on days of insurrection, gatherings of children, whether spontaneous or organised, demonstrated the identification between the riot and the destiny of the city that was desired. So one often encountered a young boy beating a drum at the head of rebel marches. Children were also involved in scenes of iconoclasm and massacre, in destroying monuments and dragging corpses or cutting them into pieces. The wars of religion provide numerous examples of such episodes in which infantile cruelty, curiosity and frustrations sated themselves. In August 1647, in rebel Palermo, the procession of scape-goats, bailiffs or *sbires,* riding on donkeys and lashed through the city, was surrounded by 2,000 running and screaming children.

The involvement of women was also traditional. They were to be found first of all in the grain disturbances, where they often formed the majority of the crowds. In other types of disturbance, they might also appear in the front ranks, where their presence was a more eloquent sign of the misery and determination of the community. Lastly, scences of bloodletting and the most frightful episodes of lynching also witnessed the involvement of a number of women. Another female role may be added to this list – the custom of some masculine rioters of dressing up as women in headdress and skirts. This rite can be found in extremely diverse historical and cultural contexts. It was not merely the most convenient manner of disguising oneself and of avoiding detection, but represented a desire to appropriate the external appearance of women, and to lay claim to its peculiar characteristics and role.

Each of these ritual moments admits of an explanation. From time immemorial, the woman was entrusted with, and was mistress of the family's daily existence – the purchase and preparation of food, the upkeep of the house and the education of children. She was the heart of the family, the guardian of its traditions and the symbol of the household. Far removed from male diversions such as the tavern or the fair, her universe was limited to the obscure but vital tasks with which she alone was entrusted. It has been noted that the entry of women into politics in our own time has always led to problems being put in more concrete form. Attached to the family home whose permanence they symbolised, women expressed the complementary values of Martha and Mary. For this reason, the riots most closely connected to survival and the most bereft of political implications were those in which women played the leading roles. Their involvement signalled a determination and a measure of distress of the most desperate kind. Because of their impunity and of the legal irresponsibility that opinion generally ascribed to them, their participation had something of a traditional stratagem about it. At the very heart of the spectacular harshness of repression which was characteristic of earlier centuries, women enjoyed relative impunity. The weakness of their sex, the embarrassment of the all-male agencies of repression, and the kind of perpetual minority and political impotence imposed on them, all enabled them to fill roles of provocateurs in insurgent crowds.

Finally, there was a carnival-like derision in such outbursts of female violence, which heaped ridicule on its victims, enemies of the community and appointed scape-goats of riots. The tipstaff, the forest-guard and the servant of the tax-farmers was no longer feared when manhandled by women; he was no longer an object of fear, but of laughter. Many folklore traditions have preserved the memory of a more or less legendary victory won by local women over the enemies of the community. Here are two anecdotes from among a multitude, both famous and insignificant. In 1580, the women of Lisbon joined in the general anxiety caused by the devolution of the throne to a Spaniard. 'I would not fail to note the remarkable fact that there was a group of women who sell their wares in the city square, who formed ranks as if soldiers under arms; the woman who served as their captain carried a pan in the place of a halberd, wishing to remind people of the ancient battle of Algibarrota between the Castilians and the Portugese in which the latter were victorious and in which they boasted that a baker-woman killed seven Castilians with her pan.' In February 1797, the women of Wales, we are told, sufficed to capture 1,200 Frenchmen landed on Hoche's orders on the Pembrokeshire coast to start a rebellion there. According to tradition, Jemima Nicholls, a shoemaker from Fishguard took twelve French prisoners single-handed. The appearance on the hills above the shore of the Welsh women in their tall black hats and red skirts, and armed with forks and brushes, terrorised the invading soldiers who mistook them for regular troops. These mocking tales were part of the paradox of the warrior image of women – protected by, and protectors of their households, they were soldiers who were also symbols of the revolts of their time.

Provocative circumstances

The outbreak of a riot and its immediate causes often appear miniscule or absurd after the event. The part played by false information and instances of panic have been quite rightly emphasised.[6] A rumour or a minor item became direct causes of violence, and a riot began to take shape. Triggered by a simple incident, events could move through different stages, whose implications were more formidable, even to the extent of challenging the working of certain institutions or an existing set of social relations.

The strangeness or futility of the original spark was purely superficial. Its capacity for danger derived from the fact that it was a response to the expectations of popular opinion or the feelings of apprehension of a community. The spark corresponded to a vague state of fear that was always apt to reawaken, or to a collective obsession rendered all the more immediate by a number of previous indications. People heard that grain would be in short supply, that the brigands were indulging in dangerous acts, that an epidemic had broken out not far away, that policies had been decided upon which would be a heavy burden on people, or that troops were already on their way towards the province. The danger was held to be imminent; a horseman seen on the road, an unknown traveller in an inn, a letter whose contents were obscure or an unguarded word were enough for a crowd to gather and violence to raise its head. In his *Trésors d'histoires admirables,* compiled towards the end of the sixteenth century, Simon Goulart, listed a large number of instances of panic, complete with a general alarm, bell-ringing, people taking refuge in castles and towns, a rush to take up arms and the formation of armed bands ready to fight against their phantom enemies. The unending threat from the Turks in south-eastern Europe, the advance of an enemy in a frontier area, the fear of papist plots in England or of a Huguenot uprising in southern France were the cause of many a rush to arms, which for the most part either melted away or at times found victims in order to satisfy their state of excitement. For example, the clouds of dust raised by flocks of sheep returning from Hungary caused the whole of Austria to take up arms. In August 1690, and later in September 1703, two cases of panic lasting about ten days, spread from Languedoc to the Limousin, claiming that the Huguenots were about to ravage everywhere. At Réalmont in Upper Languedoc on 22nd September 1703, 'the whole population emerged armed with halberds, pikes, roasting-irons and staves; they gathered with the militia on the square, the consuls had timber piled up at the gates to prevent entry, but no one turned up'. As is well known, the French Revolution began with the Great Fear of July 1789. Recourse to arms by the people of the countryside against the coming of undefined brigands corresponded to their anxiety and impatience for the great changes that the assembly of the Estates General promised.

In every age, there are myths or stereotypes of news which are immediately fastened onto by opinion, people who are ever-ready to accept them, and anecdotes — whether false, true or plausible — which are bandied about, repeated, orchestrated or reinvented. 'In the towns, men gather around merchants from elsewhere and oblige them to say where they came from and what they have discovered there; most of the time, we discuss our most important affairs on the strength of such rumours and reports – which, inevitably, we almost immediately regret. For, I ask you, on how many false rumours have people in revolt based their discussions? How many crack-brained notions, entirely lacking in credibility, have succeeded in seducing people? How many easily-detectable falsehoods induced them to adopt their fragile decisions? A report by a lackey, a mistaken impression that a spy had been sent or a mere noise led whole cities to rise in revolt.'[7]

In the range of news items awaited by people, we find simple and inexhaustible themes such as the goodness and justice of the sovereign and, on the other hand, of the evil of ministers, lords, heretics, tax-farmers and usurers, depending on the circumstances.

The end of taxation, the return of peace and the abolition of servitude in its various forms were indefatigably believed in, and anticipated from each generation to the next, as were their opposites, namely the conspiracies of evil men to invent new taxes, to trouble, ruin and drive poor people to despair. The ever-reviving and hated legend of a tax on child-births spanned the early modern centuries. People believed that men would no longer have the right to be born or to die without having to pay, and that there would be a tax on conjugal relations or on burials in christian ground. Present from Henry IV to Louis XIV, this myth may have had its source in the extension of state law and administration which invaded man's day-to-day privacy via parish registers, notarial deeds and, somewhat later, stamp paper. Obligatory recourse to them may have symbolised, as an unconscious generator of anxiety, the grip of the mysterious world of the written word on the most natural, and therefore the most sacred, events in the lives of everyman.

Here we find revealed the ambivalence of the written

document in oral and illiterate societies. Not understood, it is, at the same time, admired and feared. Men ascribe to it a direct and magical power; it proves, establishes, founds and binds, not by its contents, but by its very material form. Written proof enjoyed astonishing power in earlier societies. The tricks and naiveté revealed by falsifications of title-deeds and the severity shown to unreliable notaries, who were always punished by hanging, testify to this prestige. Every corporation, 'company' and community kept its archives with particular care, as proofs and symbols of its franchises and liberties. Those whose sole archives were the memory of their ancestors and their ignorance of written law, were in no doubt that a few scrolls contained powerful secrets, like the proofs of their liberties, of their exemption from taxation and their ownership of their land. In provinces subject to the Empire, they talked of a golden bull which declared the peasants free of servitude. The Valencian tenants in 1693 believed that research in the archives would in the end establish their rights to their fields. In 1789, some peasants asked their parish priests to show them an alleged royal letter abolishing their dues. Each time, they imagined that it was the wickedness of their enemies which had silenced and concealed this wonderful document. Contrariwise, pernicious documents were held to contain in both their characters and substance, all the misfortunes of the poor. Desperate, ceremonial burning of papers thus frequently went with revolt. Just as in burning a witch and her appurtenances, one put an end to her evil-doing, its sources, effects and memory, so the burning of charters, according to the magical legal notions of those involved, would produce immediate consequences. The Ghent rebels in 1539 believed that the 'redemption of Flanders' was hidden in the city's tower – that is, their perpetual exemption from taxation for having once upon a time re-purchased their country, which the ruler had supposedly lost in gambling. They put to death an aged magistrate accused of having hidden it. They solemnly tore up a ruling imposed on the city, eating the pieces or sticking them in their hats.

The theme of an end to taxation was not entirely legend, any more than that of the emancipation of the peasantry. In fact, the establishment of regular taxation in the kingdoms of the west and the binding of the tenants to the land in the eastern countries were both recent phenomena which occurred in the sixteenth century. Each royal succession or victorious peace led men to believe these burdens would be suppressed. Even 'sovereign' courts and political theorists still believed in the sixteenth century that it was possible and right for the state, like any owner of a family estate, to have no other source of revenue than that produced by those lands belonging to the king personally. The parlement of Paris at the time constantly opposed the creation of new taxes by the king's council. By an act of 17th January 1564, it even claimed the right to prosecute before the king the 'inventors of taxes'. This kind of jurisprudence would appear to have justified for a long time a resort to arms on anti-fiscal grounds. A discharge from taxation given to a village hit by hailstones, or an exemption to one that had housed troops were interpreted as general remissions. One-sided texts compiled in this fashion and subsequently printed with a promising title were sold at fairs and hastened the spread of the legend.

During the *Nu-pieds* rebellion in Normandy, two councillors from the parlement of Rouen saved the lives of two tax-farmers and their servants by putting them in prison. In order to free them from the hands of the rioters, they had to give the latter a copy of their decree and state that they were sacrificing to the rioters the farmer's house. (23rd August 1639). 'This well-intentioned statement was broadcast by the people, who believed that the court allowed the house to be pillaged, which was why many people who had not participated in the pillage of other houses, went to this particular one, imagining in their stupid simplicity that what they were doing was authorised by permission of the parlement.' In the summer of 1789, some of the peasants of the Dauphiné believed Louis XVI had ordered castles to be destroyed.

Documents which incited revolt more by what they threatened than by what they promised, were classified in a similar fashion. Any unusual or incomprehensible piece of paper, or any new sign appearing in a public place seemed to herald the oppression whose advent men feared. An episcopal ordinance, an action of a process-server, even if wholly unconnected to current events, or the unexpected passage of soldiers could be interpreted as sinister precursors. A cross erected at Urrugne, in the Basque country, in 1671, was seen as the end of local liberties. 'Most of the people are convinced that it is the standard of the gabelle and of a perpetual misfortune which threatens the country.'

A thoughtless remark or a misunderstood phrase was enough to uncover public enemies, to whom execrable pleasantries were attributed. Mazarin was supposed to have said that not everyone had been reduced to wearing wooden shoes, and tax-farmers boasted of only sleeping well with gold under their beds. At Metz, in August 1515, the magistrates condemned a merchant who was the author of a dangerous joke. He had demanded from the town's militia 'an impost on their booty, since he levied a tax on the re-sale of goods'. In 1635, a canon of Agen was slaughtered for having said jokingly that he levied the gabelle on the wages of the masons working for him. Before the great Neapolitan revolt of 1647, word spread and was reported everywhere that an official of the viceroy, despatched to demand that arrears of taxation be paid, had said to those who complained 'that if they could not pay, they should sell the honour of their wives and daughters in order to do so'.

Functions of revolt

The crowd was master of the streets; the middle-class militias either gave the populace a free hand or made common cause with it. The garrison, if there was one, had either left or retreated to the town citadel. It could happen that success occurred so quickly that the rioters were astonished at their easy victory. Thus, during the insurrection of 7th July 1647 in Naples, the Masaniello tumult in the market place which involved a few hundred youths, grew from one square to the next until it included 10,000 men marching on the viceroy's palace. Every revolt was characterised by legal demands, a military question and naked violence, whose importance and shape would vary depending on the degree of preparation for it, the hostility of the notables or, on the contrary, the role they played in it.

The military dimension included the construction of barricades, the organisation of armed bands drawn from the town districts or crafts, and the appointments of captains. To guard against being surprised, the rebels had to secure the gates and the ramparts, and to station groups of guards here and there. The juridical phase included the inevitable capture of the town hall, where the rebels seized the insignia of urban government; they would install one of their members or secure, by consent or by force, the approval of one of the town magistrates. They demanded from the legal authorities the abolition of hated taxes and a promise of immunity in respect of the disorders that had occurred. Lastly, in the phase of pure violence, one of their first actions was the opening of the prisons and the escape of their inmates. Ringing ceaselessly, the alarm-bell summoned the inhabitants of the neighbourhood who flocked to join the pillage, of which they would have their share if the rioters left the town gates open. The houses of designated victims were ransacked and burned. Those individuals alleged to be responsible for public misfortune were hunted down and massacred. When night finally came, the barrels were rolled out into the streets and most of the rioters ended up drunk to the world.

Owing to the practically unchanging repetition of these gestures throughout different eras and regions, revolt seems to have very general causes that are independent of the specific aims pursued in any given historical context. It is possible to speak of the functions of revolt as a routine social occurrence which was too frequent and too similar not to be part of the much wider system of social relations. It was as if institutions and hierarchies learned to live with these eruptions, and as if their balance and development managed to adapt, in the long-term, to the episodic incursions of insurrectionary violence.

If an indulgent view of an ideology of revolutionary innocence has at times led to festival and revolt being confused with one another, the historical study of events leads one to see only a limited convergence between them. In its early stages at least, revolt may have a certain resemblance to the festival, because it borrows some of its features, or encounters it through some aspects common to both of them. Mere riots, free of tragic excesses, set about copying traditional festivities or, more precisely, re-enacting the sanctions of traditional law. The expulsion of undesirables or the refusal of an obligation lent themselves to grotesque scenarios; running out a tax agent, hoaxing him, forcing him into shameful flight – all of this formed part of the rites of charivari. Dragging about, burning and drowning a dummy which symbolised the provocative demands laid on people, or else conducting the dummy's funeral were gestures which repeated the dethronement of the authorities that occurred during Carnival.

In the course of more serious events, when blood flowed and revolt reached a state of war, fragments of festival could still appear. At a propitious moment or in the euphoria of easy victory, the illusion of an end to oppression seized hold of the participants. This enthusiasm would be all the more prolonged if the power vacuum endured, leaving more scope for myths of success and even for more audacious objectives. Above all, it was drunkenness which, in these earlier societies, characterised such moments. Drinking-bouts of wine, beer or corn-based alcohol, depending on the area, were the simplest and commonest forms of popular diversion, taking up Sundays and feast-days. Drunkenness was denounced as a moral scandal, but not yet as the social pest that it would doubtless become only in the nineteenth century. Violence related to taxes on beverages was always the one which gave rise to the most convincing festive developments; and, as we saw, the inn-keepers often played the leading parts in revolt. The burning of branches and of handfuls of straw was not uncommon in France, and served as a symbol. In England, during the summer of 1736, the establishment of taxes designed to limit sales of alcohol, the Gin Act, triggered off canivalesque disturbances that were orchestrated by the inn-keepers. Alcohol was handed out free, announcements of the death of poor Mother Gin were posted up and then, just when the tax was about to come into force, her burial was celebrated almost everywhere with a funeral that was burlesque and rumbustious on 27th September 1736.

Like the festival, revolt noisily proclaimed its beginnings to the sound of bells and drums, both traditional instruments of alarm and symbols of the major collective disturbances. Like the festival, it interrupted day-to-day normal existence and led men abruptly into another system. It procured a sort of utopian time-scale in which the ordinary workings of society ceased, and in which roles and behaviour were re-distributed and modified. However, revolt was not the pure joy of a state of rejoicing, nor on the other hand the horrifying anarchy of the sack of an enemy city: it constituted a peculiar interval, and a crude kind of utopia. These analogies with the festival and with war were not unknown to contemporary observers, one of whom wrote of Bordeaux in 1650, 'that most of those who desire war and create sedition have the same humours and behaviour as the robbers and thieves who risk their lives and the scaffold so as to merrily spend a day or two in dissolution and debauchery' [8]

But the principal function of revolt, the one that was most obvious and explicit, was that of meting out justice. The rebels set about copying the practices of written law, not in order to criticise it through caricature, nor to claim to carry it further, but to demonstrate the legality and integrity of their action. They knew full well that their behaviour belonged to a different code that they took to be more fundamental: revolt belonged to a kind of subjective right in communities, one that was prior to all forms of state law. It could be regarded as a penal custom based in folklore, in which the execution of those responsible for public misfortunes represented the ultimate modes of sanction.

It could happen that sham tribunals were organised, with all the appearances of legal procedure. The ransacking of houses was often the object of a formal procedure. The victims' houses were marked out; ringleaders often saw to it that individual pillage was prevented and that booty consisting of movables was destroyed or burned. Machine-breaking, christened Luddism during the crisis of 1811–16, corresponded to similar demands. Rioters in London and in the Midlands in 1768 and 1779 embarked on such destruction by forming processions, with prior summonses and to the accompaniment of fifes and drums. When a rebellion failed to seize one of the victims singled out, his execution in effigy, or the drawing and hanging of a dummy imitated the mechanisms of formal contumacy.

Above all, it was the execution of public enemies which brought recourse to ceremonies which recalled the paraphernalia – as well as the spectacle, the moralising aspect and the eventfulness – of official executions. None of the manhunts, the marches to the scaffold, the hangings or hurling of victims over precipices, the exposure or mutilation of corpses were improvised by accident. A bridge, a public well or a post in the market place were used to inflict punishment because they were symbols of the community, located at a point of general passage, or because they were in existing places of punishment. The drawing of corpses and the refusal to bury them completed this almost timeless macabre ceremony, since its features were inherited from Roman law.

The events at Rouen in August 1639 may serve as an example of this judicial claim. Houses to be pillaged were placed on a list, and their furniture taken away to the public square to be burned there. A ringleader passed from street to street. 'This rogue claimed to have orders from a person in authority at the king's court, and carried in his hand an iron bar on the end of which was engraved a *fleur de lys,* with which he knocked three times on the doors of houses he wanted to expose to pillage.' It was noted that when knocking, he shouted 'Haro' or 'Raoul, Raoul', a reference to the cry of 'haro', with its appeal to the legendary justice of duke Rollo or Raoul. This appeal to a primitive and customary support of a specifically provincial law which pre-dated monarchical law confirmed quite clearly the legalistic intent of the revolt – its identification with popular justice.

Finally, we can detect a purifying function in revolts. Its participants did not doubt that they were fulfilling a sort of christian mission, or that they were in harmony with their conscience and their political obligations. Unconsciously, they sought through violence to restore the original innocence and purity of their community, which were prior to the attacks of public enemies seen as profaners of them. The massacres which accompanied the wars of religion could openly claim this objective. Even the anti-fiscal revolts invoked the help of the saints; most of the time, the standards of the peasant rebels carried figures of piety, Christ or the Virgin. Men had recourse to the patron saints of their locality to ensure protection against taxation. The Madonna of the Ark venerated at Naples had, through several miracles, intervened on the side of the rebels and during the 1647 revolt, it was her intercession that freed the city from the gabelles, as a collection of her benefactions compiled by a Dominican priest in 1653 testifies.

In this determination to purify, scapegoats and public sinners such as tax-farmers, usurers and non-christians appeared as the chosen victims. Foreigners or Jews were the particular targets of these excesses. Xenophobia would attack groups which were socially isolated, visibly different, easily got at, and also economically well-to-do, such as competitors or creditors. News of some disaster that was laid at their door – the beginnings of an epidemic, the loss of a ship, or an act of sacrilege – triggered popular revenge. The news of the capture of Marseille ships led to the massacre of a Turkish embassy then stationed in the city on 20th March 1620. English sailors were slaughtered in Edinburgh in 1706 for similar reasons. In London, obsession with papist plots led to periodic anti-Irish witch-hunts. The Roman lower classes attacked the Spaniards who were accused of kidnapping young men for service in their armies. There was a massacre of 2,000 Jews in Lisbon on 19th April 1596 just as the city was threatened with plague. The crucifix of a church had lit up, and a Jew had refused to acknowledge the miracle. The extermination was conducted by sailors from the port and peasants from nearby, and only stopped when bands of nobles entered the city. It has been noted that popular anti-semitism, officially sanctioned by massive expulsions, reached its peak at the end of the fifteenth century, a time which coincided with the crystallisation into states of existing national groups. Thus, a purifying xenophobia reflected a strengthening of feelings of collective cohesion and identity. Of course, witch-hunting possessed the same virtues. Extending little by little, collective psychoses of this kind were concentrated approximately in the period 1560 to 1660. They often took the form of riots in which village crowds set about unmasking those responsible for common misfortunes; they had to find criminals corresponding to, and within reach of, popular anger. Hesitation and slowness by magistrates triggered off punishments by fire and water which would, it was thought, free communities from the forces of evil.

The three functions of festival, justice and purification were latent in the actual evolution of rebellions; they referred more or less consciously to a sort of community law that was primary and customary, as well as superior to the inventions – or interventions – of state law. Their ideal was conservative, and their enemies were accused of disturbing hierarchy and custom. Their origins were re-actionary, that is they did not initiate a train of events, and were responses to aggression from above – from the state, the church or the aristocracy. They wished to heal the wounds inflicted by aggression, to right wrongs and restore the social fabric to its original condition.

However, it could happen that the twists of ideology or the cunning of history disguised the artisans of change as champions of tradition. Thus the revolutions of Holland and England constantly referred to the values of the past which they claimed to revive. Above all, time never recurs and returns to the past are illusory. Consequently, without intending it, revolts could uncover possibilities hitherto unnoticed and, without knowing it, begin new traditions. Faced with clusters of rebellion – whether ephemeral or frightful, spectacular or obscure, successful or vanquished – states and the growing legal system were obliged to mark time or alter their route. Their development splintered according to the resistance encountered to the unification of an area or in the application of a particular principle. The unevenness and specific characteristics of each nation's history still bear the scars of this.

The outcome of revolt

If the weakness or remoteness of central government gave the rebels a respite, their objectives would have time to become more explicit and to explore their implications to the full. These last phases of revolt drew only the most determined leaders, men who readily identified with a day-to-day existence and who, because of the amount of blood that had been shed, despaired of either reconciliation or amnesty. Too implicated to withdraw, they were forced to persevere in acts of violence, to pursue their aims to their conclusion, and to rush to extremes. The termination of a revolt was thus likely to bring about an extension of its objectives or, more precisely, a radicalisation of positions. The rebels would be surrounded, bottled up together and subject to siege fever. Such panic-inspiring pressure, which was well-known during this era of seige-warfare and assaults on towns, led men to see treason everywhere. The safety of all led to suspicion of all, the crushing of internal enemies and the persecution of the luke-warm. In a city besieged by enemies, whatever the cause of siege, men began by setting up extraordinary institutions which pushed aside the usual administrative bodies. The new ones should have the capacity to organise energies of all kinds, and were, therefore, representative of all the corporate bodies in the town, bringing together clergy, magistrates, merchants and craft-masters. They had the power to levy taxes, to confiscate provisions and arms, to enlist and utilise bands of soldiers. Rebellions that were tenacious in pursuing their resistance had their requisition tribunals and war councils, too, and these bodies set about cataloguing resources and mobilising everything at their disposal. They pressed everything into service, punished the recalcitrant and confiscated their property, motivated their supporters by handing out offices and honours. Through such repression and disputed redistribution of places, subversion made headway; the hierarchy of men and the ownership of property became problematic. The time-factor and the danger faced were forces for subversion. It was in the permanence of civil war that secessions took shape; it was in the spiral of violence and the panic of emergencies that revolt was explained, clarified its own silences, revealed its aspirations and discovered to their full extent the consequences of its acts and the logical conclusion of its arguments.

In 1548, the people of Bordeaux began by attacking the gabelle and ended up shouting 'Guyenne, Guyenne', that is by refusing to obey the king of France.

In 1580, the Portuguese towns preferred to support a Portuguese pretender, Antonio, prior to Crato, rather than his Castilian cousin, Philip II. In June, the duke of Alba attacked the shaky government of king Antonio with 20,000 men. In Lisbon, where they were preparing for a siege, confusion was total, with the nobility exhausted and the clergy hesitant. For two or three months, the city was in a state of siege. To extract money from every source, merchants owing money were imprisoned, and the property of those who left the city was confiscated. The sums of money and valuables hidden by these fugitives in the covents were seized. The alleged supporters of Philip II were crushed with fines and legal proceedings. 'The barbarous ordinances and the orders issued to suspend payments and annuities, to oblige everyone to remain in the city for its defence, to open up and ransack unoccupied houses, were legion.' In order to recruit soldiers, ranks, offices, titles in the military orders and even ennoblement were granted to volunteers of all kinds, including New Christians. The search for solutions, given the imminence of the danger, even led to the emancipation of African slaves. 'The black slaves, who because they are so numerous in Lisbon, do not have the right to bear arms, suddenly found themselves armed and practically free, as orders were given that all those willing to serve in the war under Moorish captains designated for the purpose, could do so, even against the wishes of their masters, and without payment to them. All the slaves assembled for this purpose, and seeing the royal order as more favourable to them than it was in reality, shook off their yoke, abandoned their owners and rushed around the city, seizing arms and horses by force and committing a thousand acts of insolence.'[9] The excitement in Lisbon ended with the rout of Antonio's supporters at Alcantara on 24th August 1581.

Other famous examples of this acceleration of objectives and drift towards extremes owing to a siege are provided by Leaguer Paris, which was more or less blockaded from April 1590 to May 1594, Naples in insurrection from July 1647 to April 1648, or Frondeur Bordeaux under the domination of the extremist Ormée party from June 1652 to July 1653. In each, it was the determination of the leaders, who despaired of 'pardon or security for their lives', which brought the re-discovery of the expedients of martial law and the institutions of terror inspired by insecurity and the emergency.

In fact, most of the time negotiations by notables or a show of force by the middle-class militia or the governor's guards sufficed to terminate a revolt. The frequency of this normal outcome was due only to the fact that the bourgeois identified with urban causes, orchestrating the anger they produced and showing themselves to be total masters of their streets and districts. Disturbances could only achieve their goals if the bourgeois militia deliberately chose to give violence a free hand, or if their unity and resolution were undermined by support for it by some from among them or by extensive factional divisions within their ranks. In the Dutch towns, the transition to secession was often made with the complicity of these militias [*Schutterij*]. It was so in Holland, in the case of the great maritime city of Amsterdam, which was full of numerous, violent sailors, and which expanded rapidly in the seventeenth century from 30,000 inhabitants in 1590 to 200,000 around 1630. The province's mobs only committed serious disorders in 1617, against the Arminian notables in Amsterdam, and in 1672, during the lynching of the de Witt brothers at The Hague. On both occasions, the pro-Orange militia freely left the streets to the rioters.

Likewise, the Mediterranean cities could be dominated by arming the master craftsmen. Rebellion came to a halt when the latter, tiring of disorder, organised their companies under arms to patrol the city. At Naples in July 1707, when sovereignty passed from Spain to Austria, pillage by soldiers or groups of day-labourers and beggars was to be feared, so the craft-masters and magistrates organised patrols and prevented street disorders.

After the crushing of a revolt came the repression, which might begin with a military defeat of the rebels. If they had ventured out into the countryside, they would, in the course of a pitched battle, have left many men dead on the scene. Beyond such blood-letting, amnesties which obliterated their crime were granted rather quickly. These documents usually contained a list of the names of the principal leaders who were excluded from the amnesty and to be punished or exiled. Rapid sanctions followed by generous pardons – such calculated tactics were genuine political maxims, repeated frequently and with effect. Repression was directed towards a corporate body, in accordance with the basic principles of society and the specific nature of the crime committed. Here too, legislators were inspired by classical models: referring to the punishment of Rouen in January 1640, a memorialist cited the crushing of the revolt of Antioch by the Emperor Theodore as recounted by St John Chrysostom.

Punishment, therefore, affected not merely guilty individuals, but an entire community, chastised in its privileges, fortune, dignity and symbols. In 1542, the people of La Rochelle, having driven out the gabelle officials, lost their town magistracies, their leaders and their arms. But Francis I restored them, 'for which historians censure the king, on account of the magnanimity that he showed towards a mutinous and seditious people who, precisely for this reason, would revert on the slightest excuse to its vomiting, for he should have punished them as an example and restrain them by building a fortress. This extraordinary magnanimity led the people of Bordeaux to revolt, too'. After La Rochelle's final revolt in 1628, it lost its ramparts, privileges and dignities.

Corporate repression could extend beyond a single city. Thus, the valley of the Leventine, a fief of the canton of Uri, expelled the Uri *bailli* in May 1755. Subjugated by an expedition from the old cantons, all of its inhabitants had to attend, kneeling, the execution of their leaders, renew their oath of loyalty to Uri and surrender their exemptions, which were only restored them in 1781.

The only revolts to leave behind an enduring nostalgia were those identified with religious or national causes. Most revolts were so clearly limited by their demands and the circumstances giving rise to them that their defeat destroyed even the memory of them. A short memory for such events did not prevent an ineradicable tradition of revolt, which is to say that while the circumstances of a revolt might be completely forgotten, the institutional triggers which provoked them remained tenacious. The fleeting character of popular enthusiasms, the apparent spontaneity of their gatherings and the ease with which they dispersed showed a contempt for such happenings among political figures. The populace was incapable of continuity or constancy; it was mad and fickle; even its most terrible undertakings did not endure long. Such opinions were common coin.

'Ignorance shields the populace from difficulty, and brings precipitate action; thoughtlessness removes apprehension from its mind, and provides it with an assurance thanks to which it throws itself into something reckless which is no more than touch-paper; yet it takes fire, and often burns first those who provided them with arms.'[10]

As an instance of popular catastrophe, English chronicles offer that of the ever unfortunate revolts of the Kentish tenants, enduring enemies of London's domination. In 1471, having taken up arms too late for the already lost cause of the Lancastrians, they had to take flight again as soon as they reached London. Their dispersal inspired sarcastic songs among the city folk:

> Like masterless men why thay wante
> Erly in the mornynge, or it were day
> Thrown halkys and hegges resorted into Kent
> They vanished away as thayre tayles had be brante.

The art of governing assumed a cynical mastery of popular movements. Princes should learn to know the blindness of the people, 'to lead it by the nose and to get it to approve or codemn the entire contents of a sack merely from its label', in the opinion of Gabriel Naudé. Botero wrote in his *Reason of State* that, in order to prevent popular disorders, it sufficed to ensure that bread was never lacking, to ensure that justice was properly administered, to lay on public games and, lastly, to keep far-away wars going which drain off the surplus of neer-do-wells in society. 'Experience has shown us . . . in Naples and elsewhere, that harsh living conditions and scarcity of bread exasperates the common people more than anything else. An abundance of bread, however, is of no avail if the violence of enemies or the wickedness of one's fellows prevent its enjoyment: and it must therefore be accompanied by peace and justice. And then, because the common people are unstable and long for novelty they will seek it out for themselves, changing even their government and their rulers if their prince does not provide some kind of diversion for them. Knowing this, the wisest rulers have introduced various popular entertainments.'[11] As for foreign war, it attracts young men and drains off their excess vitality; the Turks, the Swiss, the Spaniards and the Venetians thus export their potential sources of trouble, while the French, not having discovered the secret of this, exhaust themselves in civil wars.

The unanimity to be found in political sarcasm against the

misfortunes of revolt and the blindness of rebels was not merely the consequence of a determination to moralise men's behaviour and to pacify states, but arose from experience of the most realistic and common kind. An uprising only stood a chance of success if it attracted enough of the nobility to ensure its military capacity and of the bourgeoisie to have the support of town walls. Popular uprisings, on the other hand, were compared to uncertain or fleeting storms, or to fogs which the sun's rays — that is, the power of the prince — would easily break up. Revolts which lasted, which recurred and which played a more or less long-term part in the political process, reflected something deeply rooted, a tradition of violence that was inscribed in statutes and behaviour.

5 Traditions of violence

Certain places and groups recur time after time in the chronicle of insurrection, regardless of historical circumstances or the variations of ideology. Such recurrences and unchanging features presuppose long-term structural causes which go beyond the short-lived nature of political events. A given geographical environment or the peculiar legal status of people in an area may help to explain a propensity to revolt, and the ease with which men had recourse to arms. In fact, the rejection of violence in day-to-day relationships, its exclusion from normal life, and the state's appropriation of the exercise of force are by no means simple matters of fact: they are social events with their own history, their stages and their causes. In a society in which solidarity was confined to the family and the village community, the development of sociability beyond them was a prolonged affair. Progress towards the generalised acceptance and internalisation of law, its extension to the very limits of sovereignty, its entry into spheres that are more complex and private was jerky and irregular, leaving whole stretches of history and masses of people outside its field of action. The theoretical equality of subjects and of different areas before the sovereign is a recent idea. In older societies, it was the complete opposite which was the fundamental principle; they were an amalgam of particularism and privilege, that is of individual conditions that were unique. Such established and recognised differences brought their own mystique, jealousies and provocation. The retreat or advance of privileges like these were charged with bitterness, anger and hope. War played a very important part in their formation and fluctuations.

The liberty of armies

War influenced socio-political struggles considerably, either because former soldiers provided leadership for popular revolts, or because military recruitment served to provoke recourse to arms, or because military operations shattered the power of states and led to power vacuums in which various latent tensions and aspirations surfaced. Thus armies represented a model, or a hope of escape; even if the majority of soldiers were destined to fall victim to camp epidemics, joining up meant being removed from poverty, with the expectation of bounty and adventure. Recruitment held out the promise of flight from village horizons, the emancipation of serfs, exemption from royal or seigneurial obligations, and even the distant mirage of a social mobility reserved for a few veterans and low-ranking officers. The careers of the officers who were produced by the Revolutionary and Napoleonic armies were to be the ultimate embodiment of the advancement in fortune afforded by a military career.

Uprooted, led off to foreign lands, united by the uncertainty of battle, and sharing expectations of pillage, shortcomings in supplies and arrears of pay, the soldiery which criss-crossed Europe from the sixteenth century onwards were microcosms of both rancour and hope. The brotherhood of arms and the licence of the camps were not idle words, since both the command structure and discipline would not be fully perfected before the second half of the seventeenth century. Regiments knew no rules apart from the laws of war, practices which were not written down, but which were accepted by all armies on campaign and which covered the conduct of sieges, assaults, pillage and the fate of prisoners. Mutinies in regiments were frequent, and reflected the autonomous behaviour of these groups of adventurers.

The chroniclers quote as the first example of a mutiny the insurrection of King Ferdinand of Hungary's troops in 1532. Fed with mouldy bread and deprived of their wages, they set out in good order to march back to Italy, capturing and ransoming towns along the way. The Dutch Wars were the high point of such insubordination. Mutinies in the Flanders armies numbered forty-five between 1572 and 1607, with at least twenty-one after 1596. Their main cycles coincided with high prices which exacerbated the normal difficulties encountered in supplying armies. Hardened in war, surrounded by hostile inhabitants, united in their frustration and waiting, the 70,000 men of all nationalities stationed for so many years in the Netherlands were an ever-ready source of disturbances. The most serious of these occurred around Alost-Antwerp, and lasted 272 days between 2nd July 1576 and 31st July 1577; it involved 53,000 soldiers and cost 633,000 crowns to pacify. The longest mutiny was that of Hoogstraten, which involved 2,200 soldiers, lasted 990 days between 1st September 1602 and 18th May 1605, and cost 430,000 crowns. The assembled body of insurgents would elect its leaders who enforced very rigorous discipline. A 'tree of justice' was provided for the submission of grievances, and discussions were held in a sort of egalitarian general assembly. Their demands were strictly professional in character. The mutineers had banners displaying the Virgin and mottoes of 'For the Catholic faith and our pay.' Green was their typical colour, to distinguish them from the red of the Spaniards and the orange of the Dutch rebels. They were not motivated by any spirit of treason or idea of subversion, and thus represented a pure case of protest in arms – moderate and legalistic – that was the most frequent and typical form of revolt in *ancien régime* society.[1]

Numerous mutinies were experienced by the imperial armies fighting the Turks, the Swedes during their campaigns in Germany, and the English in Ireland or in their navy. We saw earlier the dynamic role which the armies played in the unfolding of the English civil war. Delays in paying them provoked agitation on this issue between May and September 1646 and then, after a year of inaction and failure to pay arrears, between April and August 1647. The competing propaganda of the sects, Levellers or Millenarians, was to surface in its wake. The activities of the standing regiments of archers, subsequently musketeers [*streltsi*] in seventeenth-century Russia exhibited the same professional demands. Established in 1550, these regiments numbered over 50,000 men at the time of their most frequent mutinies. Peter the Great broke them up, and executed 1,000 of their leaders between August and November 1698.

After the second half of the seventeenth century, the organisation of bureaux of military administration, the increasing technicality and hierarchial character of military command, the improvement of transport and supplies, and the building of barracks would, at least in the west, eliminate these centres of war-related subversion. In the East, on the other hand, the continuation of the Turkish threat for a further century brought about a localisation of the privileges created by a state of war; in addition, it provided a geographical base for a provocative model of military liberties

The military borders

The diversity and contrast in the status of individuals peculiar to south-eastern Europe was, to tell the truth, much older, and should, no doubt, be sought in the conditions of settlement and conquest of the region during the Middle Ages. In the path of invasions from the east, these areas endured their ravages and received each successive addition of migrants. Christianised and settled, the invaders either founded kingdoms or scattered in communities across plains and valleys. Rulers also invited labourers from the west to clear uncultivated lands or operate their mines. Invaders attached to their martial traditions or western colonists attracted by the grant of exemptions had thus formed isolated communities there; they preserved their ethnic, linguistic, religious and legal unity, in the midst of indigeneous rural populations with different origins, traditions and customs. Thus, from the thirteenth century onwards, Transylvania was a mosaic of peoples in which individuals were classified not merely in social 'orders', but also in ethnic 'nations'.

As an example, we may take the Hungarian minority in Transylvania, called the Szeklers [*Siculi* in Latin]. They had their own courts of justice, their magistrates and codes of private and public law. They shared certain basic characteristics with the nobility – personal liberty and the obligation of military service. However, their egalitarian customs and the equal sharing of inheritance prevented the growth among them of large estates, as a result of which that they could never match the economic power of the lords. From the fifteenth, century onwards, in the conflict with the Turks, they supplied military units and captains. Dosza, the hapless 'king of the peasants' in 1514, was one of them. Specifically Szekler revolts were ignited by a tax on cattle in 1506, 1519 and again in 1596. The last of these is described in detail by Palma Cayet. Sigismund Bathory, prince of Transylvania, was obliged to confront attacks by the Poles and the Turks. He sought the Emperor's help, raised troops and taxes and, in doing so, violated the privileges of the Szeklers. 'These people say they are descended from the Scythians, and are still attached to their customs and laws, even though subject to the prince of Transylvania. Among them, everyone considers himself noble, even though they be carters or cattle-minders. They are a people wholly given to arms, which is why princes previously conferred great privileges on them, of which the last Diet deprived them.' Anticipating their banding together, Sigismund attacked them when only 2,000 men were under arms. He led them in chains to Alba Julia on 20th January 1596 where they were punished 'according to custom', that is, they were impaled, beheaded or merely had their ears cropped, 'as a mark of their rebellion and sent back home'.[2] The Szeklers' legal privileges were preserved until 1848.

In early modern times, the Balkans endured endemic warfare. To meet the permanent military investment this demanded, states had to divest themselves in large part of their authority, transferring it to extra-ordinary agencies, which were clearly above the common law. Croatia was at the centre of this confrontation. During the sixteenth century, it was contested, invaded, burnt and deserted. The king of Hungary, Ladislas II (1471–1516) made fiscal demands of it that were less than half those required of the Hungarians, a proportion that was to be maintained until 1848. The villages threatened by Turkish raids paid nothing. Under Ferdinand I (1526–64), the most exposed cantons became autonomous entities (*Konfin, vojna Krajina*) not subject to the domination of the noble Diet. The frontiersmen, or Grenzers, were generally outsiders, refugees from lands subject to the Turks, and mostly Serbs – Orthodox, pastoral and nomadic – described by the general, but erroneous label of Wallachians. The Diet viewed the autonomy of the Borders as a reduction of the state's territory.

The turbulence of the Grenzers was condemned, feared and envied by the neighbouring inhabitants of Carniola and

Hungary, Those settled on the Dalmatian coast and engaged in piracy against the Turks were called Uskoks (i.e. refugees). Their base was the port of Senj on the Adriatic. Their uncontrolled raids on Ottoman fortresses, which provoked reprisals, led to them being denounced by the Dalmatians, the Venetians and even by the Imperialists, in whose pay in theory they were. The Border as a military institution sparked off revolts by the Sultan's subjects, emboldened by their expeditions. These insurrections were most frequent in the fastness of Montenegro, where the will to resist the Turks survived at its most tenacious. The 1606 treaty did not bring peace to the Borders. Slovenia and especially Western Croatia lived on a permanent war footing, their territories invaded by wilderness and forest.

At the end of the seventeenth century, with the victories of Leopold I who advanced as far as Bosnia, efforts at insurrection revived in Bulgaria (1688) and Serbia (1690). Pushed further south, the defensive line of the Border, 1,600 km long and thirty-five to ninety-five wide, improved, and stretched from the Adriatic to the Carpathians. This territory was the direct property of the crown, and was subject to the War Council (*Hofkriegrat*) in Vienna. The seigneurial system with its forced labour, its servitudes and obligations, did not exist here. The peasant-soldiers who inhabited it were free, exempt from taxation, and subject only to military service under the command of fortress captains and generals. Serbian family structure, the *Zadruga,* a community based on the enlarged family and analogous to the French *frairies,* lent itself to this kind of organisation. Plots of land were designated in perpetuity for possession by families living under a single roof and cultivating them without sub-division. The captain's orders were relayed through the head of the family. The Border system was strengthened by a decree of 1807, and this was the condition in which Marmont, the French commander in the Illyrian provinces, encountered it. He wrote to Napoleon: 'Croatia should not be seen as a province, but as a huge "company" whose population is an army which provides its own means of subsistence.' During the nineteenth century, Hungarian and South Slav nationalism were angered by this Imperial enclave, so that in 1878, when the conquest of Bosnia removed the Turkish threat completely, the Border was incorporated into the kingdom of Hungary.

The method employed by the Imperialists met the needs of war as well as the aspirations of the different peasantries which desired freedom and the preservation of their family traditions. Many similar institutions appeared under the Ottomans. Their cavalry troops (*spahis*) were granted lands (*timar*) whose inhabitants were obliged to support and arm them. During the eighteenth century, however, these concessions tended to become hereditary, with the mounted horseman becoming lord of a fief (*chiflek*) whose peasants lost their freedom. This development did not, however, affect the mountain regions in which the villages' exemptions survived.

Many Christians who came to support the Turks in the early sixteenth century obtained privileges. They formed military associations with a family structure to them, which at this time may have included up to fifteen per cent of the Balkan population.

Finally, the elite unit of Janissaries, who guarded the Sultan, was composed of soldiers of Christian origin, who were either renegades or men taken away as a blood-tax (*devchirmé*). They numbered 26,000 men in the late sixteenth century, rising later to 60,000 and beyond. They had their own jurisdiction and system of payment; creating and removing sultans, they shaped political events. It was their custom to start fires in order to manifest their discontent, and their mutinies were frequent. Their exactions in the provinces were acts of provocation to the subject peoples. The Serb uprisings of 1798 and 1815 were directed against the Janissaries, whose last revolt in 1826 brought an order for their massacre from Mehmet II.

The Roumanian provinces also had their privileged military units, made up of refugees from the Balkans. Under Michael the Brave, they may have numbered 15,000 men. Having revolted several times, they were disbanded or killed in 1665.

Beyond the Carpathians, in the steppes of Moldavia and as far as Moslem Crimea, lay the extensive lands of the Cossacks. Nomads who lived by pillage, cattle-raising and fishing, they are mentioned from the late fifteenth-century onwards. Some Polish nobles formed regiments among them around the Dnieper rapids. In 1578, king Stephen Bathory 'registered' these regiments, and recognised their extensive privileges in formal documents. Because the attractions of Cossackdom constantly swelled the number of irregulars among them, their liberties soon clashed with the southward expansion of Poland. Revolts in 1596, 1629 and 1639 demonstrated the subersive power of these military communities. The great Ukrainian and Russian peasant uprisings were, as we shall see later, for the most part Cossack wars.

Guerilla war

Because of the great open spaces suitable for cavalry and because of the combat tactics of the Turks, which involved savage, lightning raids, military operations in the plains and steppes did not resemble the techniques and tactics of western armies. The permanence of military theatres in central and eastern Europe led to the discovery there of light cavalry tactics which astonished French observers. In reality, the latter were not ignorant of the activities of the scouts, adventurers or 'forlorn hopes' (*enfants perdus*), the names by which the foragers and men engaged in reconnoitring were previously known, but they found during the wars of Louis XIV that the French light troops were always inferior to the Imperial units of the same type. It was in order to imitate the Hungarians that the first French regiment of Hussars was established in 1692. Returning from the War of Austrian Succession, a French officer, Captain Grandmaison, published in 1756 a treatise called *La Petite Guerre*. 'If the value of troops and faction leaders for guerilla warfare has been so generally recognised in every age and nation, the necessity of having them is much better shown in our own time, when the queen of Hungary's horde of light troops overran Bohemia, Bavaria and Alsace at a time when France was without this type of military unit.'[3] It amounted to the rediscovery of a very old model which had been forgotten during the peaceful reign of Louis XV. Civil war had disappeared since the Fronde and its prolongations and, since 1712, the country had experienced nearly thirty years of peace.

In fact, guerilla war is a mode of combat which transcends period; it was practised during early modern times in the normal course of war between states, whether in engagements involving few men, or at moments when the population took part in operations; and, of course, it was part and parcel of peasant revolts.

In wars between rulers, massed battles and full-scale sieges were rare. During the course of a campaign, each unit was determined to avoid large-scale clashes, the outcome of which was always uncertain. They preferred to seize bargaining-counters, and to gain control of the large villages and medium-sized towns which supplied them. There was, therefore, scope for surprise raids, ambushes and harassment of the enemy. Monluc's *Mémoires* are full of accounts of towns captured with the help of three ladders mounted on a cart, and of attacks on convoys by small troops of horse. Popular participation is also evident in the salvos loosed off by the bourgeois stationed on the walls, in the intelligence supplied by inhabitants, and in the massacre of fugitives left to the mercy of the peasants.

In fact, everyone was armed and took part in warfare. Towns had their well-equipped companies of bourgeois and their own artillery. In the event of danger, local nobles would assume leadership of these companies, and provide a military command. Country people, without walls to defend, themselves took refuge in their church, with musketeers in the bell-tower, barricaded the village streets with barrels filled with earth, or lay in ambush along the forest roads.

The maintenance of public order was, like war, a matter of common interest. Central government did not have its own forces entrusted with implementing its decisions. Heralds, provosts, sheriffs or *barigels* with their archers, tipstaffs from the courts, *sbires* or the mounted police of the *maréchaussée* in France were very few in number, because their actions were purely symbolic. They wore the sovereign's livery, personified the state and their appeals for support were supposed to get the local inhabitants – the 'commoners' as they were called – to come to their assistance. The bourgeois militia might be needed in the towns. In the countryside, the nobility were supposed to saddle up and the 'commoners' to march off at the sound of the alarm. It is clear that popular revolts were no different in their military characteristics from the practice of warfare, the formal legitimacy of which was sanctioned by royal ordinances. Instances of popular involvement in wars which were patently insurrectional could be multiplied endlessly. Thus, in 1518, soldiers of the duke of Saxony, entered Guelderland, 'where they cruelly pillaged the villagers'. The duke of Jülich barred their way, and his peasants finished off the rout by massacring the soldiers. In 1568, in Hainaut, a Calvinist column was scattered by the Spaniards. 'The runaways, thinking they had successfully escaped butchery by their enemies and that they were now safe, fell into the hands of the peasants, people with neither pity nor mercy, a swarm of angry wasps among whom there were a few uncouth nobles, who first robbed them, then massacred them appallingly, killing over 1,200 in all.' Peasant communities' defence of themselves, which was constant, universal, vigorous and which revived with every conflict, illustrates the overlap and convergence between war and rebellion.

The War of Austrian Succession saw a rebirth of methods of mobile warfare. The Hungarian and Croatian cavalry trained in the Turkish wars excelled in isolated actions and harassment. Their incursions into Bavaria and Bohemia between 1742 and 1744 spread terror among the Prussian and French troops as they crossed hostile regions where the Austrians employed the old scorched-earth tactics. Frederick II, who encountered such difficulties when he invaded Bohemia and later during his retreat through Silesia, testifies to it in his Mémoires: 'The Austrian government ordered the inhabitants to leave their houses at the first sight of the Prussians, to conceal their grain and to repair to the woods, promising to indemnify them for their losses. Foraging required protection by detachments comprising thousands of men. Every bale of straw cost blood.'[4]

Although success always depended on defensive fortresses, artillery parks and big battalions, henceforth every army wanted to have its light cavalry units, as well as its free companies of infantry skirmishers, whose actions resembled peasant guerilla war. The effectiveness of the partisans, called 'foot-dragoons' or 'free shooters', raised by the Swedes in Karelia, was quoted as an example. Advancing through the forests on snow skis, the Finnish peasants provided 4–8,000 men for every war waged against the Russians or the Danes. The signs of a renaissance in the art of war which enlightened opinion was fond of discerning were, in fact, campaigns whose military scale was small, but ones in which the appearance of national conflicts led to the stakes being high. They liked to quote the Corsican revolt against the Genoese, Poland's resistance and, of course, the American War of Independence.

'Insignificant from a number of points of view, the American War of Independence', wrote the Prussian general von Bülow in 1801, 'was absolutely remarkable as the beginning of a new political and military era. No battles, only small engagements; a war fought by light troops – this is what we shall see in future. . . . From it dates the first use of sharpshooters, which was the manner in which the Americans deployed their militia'.[5] It seemed that victory must go to the nation that was totally involved in a cause. However, as Jomini more perceptively remarked, insurrections that were purely popular would inevitably be put down. Jomini had served in Spain, and could remember the disappearance in a single night of the Ney division's artillery train: 'The difficulties are particularly great when the people are supported by a considerable nucleus of disciplined troops. The invader has only an army: his adversaries have an army and a people wholly in arms . . . he holds scarcely any ground except that on which he encamps; outside the limits of his camp every thing is hostile.'[6]

The impact of Napoleon's Spanish and Russian campaigns, and their encounter with the intoxication of romantic nationalism, sanctioned the birth of the idea of a people's war, in which everyone is a combatant, and the defence of one's homeland is at issue. Heroic or fierce, the guerilla and the brigand turned patriot become heroes of novels and objects of genre painting, as particularly illustrated by the Englishman David Wilkie (1785—1841). From being a marginal auxiliary, the guerilla is raised to the dignity of an engine of history. He brings popular legitimacy to the cause he defends, and the laurels of victory in the Greek War of Independence are awarded to the rebel Greek child in preference to the canons of the English fleet. The image of the guerilla has been ceaselessly embroidered, its latest phase being the contemporary myth of 'revolutionary war'. We should note that, as early as the 1740s, guerilla war appeared novel. The endurance of this illusion is due, no doubt, to its daring and risky character, and to its resemblance to a dangerous and heroic game.

Insurrection's reservists

We have seen how a tradition of revolt corresponded to personal privilege and to the military vocations of certain groups or, as in time of war, to the whole of society. The perennial character of violence has its territorial roots, too. At the origin of this we find the same reasons as those lying behind the grant of personal privileges. An area's peculiar importance at a specific moment in history compelled a ruler to attempt to bind it to him by the grant of a favour or an official recognition of an actual state of affairs. The location of a province on a disputed frontier, the uncertain loyalty of its inhabitants and the defensive potential of its terrain justified the fragmentation of power, and the acceptance of autonomy or of a regime based on privileges. As with the condition of persons, such inequality and contrast between areas created bad feeling and allurements. A privileged place would always be ready to defend jealously, by revolt if necessary, a legal patrimony which seemed eternal and sacred to it, while neighbouring places would be tempted to follow the example of such revolts or, in their turn, to claim the same advantages and exemptions.

A study of popular uprisings in the south-west of France in the sixteenth and seventeenth centuries revealed the existence of such roots, and of local recurrences of rebellion. The areas so catalogued – the marches between Poitou and Brittany, the southern castellanies of Saintonge and the Angoumois, the Paréage region of Périgord, the viscountcy of Turenne, the Pyrenees valleys etc – all had in common the possession of fiscal immunities sanctioned by royal decree and the power to protect them with impunity from aggression by the state, because of their marshland or mountain terrain. Law and fact were not readily distinguishable: the difficulty of access to these regions and the dangers of frontier zones ensured either that they received privileges more extensive than those of other places, or that they had the power to defend them much longer.

Only detailed research enables us to discover such local roots to revolt. They can be all the more difficult to recognise in the the frontier phenomenon and the juridical particularism which gave rise to them are not necessarily obvious from their geography. The frontiers of states, of jurisdictions, of customs and of fiscal regimes were capriciously drawn, with over-lapping, blanks and enclaves which resulted from seigneurial rights or the fortunes of war. Such tiny distortions determined the exemption of a particular village or the political allegiance of a particular valley. Ease of passage across frontiers offered the possibility of escape, of avoiding the constraints imposed on either side and, also, of engaging in fraud and contraband. The fate of certain villages moved in a centuries-old groove, ensuring that each inhabitant would necessarily be frontier-guard, peasant soldier, and smuggler.

The region known as 'the common marches of Poitou and Brittany' reflects both the accidents of history and geographical determinism. The centuries-long overlapping of the two territories stretched about sixty kilometres from the Sèvre Niortaise to the marshes of Retz. It contained some thirty parishes of scattered settlement that straddled provincial boundaries. Concealed by hedgerows and marshes, these villagers were free of all authority. The proximity of Brittany with its fiscal liberties induced the state to abandon levying taxes which it would have been impossible to collect. There were innumerable riots against the *taille,* the *aides,* and the *traites* in this area during the seventeenth century. The villages of the Challans and the Machecoul marshes in the west enjoyed an impunity guaranteed by their network of waterways and streams. As for the parishes of the free Marches, around Montaigu, all had interminable court cases at the *Cour des Aides.* In the major revolts of 1637, 1643 and 1648, these Poitevin borderlands were the first parishes to rebel and the last to submit. In March 1793, it was just here that the Vendée uprising broke out. One of its first proclamations, of 12th March 1793, was issued 'in the name of the people of Machecoul, Retz and its adjacent locality, assembled of their own will in a national body in order to put a stop to brigandage, to throw off the yoke of tyranny and to reconquer its rights and property.'

The frontier between Mayenne and Brittany was another centre of the great western revolt of 1793; here, too, it was a matter of an area where a historic frontier had localised the profits of smuggling and traditions of evading the law. 'In all ages, fraud was a craft and almost a state of existence for the inhabitants of those same parishes that engage in it to-day. . . . We must therefore stop believing that it is the consequence of certain peculiar circumstances influenced by calamity or the penury of certain years. It is practised because of people's style of life, the ancient custom of the parish and, lastly, by the sons of those whose fathers practised it there, too.' An analysis of the condemnations issued by the salt-tax court at Laval confirms this view.'[7] Over half the 4,788 smugglers tried between 1759 and 1788 came from eight parishes. One of these salt smugglers (*fauxsauniers*) was Jean Cottereau, alias Jean Chouan, son of a woodman and shoe-maker from St Ouen-des-Toits; he was to become one of the most popular leaders of the Vendée revolt.

At the other end of the kingdom, the province of Dauphiné formed another centre of frequent revolt, which derived from its legal patrimony. The movement for the emancipation of peasant lands occurred early there; from the late thirteenth century, it was closely connected to the authority of the Dauphins, who granted charters to the village communities in return for immediate fiscal or military contributions. The short reign of Jean II (1307–19) was more decisive than any other. When, in 1349, the Dauphiné was ceded to France, a contract known as the Dauphiné statute, laid down the emotional and juridical framework for relations between the ruler and his subjects. This charter of its liberties embodied the province's path to autonomy which had already taken shape, and guided its future constitutional development. From then on, its inhabitants constantly referred to the 'natural liberty of the lands of this country'. An allodial province, like all those of the south and the east, the Dauphiné in addition allowed for the possibility of someone becoming an *alleutier* by prescription, even at the expense of the king's domain. The parlement at Grenoble and the province's lawyers loudly proclaimed these spectacular exceptions to the common law of the kingdom. A conviction about the original character of their liberty guided their insurrections as much as it did learned defences of it. The critical events of the pre-Revolution were enacted here in the name of provincial autonomy and, in 1793, the province distinguished itself in south-eastern France as a bastion of the Convention, the centre of 'southern sansculottism'. Dauphiné's revolutionary vocation can thus be fitted into a pattern that spans five centuries. Throughout this period, and via a succession of contraditory theses ranging from autonomy to centralisation, the people of Dauphiné seemed predestined to a kind of subversion.

In the above example, the idea that the institutionalisation of a specific right could provide legitimacy for revolt and a tradition of recourse to violence, was not localised in a few villages or districts, but embraced a whole province. This is because law, itself a product of history, in its turn influences the course of events, not merely by orienting human actions in the direction of legality, which is a truism, but also in modifying and originating behaviour outside of the field of law. This idea has been supported by another hypothesis. It has been noted that in the anti-seigneurial disturbances of 1789, the peasants either burned title deeds or extorted written renunciations of them, and that these two approaches were differentiated by geography. In this view, the demand for a renunciation occurred in non-allodial provinces (no *alleu* without a title) or in those with 'censual' legal customs (no title without a lord).[8] As the burden of proof in the courts in these western and northern provinces lay with the tenants, their aim was to obtain from their lords a document in proper legal form abolishing it. On the other hand, the burning of deeds corresponded to allodial provinces (no lord without a title), where emancipation from seigneurial obligations presupposed the destruction of the proofs in his ownership.

To carry more conviction, this analysis needs examples other than those from France. English experience testifies to the irreducible character of the regions furthest removed from the capital and most difficult to get to, such as Cornwall or the northern provinces. Kent, on the other hand, no more than two days' march from London, is a case of a well-developed

141

particularism at the capital's doorstep. The commons and gentry of Kent were involved in successive revolts against the power of London in 1381, 1450, 1471, 1483, 1554 and 1648. A county of very early settlement, the religious centre of England with Canterbury, the gateway to Europe, and an area of long established maritime activities with the Cinque Ports, Kent was full of history, and its towns and villages rich in privileges and distinctions. London's proximity and prestige engendered jealousy, while the isolation of the hedgerows and woodland of the Downs and the Weald began not far from the Dover road. Its small towns had experienced decline from their medieval glory, owing to the huge growth of the capital and the extension of maritime trade-routes. Survivals of the past and contemporary frustrations produced images of Kent's heroic calling and of its inhabitants' native independence. These feelings appeared in a torrent of ballads and common rhymes acclaiming the royalist rising of 1648.[9] The powerful attraction of London and the intensity of migratory movements in the long run altered the population balance and consigned this particularist tradition to oblivion.

The old Swedish province of Dalarna may provide us with another example. Blanketed with forests, this upland area possessed copper mines worked since the thirteenth century, and silver mines started in the fourteenth. The mining district constituted an autonomous juridical entity, governed by privileges of German origin which were established in 1347. Workers were attracted by grants of land, and its inhabitants were exempt from billeting troops and taxation; their tribute consisted solely of furs. Kings only entered the area after delivering hostages to them as a guarantee of their privileges.

Following the union with Denmark, the Swedes were angry at seeing posts of honour go to foreigners and at taking orders from Danish governors (*baillis*). Rebellion began in Dalarna in 1434, and its success brought the regency of the kingdom to a wealthy miner from Dalarna, Engelbrekt. Yet again, in 1471, 1497 and 1500, Danish authority reeled from the uprisings of Sten Sture, who was supported each time by the archers of the Dalarna militia. In 1520, the new champion of Sweden's liberties, Gustavus Vasa, sought refuge in Dalarna to escape being pursued by Christian II. It was there, in January 1521, that his revolt 'for public liberty' began. Acclaimed as king in June 1523, Gustavus Vasa had, in his turn, to deal with violent uprisings in 1525 and 1532 by the Dalesmen, who were stubbornly attached to the defence of their fiscal immunities. The privileged foresters, smiths and miners of Dalarna thus personified the liberties of the kingdom, and their isolated province was for a century the epicentre of every rebellion against the power of Stockholm.

The defence of the juridical inheritance of its regions has a central place in Spanish history. In relation to the Catalan revolt of 1640, a contemporary rightly observed that military levies appeared more intolerable in this province than elsewhere. 'These people are accustomed to living in almost complete liberty, because privileges were granted them by their lords of old and were always preserved inviolate – and because they are by nature fierce; because the harshness of their land makes it easy to defend for a long period and with few men; and lastly, because their province is situated on a frontier with another very powerful king.'[10]

In the above quotation we find the elements essential for a centre of rebellion, in theory and in practice. In theory, a conviction of the legitimacy of a movement designed to defend a very old inheritance; in practice, the habit of recourse to arms in its defence and the possibility of success in so doing, given the advantages provided by terrain or by frontiers. Theory and practice are so closely tied to each other that it is tempting to reduce everything to geographical determinism. Mountainous terrain sketched out frontiers and the fate of provinces, brought about the grant of privileges, and provided the means to defend them. But if this definition were strict, then all mountain and marsh folk, all seamen and frontiersmen should also have engendered rebellion. But of course, explanation by geography alone is unacceptable, so we must think instead of encounters and interaction between the facts of geography and aspects of cultural behaviour.

We may take the example of the Camisards fighting the guerilla war of the 'children of God'. Their operations between July 1702 and autumn 1703 were confined to the forests of the Cevennes uplands. To get them to move from there required recourse to Catalan irregulars who, accustomed to similar terrain, served as scouts for the troops. From winter 1703 to May 1704, the scenes of the last battles were the scrublands and stony ground of the Euzet moor. Forests and wasteland dictated the different tactics used, and the course of the rebellion depended on them. We could add that the Cevennes landscape played an important role in localising the uprisings, as did the hedgerows (*bocage*) in the history of the Chouannerie, its genesis, its character and its duration. Likewise, in every country, the great forests were suitable for the attacks of, and as refuges for outlaws.

Many forests fell victim to repressive retaliation, which was a matter of depriving brigands of their hideouts or, at the least, of widening roads in order to limit the risks of ambush. The Convention wanted to tear down the hedgerows of Lower Poitou. Control of space implied an alteration of the landscape.

However, not all forests or mountains harboured the same dangers; what determined their 'perilous' vocation was their location astride lines of communication or proximity to a frontier. The Appenines, for example, were not full of brigands; their occurrences were limited to the borders of the Papal States and of the kingdom of Naples, where they were able to move smartly from one state to another in case of danger, or else along important roads like that from Rome to Naples. In short, the environment is inadequate to explain behaviour; it is rather the activities of men who utilise, adapt and distort their surroundings which confer on an area its peculiar historical role.

Brigandage

Mention of the influence of geography and of peripheral locations brings us to a final form of endemic violence, brigandage. It is a well-defined phenomenon which can be described and circumscribed in its manifestations, and in its temporal and spatial appearances.

Brigandage is not to be confused with criminality. The brigand was not regarded in his place of origin as a dishonourable individual inspiring horror and contempt. Nor should brigandage be confused with revolt. During an insurrection, communities chose their leaders from their midst. Moreover, brigands were unconcerned about the demands of the settled population. Of course, when civil war became widespread, brigands were drawn into it, like everyone else; they could be tempted by the opportunities of the day, and their military abilities were valued by those in revolt. Thus, pillaging brigand leaders joined in the major Russian revolts. Brigands enlisted in the Neapolitan uprisings of 1647, 1799 and so on. Bulgarian haïdouks and Greek klepthes took part in the independence revolts of the nineteenth century. Leadership of these revolts actually lay with the merchant cattle-farmers of the uplands and the traders of the port-towns, that is to the elites who were susceptible to western influences through commercial links. The brigands' involvement captivated the curiosity of the Romantics, but it was in reality very occasional and secondary, and in no way typical.

The brigand chose to live freely outside of his community. In the concentrated settlement of Mediterraneon countries, villages were perched on sheer rocks, with steep approach roads; the walls of houses served as ramparts, merging with the cliff face; at night the heavy nailed gates of the village were closed once the last cattle had returned to their sheds. It was the brigand who remained in the danger of isolation on the outside. His depredations were perpetuated at the expense of the strangers to his community; he remained confined within certain limits of village conventions and honour. Neighbouring peasants sold him food and munitions, and purchased his loot from him. In winter, he would find shelter in a hospitable house; he might even turn up in the village for a festival, a wedding or a pilgrimage, or retire there in his old age.

The life of the brigand was celebrated in ballads and lays, whose couplets were composed by the local bards. They boast of his liberty, his daring, his roistering and his ostentation; the brigand was abundantly supplied with food; he had the best wine and was loved by the prettiest girls; he showed off sumptuous items of apparel and expensive jewels. The popular imagination delighted in attributing to him a life of ease, abundance and permanent festivity amounting to a sort of village utopia. Escaping from the routine accepted by all, the brigand thus became the projection of their desires and the realisation of their dreams.

Men might choose the life of the brigand or be forced into it. The transition and change of status was visible in language – as in 'to take to the bush' (*prendre le maquis; darsi alla macchia*) or to adopt the life of haïdouk (*haïdutsvoto*). Local custom recognised a sort of brigands' 'estate'. This kind of sanction implies some collective utility, at least unconsciously – for example, the elimination of useless young men. In contrast to cereal farming, pastoral farming does not need much labour. Here we have an element of the special relationship of brigandage to the pastoral world of the Mediterranean. The numbers of brigands, however, cannot ever have been considerable – not more than 0·1 per cent according to Hobsbawm.[11] Joining them had no demographic significance, unlike traditional migrations, but was rather a qualitative purge of excess social turbulence.

An act of bloodshed, which obliged a young man to flee punishment by the courts or family revenge, was often the source of a move into brigandage. Such a flight unveiled a conflict between village custom which acknowledged the possible legitimacy of assassination in a matter of revenge or the murder of a public enemy – such as a Turk or a tipstaff – and, on the other hand, public law which demanded the head of the guilty person. Customary practices of violence belong to a form of law which theorists have labelled 'natural, primitive, popular, *folklorique* or social'. Multiple layers of law exist in every society, but in the Mediterranean region the separation is much clearer between public, state law and the popular, oral one in which legislators would see only barbarism and utter delinquency. This divorce can be attributed to the alienation that occurred in state power, which passed to invaders (the Turks) or to distant overlords (Spain or Northern Italy). Over the centuries, central justice had accepted its inability to discipline men and supervise the localities. By adjusting to this remoteness, it worsened and even institutionalised the violence of customary law. Local administration of justice was turned over in the Balkans to peasant communities and in southern Italy to the barons' courts. Subsequent attempts by the state to intervene in the social order would be unwelcome and regarded as infringements of their liberties. The state also accepted the collective responsibility of families or communities in acts of brigandage. It gave up any exact administration of justice, and preferred the purely provisional effectiveness of pragmatic approaches to pacification. This means that the investigations and sentences of common law gave way to arbitrary methods, compensations, ransoms, guarantees, safeguards, grants of personal immunity and of various favours.

Brigandage experienced a peculiar expansion all round the Mediterranean during the sixteenth century, coinciding with the turning points that were the Turkish invasions and the growth of activity in the Atlantic. Every subsequent expansion in the numbers of brigands corresponded to cycles in the world of pastoral farming and its excess supply of young men. The critical moments were the end of war when the closing off of the safety valves that armies represented sent back demobilised soldiers to their native places. The successive stages of the very slow decline of pastoral farming exacerbated its violence by gradually restricting pastoral communities to the higher ground, as in the case of the Sardinian shepherds pushed back towards the mountains of Barbagia in the centre of the island.

Occasionally, brigandage did actually influence events, as during the period 1585–90 when the centralising efforts of states faltered as the particular misfortunes of years of scarcity were encountered. The veritable private armies of Marco Sciarra, who was killed in 1593, and of the duke of Montemarciano, killed in 1591, sometimes numbered more than 1,000 men. At the end of the seventeenth century, the worst years, during the War of Messina (1675–8), led to over 1,000 brigands being listed for the entire kingdom of Naples. But the establishment of permanent bands was uncommon. It was as if the number of men involved, the time-scale of their insubordination and the ferocity of their actions represented a threshold of tolerance beyond which local complicity no longer functioned and military expeditions, organised from Palermo, Naples or Rome, led to their being scattered. In his *Voyage pittoresque* of 1781 the abbé de Saint-Non noted the impossibility of distinguishing brigands from the constables employed by the Sicilian barons. Their impunity was almost wholly guaranteed 'either because men are circumspect towards lords of whom they are vassals and to whose fiefs the brigands have

147

retreated, or because the brigands' relatives settle their problems for them through money, protection or the waivers of their victims'.[12]

In the Balkans, the proliferation of brigands also coincided with war, the opportunities it afforded and the uprooting it occasioned. The great campaigns of the late seventeenth century favoured the establishment of the *haïdouks* in Wallachia, where they spent the winters in safety. In the spring, they would cross the Danube to operate during the dry season as brigands in the Bulgarian mountains. Turkish convoys were their favourite targets, but their choices were entirely dictated by opportunities for pillage.

Brigandage is thus confined within precise limits of place and period. It is part of the customary practices of violence characteristic of the regions of the Mediterranean littoral. As with the guerilla war of the peasants and the insurrectionary traditions of provinces possessed of privileges, it is evidence of a propensity and an easy transition to violence, as well as of its very familiarity, in older societies. This commonplace has been lost from sight owing to historians' exclusive concentration on acts of violence which produced social and political change. When restored to this framework, many acts of rebellion lose their strange character, and recover their 'ordinary' brutality and the natural legitimacy that those involved claimed for them.

6

Peasant wars I:
the sixteenth
and seventeenth centuries

Peasant disturbances must form part of any typology of early modern revolt, since in a world that was overwhelmingly rural, they were the kind of social disorder capable of spreading on the widest scale. Crowds are a rare experience for country people; news is slow and unreliable. However, when discontent takes root or when a cause succeeds in winning over a province, its accumulated force assumes the proportions of civil war, the breadth and tenacity of which contrasts with the fleeting character of urban riots. Despite its potential seriousness, this type of event is poorly understood, as it does not fall into the purview of what is called important, this is to say, political history. Occurring far from towns and sharing none of their feelings, the reputation of such revolts at the time was either pitiful or shameful. When, in the nineteenth century, they became precursors and distant forerunners of national rebellions, and have, in our own time, been inserted by socialist historiography into the prolonged unfolding of a class struggle that was not yet conscious of itself, the opposite danger of magnifying them would yet again distort them. We must therefore narrate their history with care, and attempt to measure, number and date things in a domain which is badly served both by the sources and by the historiography, and vulnerable to approximation and mythology. For this purpose, we have grouped these movements together into several models which are more chronological than methodological – the resistance of the eastern peasantry to the second serfdom throughout the sixteenth and seventeenth centuries; the opposition, which was characteristic of the seventeenth century, to centralisation in the west; the disturbances that accompanied the collapse of the seigneurial system in the eighteenth century; and, finally, the struggles for survival by *ancien régime* agrarian communities as they fell apart at the beginnings of the modern era.

149

Resistance to the 'second serfdom'

The fourteenth and fifteenth centuries were characterised by the sudden arrival of plague which became endemic, and was to remain so for three centuries, as well as by the prolonged disasters of war. Europe's kingdoms emerged from these trials with fewer men and more empty spaces; land was there for the taking, while labour was scarce – ideal conditions for agricultural producers. Freed from the bonds of personal servitude for a greater or lesser period of time, Europe's peasantries cleared land, sowed and reaped, and could even sell their goods and prosper.

Meanwhile, the nobilities saw the yield of their dues payable in money lose their value because of centuries of inflation, which was later sharply increased by the arrival of precious metals from the New World. In view of that, noble landowners attempted to make profits from the sale of grain from their estates, rather than from the collection of devalued peasant dues. This turn-around was easier in countries where, unlike France or Spain, there was no prejudice about the loss of noble status (*dérogeance*) to prevent them from engaging in trade. Grain production required a labour force which the owners obtained by reviving and extending old labour obligations which they had in earlier times demanded of their tenants. Increasing demands for service in the form of work-days could only be asserted successfully in countries where the nobilities held enormous political prerogatives. In Denmark, Poland, Hungary and some German lands, the powers of rulers had been circumscribed by Diets dominated by the nobility. The absence of a law of succession capable of facilitating the hereditary transmission of a crown, obliged kings to negotiate their election to the throne. Furthermore, the urban middle classes were incapable, unlike those of the west, of forming a counterweight, or of providing a basis for monarchical centralism. They were prevented from doing so because they were weak and impoverished, firstly by the breakdown of trade routes to the east following the Turkish invasions, and later by the shift in trade towards the Atlantic. Lastly, the military and financial demands made by almost permament war against the Ottoman Empire subjected rulers to the goodwill of their nobles. These various series of causes had the effect of making the landowning seigneurs masters of the political destiny of their kingdoms. Thus, the eastern nobilities possessed the required political and institutional means to increase their grip on society and to extend peasant labour services. This occurred progressively over two centuries, with chronological stages and features that varied from one region to another.

Easily navigable rivers, the capacity of the Hanseatic ports, the rise in Atlantic prices, and western demand, were all factors in the success of the huge trade in eastern grain; the price of rye at Danzig increased nearly four and a half times between 1550 and 1600. The great cattle-herds of Denmark or of the Hungarian plains witnessed similar rapid and profitable growth, whether exported by the North Sea or overland up the Danube valley; the price of Hungarian cattle rose 2·3 times between 1520 and 1600. Thus landowners were no longer *rentiers*, but businessmen. Fully part of the money economy, they were in a position to benefit from short-term crises. The peasant smallholders, surviving in self-contained subsistence and barter-exchange, inevitably became their debtors. In debt and dominated, they were obliged, whether they liked it or not, to surrender their lands sooner or later, and to give way before noble appropriation of the land which, by the late sixteenth century, had become hegemonic.

For decades, many peasants succeeded in escaping the growth of seigneurial power by moving elsewhere. The huge plains and the mediocrity of their limitless acres had accustomed men to an eastward-moving style of colonisation, and to nomadic and extensive agriculture. Where they once left exhausted lands for virgin soils, they now abandoned estates subject to labour services for the freedom of the steppes. The Poles left for the forests of Mazovia or the huge prairies of what was to be the Ukraine, marcher lands that were empty of men and governments. The Russians also fled to these steppes, following the course of their rivers southwards, or traversed the Ural pine-forests and began trying their luck in the immense spaces of Siberia. The Hungarian plain, the Transylvanian forests and the valleys of the Danubian principalities provided other exiles and refuges for Hungarian or South Slav peasants. To dominate this scarce and unstable labour force, the Polish Diets progressively established more or less explicit rules which in practice amounted to tying men to the glebe of their lords. In Poland, Prussia, Bohemia and, later, Russia, the peasants were gradually restricted in their movements, forbidden to quit their holdings, registered on a given estate and tied once for all to the land.

Subjected to labour services, deprived of the profits accruing from the sale of their harvests, and tied to the land, these eastern peasants became genuine serfs in the course of the sixteenth and seventeenth centuries. While the institutions of servitude collapsed in the west from the thirteenth century onwards, later developments in the east moved in the opposite direction. The once free rural communities, obliged only to pay their dues, now found themselves subjected to obligations (*Erbuntertänigkeit*) to which historians have given the general label of 'the second serfdom'.

The Hungarian crusade

The first and most brutal revolt of the sixteenth century brought bloodshed to Hungary in 1514. Faced with a Turkish advance, the Cardinal-Archbishop of Esztergom and Primate of Hungary, Tamas Bakocz (1442–1521), who was also chancellor to the weak king Ladislas II, obtained from Rome a bull summoning a crusade in November 1513. Owing to the opposition of many barons who feared their estates would be deserted, its publication was only authorized by the royal council on 8 April 1514. Sure enough, the peasant rush to join was immediate. The first recruits were the soldier-shepherds of the great plain, where stock-raising, as yet remote from its growth in the 1550s, suffered from the hardships of the neighbouring war. 'When news of this circulated more widely through the marches, a countless throng of peasants left their villages and took up arms, refusing the toil of working in the fields, as they were then full of hatred of the nobles; the majority of them, inspired more by dissatisfaction with such a life than by devotion to the faith, arrived en masse before Pest. . . . The first to have been thus persuaded to leave their homes got others to join them along the way.'[1] Between April and May, they formed an army of 40,000 men, bearing a red woollen cross on their tunics, and living off the nobles and the towns. Then the crusade was discredited, and the disbandment of the army demanded.

At this point, the crusade became a civil war, in conflict with the barons' military forces. Its leader, Gyorgy Dosza, was a captain from the privileged frontier garrisons who was famous for his exploits against the Turks. His flag bore the cross and war against the 'infidel nobles'; he took the title of 'prince and supreme captain of the blessed army of crusaders, obedient to the king of Hungary alone and not to the nobles as well'. The revolt spread across the entire plain, and then eastwards to Transylvania. Its leaders were men from the garrisons, clerics and even nobles from Marmoros. The overcome them, near Temesvar on 15 July, it required the army of the voïevod of Transylvania, John Zapoloya whose soldiers, 'superior in valour and experience in the use of arms and in military affairs', shattered the ranks of the 'inexperienced multitude'.

The repression which followed was appalling, replete with martyrs and massacres. The archbishop and the king, threatened openly by the barons, sought the assistance of the king of Bohemia. 'Claiming to be defending the king's honour and to be taking the king's revenge for what he had lost through the fraud and theft of his barons, the Bohemians halted the incipient civil war ... and restrained the ferocity of the nobles.'[2]

The Hungarian crusade was an uprising against noble demands which were still rudimentary; noble domination would not reach its peak until the beginning of the next century. The Hungarian code of customary law, Istvan Werböczi's *Opus Tripartitum*, was published in Vienna in 1517, but it was not until long afterwards that its interpretation reached the point of abolishing peasant ownership. Peasant rights to own, sell and move about were not questioned until the 1570s. The crusade was thus clearly linked to a long process of noble economic domination, but occurred in its early stages, when the customs of the free communities were still flourishing; it included non economic grievances, such as religious and political motifs. In particular, it derived its ideology and ephemeral strength from the leadership provided by the lower clergy and frontier troops.

The German peasants' war

The German Peasants' War of 1525 has been considered by some as an attempt at revolution because of its extraordinary geographical range, the near unanimity of the peasants involved in it, and the convergence of their demands notwithstanding differences from province to province. Its similarly extensive historiography, ranging from Engels' work of 1848 to the studies that marked its 450th anniversary, enable us to concentrate on essentials here.

The fundamental cause of the war was the reinforcement of the seigneurial system which was transforming peasant subjection into serfdom. This provocative change is visible in long-term social and institutional developments, in the immediate causes of the insurrection and the demands it published. By virtue of some very ancient claims, the German princes were attempting to exercise certain regalian prerogatives such as the authorisation of fairs, town walls, minor privileges or tolls. This trend was accentuated with the reception of Roman law, which emanated in the fifteenth century from the Italian universities. Many lords established themselves as territorial princes, and because of such ambitions, they enforced their judicial rights to the full. They reorganised local courts, and replaced the village elders who had ensured respect for customary law by magistrates steeped in written, academic law.

The conflict between two legal systems did not have merely political reasons. The slow devaluation of their monetary dues hampered the princes in their military undertakings; even the Habsburgs were unable to put an end to the revolts of their Tyrol domains without the assistance of the Swabian League towns. Domination of the village communities was thus part of a search for revenue. Seigneurial judges seized cognizance of cases involving grazing rights, irrigation, forest usages and divisions of inheritance, that is, they attempted to strike at the very heart of customary jurisprudence; they attempted to impose on alleged transgressors fines that were profitable for the lord's treasury.

Peasant customs were also taking a hammering from demographic growth. In less than three-quarters of a century, the population of Swabia doubled. The villages were over-populated. Too numerous, the labourers who did not have enough land of their own made it impossible to utilise peacefully and profitably the common lands, woods or pastures. The enclosure of these open spaces or their conversion by the lords into new tenancies, deprived existing tenants of a share of their income which was only marginal in appearance. The ingredients of a revolution were present in a social group that was still prosperous, aware of its strength and traditions, as well as of the threat hanging over its future.

It is well known that the peasants' demands were summarised in Twelve Articles, which were copied, added to and changed; this has made it possible to record the differences between the various versions of the document. Of the grievances registered in them, ninety per cent demanded the abolition of serfdom, thirty-seven rejected the dues demanded by lords when tenants died, which had the effect of preventing the growth of wealthy peasant holdings. Twenty-seven per cent denounced fines imposed by lords which obstructed the exercise of ancient use-rights, and twenty-four per cent attacked the restrictions imposed on freedom to marry, and so on. This amounted to a rejection of a recently-introduced seigneurial fiscality; the peasants wanted a return to ancient custom, the memory of which was still quite fresh. The importance of their demands over use-rights is, incidentally, vouched for in a tradition which claims, significantly, that the first revolt, in June 1524, was that of Swabian peasants who had been required to pick snails for their lord's benefit.

The Peasants' War came at the end of a long line of resistance to the lords, stretching from the Alsatian Bundschuh of 1439–44 to the Joss Fritz revolts in the Black Forest in 1513 and that of 'Poor Konrad' in Wurttemberg in 1514. It inherited their banners, with their symbols of Christ, the Virgin, the arms of the pope and emperor, and the peasant shoe tied at the ankle (*Bundschuh*), a pun on the word *Bund*, which was both a shoe fastener and the alliance of the communes in insurrection. The pope and the emperor were the only authorities recognised by them, as they were superior to their lords. The arms of pope Julius II della Rovere, an oak and an acorn, were a further symbol of unshakable strength or of future dynamism, as in the acorn which germinates and grows. While we are in the sphere of representation, it should be added that the propaganda of the Reformation had altered the image of the peasant, replacing the ridiculous and ponderous figure staged during Carnival with that of Karsthans, the evangelical peasant. Popularised in wood-cuts from 1520 to 1525, this figure holds a flail or a hoe, he is intelligent, devout and self-confident; articulating simple truths, he contrasts with the verbosity of the papists.

The force of the Reformation movement, and the passion of the young clerics who spread the new ideas, were to permeate the peasant demands. The arrival of religious liberty meant the end of oppression; God's law was identified with the peasants' cause. In conflict with ecclesiastical lords, the peasants discovered they had the same enemies as the urban middle classes who had adopted the Reformation. Lastly, the neighbouring utopia of Switzerland, with its liberties and legendary victories, completed the job of persuading the peasants.

Their leaders were artisans rather than peasants. Armed units came together little by little after meetings or conspiracies. Delegates travelled around to villages which assembled at the sound of the alarm, in order to have them swear adherence to the alliance and mutual assistance. Confiscations from abbeys and contributions from the smaller towns that joined them composed their treasury, which was administered by village notables and mayors of small towns.

Beginning in Swabia in June 1524, the revolt spread to the entire south and west of the Empire by the spring of 1525. It comprised several military units, devoid of mutual contact or co-ordination. In five different battles during May and June, these units were crushed by the armies of the princes and the leading Lutheran cities. Taking place in open country, where the peasant leaders, ignorant of military affairs but believing they could fight by trusting in their numerical superiority, some of these engagements turned into bloodbaths. At Saverne on 16 May 1525, the troops of the duke of Lorraine massacred several thousand Alsatian *Rustauds*. In Upper Alsace, engagements continued until October. Judicial repression led to hundreds of condemnations, and the impositions of heavy collective fines.

The complete loss of political power by the German peasantry was for a long time thought by historians to be the result of the 1525 defeats. To-day, other scholars such as Peter Blickle emphasise that over one-third of the rebel areas succeeded in preserving the agreements signed between the delegates of the peasant armies and the landowners. During negotiations and truces, and thanks to the support from the towns, agreements inspired by the Twelve Articles were drafted during the spring of 1525. Despite military defeat, economic concessions and the rudiments of communal political representation survived, for example in Tyrol and Baden.[3] The Germanic areas of the north and east of the Empire, where the condition of the peasantry had already considerably worsened were, with the exception of Samland in north-east Prussia, little affected by this movement of revolt. By contrast, the south-western provinces which were its core, would in large measure escape the effects of the 'second serfdom'. Such local preservation of peasant status and the survival of use-rights ought, in such a hypothesis, to be credited to the revolt which, despite its tragic battles, achieved indirect success.

The decisive factor in eastern Europe's destiny for nearly four centuries was the dreadful permanence of the Turkish threat. The Ottoman empire's dominance seemed irreversible, owing to its accumulated victories and conquests. The Turks' unending harassments and the periodic revival of their advance westward and northward worried the neighbouring Slav, German and Italian states. The Balkans were subjugated, the Orthodox lands reduced to vassal status, Hungary dismembered, and the Venetian outposts captured one by one. For two centuries, Turkish invaders could launch attacks as far as the walls of Vienna and the central Mediterranean. Neighbouring states were obliged to live on a war footing, with their lands frequently devastated and abandoned, their peasants over-burdened with taxes and military recruitment, and their strongholds defended by soldiers enjoying privileges. These three economic and social consequences of endemic hostilities bred revolt. Indeed, a decline in the labour force, caused by massacre or flight, led landowners to stiffen measures which tied peasants to the glebe-lands. Oppressed by such subjection, whose burdens were still new to them, and also subject to an embryonic central fiscal system, the peasants could see before them models of exemptions and privileges as enjoyed by the frontier garrison-men. Here, then, was provocation by competition – their own worsening condition, and the preservation of models of liberty. The contrast gave rise to revolts whose sequence corresponded roughly to periods of Turkish offensive action.

The Croatian revolt of 1573 belongs to this context. Each year since 1560, the Turks advanced into the Bosnian lands, gradually seizing the valleys and the towns. Neighbouring Croatia was not spared; after a half-century of invasions, its population fell to one-eighth of its size, and in some places, it seemed deserted. The peasants had either taken refuge in walled towns, or fled to Carniola and beyond. From 1566 to 1579, systematic emigration by entire villages with their lords, their elected leaders (*Knez*) and clergy, their arms and their cattle, led to the departure of 40,000 inhabitants. The empty lands were granted to Hungarian lords, and this type of transfer was the point when an increase in the bonds of serfdom afflicting the few peasants who had remained, would occur. The revolt of the winter of 1572–73 was a reaction to such changes. Its leaders, such as Matthew Gubec, had distinguished themselves in the Turkish wars. Shouting 'Down with the lords' and 'For our ancient rights', they demanded the status of frontier solders and the emperor's protection. The revolt may have attracted 20,000 men from the Sava valley and the area around Zagreb. It is said that 5,000 peasants were defeated, and their leaders immediately put to death, on 15 February 1573. On a petition from the bishop of Zagreb and the archbishop of Eszertergom, both of whom were Croatians, the emperor sent a commissioner to hear the peasants' grievances. It appears that the rising was not extensive, either in the area it covered or in its duration, and that its historiographical good fortune derives from the Tito regime's desire to commemorate it. The exodus continued and a new Turkish advance, beginning in 1584, transformed western Croatia for over a century into a strategic buffer, where only privileged military communities survived.

The Austrian peasant revolt of 1596 was very similar. The

Diet was dominated by the two noble orders of lords and knights, and the emperor's authority was very remote. Seigneurial farms run by forced labour had been developing. The right of pre-emption, which obliged the peasant producer to reserve the sale of his harvest to his lord, thereby leaving him with the profits of a favourable agrarian economic cycle, had recently been introduced. These innovations were more rapid and more noticeable on estates which changed hands either through lack of heirs or being sold. The spark which ignited the province was a demand for military recruits against the Turks. The first revolts began in October 1596; the villagers swore oaths and chose former soldiers from the Hungarian army for their captains. In February 1597, they seized four castles and three small towns. Such easy success led them to break up, in the expectation that their complaints would be examined by the emperor, who was then resident at Prague. In late March, a military expedition put an end to peasant agitation, without a single battle. About forty of their leaders were executed between March and May 1597.

The Cossack revolts

In Russia, restrictions on peasant mobility began as early as the decline in Tatar power. Avenues for migration opened up to the east and the south, shattering for a long time to come the existing balance between man and space in the forests and clearings of Muscovy. To arrest the unstoppable flight of peasants towards the virgin lands, measures to restrain them multiplied in the late sixteenth century. The succession disputes and civil wars from the death of Ivan the Terrible (1579) to the accession of Michael Romanov (1614) known as the Time of the Troubles, brought into play thousands of fugitive and uprooted peasants. They were led by soldiers enjoying privileges, who supported this cause or that – gunners, musketeers (*streltsi*), western mercenaries and, especially, Cossacks. The latter were horsemen who fought in the southern steppes on behalf of the king of Poland or the tsar of Russia. The various pretenders to the tsar's throne themselves belonged to these free, armed groups which had been formed during the prolonged territorial expansion of the Slav peasantries.

Bolotnikov, a serf from a prince's estate who had taken refuge among the Cossacks, was captured by the Turks, and returned home through Venice, Germany and Poland. Fomented by the boyars, his adventure took on the appearance of a claim to the throne on behalf of an imaginary tsarevitch, Dmitri the Silent, but support for the 'true tsar' by 100,000 men itself amounted to a genuine revolt of the periphery against injustices emanating from Moscow. Its supporters did not come from central Muscovy, where serfdom was by then well established, but from regions still free of it; these were, approximately, the *zemtchina*, that is the south-western provinces which had retained their ancient land-holdings intact when Ivan IV imposed from above massive re-distributions of estates. The centre of the revolt was the Komaritskaya district, a black-earth area producing good grain whose peasants were capable of uniting against the threat of an extension of serfdom that would include them. It provided units for the first false Dmitri in 1604, and it was from here that Bolotnikov started out in 1606. He was joined by fleeing peasants who were now being refused the right to change their lords. His march on Moscow was accompanied by the burning of estate rolls on which peasants were registered and their subjection established. Having failed in his siege of Moscow in December, Bolotnikov held out for another year around Tula, thanks to the army of another military usurper, Gorchakov. The latter, son of a Moscow shoemaker, had also sought adventure in the south and joined the horsemen of Terek. He had returned from there, advancing up the Volga in early 1607 at the head of a similar army of Cossacks, *streltsi* and peasants who had fled from the estates they had been attached to.

Cossack revolts against their protector states, which found support along the way from Slav peasants and foreign nomads, increased during the second half of the seventeenth century, when serfdom had become legally established in Russia by the law-code, the *Ulozhenie*, issued by tsar Alexis in 1649. The gradual colonization of the Ukraine dates from this time. Polish and Russian sovereignty advanced along the waterways, extending seigneurial areas at the expense of steppe freedoms.

To the west, in Little Russia, conquest and a slow social

transformation were accompanied by a clash of civilisations. The settled colonists who cleared these rich soils were Ruthenian-speaking, Orthodox Little Russians, while the territorial lords were Polish and Catholic. Resistance to Polish settlement took shape among the privileged groups which the Polish kings had, in the late sixteenth century, established to fight the Crimean Tatars. The strongest Cossack settlements were in the Dnieper islands and the rapids below Kiev; the Dnieper Cossack horsemen, known as Zaporoghes, had become wealthy from cattle-raising and, especially, fishing. One of them, Bogdan Khmelnitski, who had been issued letters patent by the king of Poland in order to fight the Turks, rose in the spring of 1648 'in order to defend ancient privileges acquired by force of arms and to reject the yoke of the Polish nobility and the far too heavy chain fastened to the gallant feet of the Cossack militias.'[4] He first attacked the soldiers of the Polish nobles and the Jewish communities settled on their estates, and which frequently served as their estate managers. The revolt grew in size because of a succession crisis. King Ladislas IV died on 20 May 1648, the news of which was interpreted by the clergy as an act of God who wished to restore their liberty to the Orthodox people; there was a new Red Sea to be crossed, that of the blood of the Poles who kept them in servitude. The revolt assumed the dimensions of a huge civil war in which Khmelnitski was sometimes at the head of 300,000 men or, more precisely, of gatherings for, as Bisaccioni says, 'not everyone involved in war deserves the name of soldier'. Polish power collapsed in this massive civil war.

The Dnieper Cossacks went over to the side of Russia in 1654, in what was to be a prelude to other changes of alliance and loyalties. The Cossack communities and their hetmen exploited the rivalries and remoteness of the central governments – Poland, Russia and Sweden, the Khanate of Crimea and Turkey. They enjoyed a *de facto* liberty, the reputation of which attracted exiles and fugitives by the thousand during the 1670s and 1680s. Cossackdom at that time was more a question of life-style than a well-defined juridical condition; all that was needed to join the Ukrainian *sotnias* was a horseman's equipment. The hetman Dorotchenko agreed to serve Turkey in 1668, Mazeppa allied himself with Russia in 1687, while Simon Paly tried to raise a revolt against the Poles on the right bank of the Dnieper in 1699.

The most famous Cossack adventure of the whole seventeenth century, bringing together all the centrifugal forces of the Russian world against the power of Moscow, was that of Stepan or Stenka Razin. He was a hetman-brigand like so many others, enlisted by the governors of the most forward Russian positions to fight the Persians around the Caspian Sea, and also ready to employ his men in piracy on the lower stretches of the rivers Iaïk (in the Urals), the Volga and the Don. His many successes encouraged him to seize the tsarist fortress in the Urals in June 1667. In the spring of 1670, he had tens of thousands of men under him, and succeeded in capturing Astrakhan on 24 June. Then he set about moving up the Volga in order to free the tsar and Russia from the exactions of the evil voïvods and boyars. The towns opened their gates and peasants rushed to join him. He reached the middle Volga, where he was defeated in October. His conqueror, Prince Bariatinski, led the nucleus of a modern army which tsar Alexis had been building, with European equipment and led by foreign officers.

Razin revived the imperishable myth of the good tsar who, forced into hiding by the evil boyars, at last hears the complaints of his subjects. Its development was very close in time to the persecution of the Old Believers (*Raskolniki*). We know that the efforts of Alexis and patriarch Nikon to reform the orthodox liturgy in 1645 led to an upsurge of religious primitivism. Popular piety was scandalised by the novelties introduced into worship, and thought it recognised in them the work of Antichrist; the true tsar could not have wanted such a perversion of the true faith.

Thus, all the unhappy people whom fate drove to despair saw in Stenka and his following the end of their torment. The young tsar and the patriarch whom, true or false, he claimed to have in his entourage, were the true representatives of the church and of the crown. The schism of the Old Believers worsened and henceforth put a religious seal on the divorce between the Russian peasantry and the government, the capital and learning. The subversive potential of this internal exile would contribute to more than one peasant insurrection, and would lead the populist intellectuals of the late nineteenth century to attribute a revolutionary mission to the Old Believers, something which was, in reality, the very opposite of their intention of restoring the primitive church.[5]

The terrible repression which followed Razin's defeat lasted several months, with tens of thousands of victims; in some areas of the Middle Volga (Arzamas), it appeared like the end of the world. The Razin epic survived in popular memory through stories and songs (the *bylines*) which related the fate of the unfortunate hero and confirmed the sacrificial fervour evident in so many episodes of Russian history.

Revolts against state centralisation

In the west, the major historical feature of the sixteenth and seventeenth centuries was the establishment of centralised states. Governments were faced with struggles on a hitherto unknown scale. The first conflict of continental proportions was the Thirty Years' War (1618–48). To meet them, it was thus necessary to dispose of ever larger financial resources, and to develop fiscal and administrative institutions that were more complex and oppressive. This expansion of early modern states was at the expense of earlier local powers. As they grew, sovereign institutions swept away privileges of place and person, and the particularisms and liberties created in the Middle Ages. These ancient authorities could no longer survive except in out of the way provinces which, because access to them was difficult or because of the political dangers inherent in their frontier location, were protected against efforts at centralisation. Taxes were no longer exceptional contributions designed for specific needs; recurring each year, they became standing demands; in the attempt to reach every category of subject and source of revenue, they became a permanent and universal duty. However, more archaic subventions survived in competition with them: the generalisation and improvement of fiscal institutions did not stop payments in kind, the most demanding and common forms of which were the recruitment of soldiers, the supply of provisions, the confiscation of harvests, forced labour for bridge-building, levelling of terrain, carting and, above all, billetings.

These obligations were also viewed as the most scandalous by popular opinion, which was angered by their frequency, violence, lack of co-ordination, absence of proper procedure and disregard of common law. Thus we find billeting at the origin of many popular insurrections in the seventeenth century.

The basis of revolt was the parish, the community of inhabitants which was the unit of both tax assessment and of solidarity in rejecting it. Tipstaff, sergeant or solicitor attached to a tribunal, the collector was an outsider who was easy to identify and convenient to hate. As an intruding, unwelcome foreign body, and as a source of novelty, he was doubly undesirable, bringing about unanimous and spontaneous rejection of him by the people. The transition from riot to revolt followed an unchanging pattern: peasants would gather from one place to the next, either by means of letters of assignation or of itinerant detachments bearing summons to meet. Once banded together, they marched off to the nearest town, the simplest and most immediate target, a sanctuary for enemies, a centre of trade and public life, an instrument of power sheltered by its walls and artillery, a place that was both envied and detested. These peasant armies believed they would find in them the end of their sufferings, the triumph of their cause, and an arena where they had for so long hoped to be heard.

The Croquant uprisings

A large number of early modern revolts fitted into this model. In France, the insurrection of the Aquitaine provinces against the introduction of the *gabelle* – the tax on salt – in 1548, may be seen as the first of these veritable peasant wars. These provinces, which produced salt from their own salt-marshes or which could be easily supplied with it by river, were until then untouched by the *gabelle* which the growth of the royal budget and the logic of unification wished to impose on them.

The 'communes' – that is, the parishes when on a war footing – of Saintonge and the Angoumois started the movement by massacring men, called *gabeleurs*, entrusted with collecting the tax. The cause of provincial privileges also led to armed revolt by the urban 'communes', especially in

Guyenne, where the subversive idea of ancient English liberties had taken root. Thus, for a few days, the streets of Bordeaux were in the hands of the rioters. Although there was a complete restoration of order by local authorities, Henry II insisted on sending an army in order to increase the punishment of the guilty provinces. While justice was satisfied in a bloody fashion, the revolt was nevertheless successful, since the *gabelle* was abolished in Aquitaine.

The Croquant risings which recurred in 1594, 1624, 1636–37 and 1707, covered the same geographical area. The word 'Croquant' was an insult, and the rebel Aquitaine peasants for the most part called themselves 'Latecomers', a term which well accounts for the long periods of sporadic violence, as well as for the slow development and maturing which preceded peasant wars. The 1594 revolt began as an act of self-defence by the 'communes' of the countryside; they took up arms to counter the ravages of the competing leaguers, protestants and royalists who, failing to respect truces, fought for the right to exact provisions and contributions from the inhabitants. The object of the revolt was thus clearly political and, more exactly, anti-fiscal. Because of the committed involvement of many noble families in the different parties, the rebels also evinced anti-noble feeling. By its nature, participants, scale and objectives, civil war provided a leading role for the provincial nobility. A demand for peace merged with a challenge to the *de facto* powers which the nobility had acquired during more than thirty years of internal warfare.

Subsequently, the extraordinary growth of state fiscality, which in France coincided with the ministries of Richelieu and Mazarin, conferred an unambiguous significance on the revolts of the peasantry. They were a radical rejection of the finance state, which was emerging for and by war, and they believed they could preserve the tranquil autonomy of their localities. In their ideal state, the king's function was limited to that of ultimate justiciar, and to distant suzerainty over a collection of towns and regions. The social order was thus not at issue in these revolts, except to the extent that political changes might affect it. Thus, the Croquants' enemies were only those individuals or groups which were brought into prominence by new administrative practices, and out of which they generally made a profit. These institutional parvenus invested the profits from land or trade of one or several generations in state funds, the most secure form of investment in the seventeenth century. Tax-farming and contracts for supplies to the army opened up avenues to speculation for them. Then the sale of offices provided them with a market in 'dignities'. Through office-holding, they could begin to enjoy a share of noble status which was, and would long remain, the dominant social ideal. The *gabeleurs* were not nobles, at least by origin. Moreover, it was the humblest among them, the simple sergeants or agents of the tax-farmers, who were most exposed to popular identification and obloquy. The anti-fiscal feelings of the peasantry and the bitterness of the nobles whose authority and prestige were being undermined by the rise of these newcomers, thus easily made common cause. The Croquants often elected their captains from the minor nobles of their district. This conjunction was no accident; it followed from the nobles' military experience, but also from the convergence of political bitterness and, above all, from the traditional bonds of military solidarity uniting individuals within the same lordship.

The most dangerous and famous of the Croquant risings mustered over 30,000 equipped and armed peasants near Périgueux in May 1637. Their military strength was destroyed at the battle of Sauvetat on 1 June 1637, which left 1,000 men dead on the battlefield.

The revolts of the *Nu-pieds* in Normandy from July to November 1639, of the *Sabotiers* in Sologne in July and August 1658 and of the *Lustucrus* of the Boulogne area in May and July 1662, were equally serious. All belong to the same period of uncertainty about the development of the French monarchy at a time when, on either side of the Fronde, the kingdom embarked, through revolts and civil wars, on the long road of early modern centralisation. They shared the same peasant recruitment, the same leadership by village notables or minor nobles, the same fiscal causes and demands centred on the defence of provincial privileges. They generally ended after a few months with the arrival on the scene of army regiments, and the more or less bloody scattering of the peasant forces. In the case of the Boulogne peasants who demanded the preservation of their state of fiscal exemption because of their frontier position, repression reached a new ferocity. The hundreds of prisoners taken were never pardoned, even years later; all were sent to the galleys, where they were left to die. Such inflexible cruelty by the state was the work of Colbert and the young Louis XIV. The crisis of the state's growth was over; the government no longer tolerated outbursts by intermediary bodies, and assumed the means of crushing and deterring them. It had resolved to eradicate a tradition of social violence which, for a century in the France of the time, had appeared perfectly ordinary.

The growth of the English and Spanish monarchies manifests similar stages in which the process of modernising institutions was more or less seriously hampered by forms of resistance on their peripheries of primarily peasant character.

British irredentism

It is true that British history contains few peasant wars. A precocious and dense urban network, very easy communications, the limited dominance of the aristocracy and, above all, the absence of peasant smallholders prevented the growth of a numerous peasant class capable of attaining a form of rural consciousness. Furthermore, absolutist monarchy failed to strike root there, but the construction of an effective, modern state was achieved by other means. If the control of church institutions, the secularisation of religious property and the advantage gained by the temporal power in the unending conflict between the *sacerdotium* and the empire can be regarded as assertions of central power, then resistance to the Anglican Reformation and to the establishment of a national church clearly possess the characteristics of peripheral movements, hostile to the completion of the state. We may take the case of the Pilgrimage of Grace which between October and December 1536 united the 'commons' of the northern counties of Lincolnshire, Yorkshire and the Lake District. The nobility there was more independent than elsewhere, because of the proximity of the Scottish border. The inhabitants were very poor, with many of them dependent for their survival on the clergy's charity. Henry VIII's break with Rome and Thomas Cromwell's ecclesiastical reforms angered these people. The most painful measure for them was the confiscation of monastic property, the re-distribution of which benefited the royal domain and the gentry. The activities of the religious orders – hospices, schools, tenure of parishes, alms and religious ceremonies – had ensured popular affection for the monks. To attack them was to attack Christ and the poor. The 'commons' carried banners bearing the five wounds of Christ and a sacred host in its full glory. On 16 October 1536, 10,000 men entered York. They were in no way intent on revolt, merely desiring to make their grievances known to the king; to the very end, their movement, which declared itself to be a pilgrimage, remained wholly peaceful. The Pilgrimage did not spread beyond the northern counties, and the crowds dispersed in December at the news of a royal pardon which they interpreted as acquiescing in their cause.

The continuation of state protestantism during the reign of the boy king, Edward VI, triggered another insurrection charged with the same demands. This time, it erupted in another corner of the kingdom, Cornwall. Gathering in May 1549, the rebels marched eastwards into Devon. They entered Plymouth, whence they set out to besiege Exeter. It was there that regular troops from London defeated them twice on 4 and 16 August, killing at least 4,000 peasants. The rebellion was clearly religious in essence; it revived the banner with the five wounds of Christ, and the councillors of Edward VI denounced it as a product of 'papist superstition'. However, local political circumstances were decisive in its outbreak: the distant government in London, which was in the hands of ministers who were regarded as usurpers, had persecuted the church, shared out its property among the evil rich and imposed new taxes on sheep, Cornwall's only source of wealth.

Thomas Wyatt's rebellion of January 1554 in Kent on the protestant side, and that of the northern earls in November 1569 on the catholic side, repeated the same pattern of a peripheral revolt attempting to march on London in order to restore liberties that were threatened there. By contrast, the seventeenth-century revolution was overwhelmingly foreign to the rural world. The communist agrarian policy of the Diggers was the work of an urban sect. The tenants and labourers of the countryside remained passive from 1640 to 1652, avoiding recruitment by the different armies, and confining themselves to self-defence reactions and to meetings of clubmen in the final years of the civil war. On the other hand, the revolts of the Irish (1641–52, 1689–91) and of the Scots nations signalled a refusal of unification with England and a struggle for a national identity which at that point lacked any state-based momentum. Events brought them on to the side of the party which appeared most hostile to the power of London and English supremacy, that is the luckless armies of Charles I and, later, of James II. The Jacobite cause extended their hopes for another half-century. The Jacobite uprisings of 1708, 1715, 1719 and 1745 always commenced in the Highlands, and the bulk of the troops comprised Scots peasants who with primitive arms and unreliable discipline, flocked to join in answer to the summons of their clan chiefs. They were convinced they were fighting for a prince's legitimacy, for the liberties of a Scotland separate from England, and against the new taxes (on malt and salt) that the English were imposing on them.

Spanish irredentism

Spanish conditions are more easily compared to the social hierarchies and political models of France. The great revolt of the Castilian towns in 1520 was the first reaction of rejection sparked off by the extraordinary growth of the Spanish monarchy. The resistance of Portugal in 1580 and of Aragon in 1591 was easily overcome by the thrusting power of Castile. The prolonged tribulations of the Thirty Years War, which shook the whole of Europe, put Spain to a severer test. From the 1620s onwards, and then after the declaration of war by France in 1635, Madrid's forces had to cope on several fronts. It had to organise a sometimes desperate mobilisation of the resources of all its territories. The invention of new taxes and innovations from above contradicted the privileges of the king of Spain's many kingdoms. In order to raise taxes in the proper way, the consent of the Estates and Cortes of the various dominions was necessary. When they were not forthcoming, the extreme pressure of events made the government choose the expeditious and peremptory billetting of troops.

The French invasion of Roussillon in 1639 placed Catalonia in the front line, making it experience the incessant passage and quartering of troops. It was the repetition of these ruthless contributions and the ensuing riots that led to revolt by the peasantry. The irregulars (*miquelets*) from the upland valleys, and the harvesters from the hill country were so numerous that they hampered all military movements in April and May 1640. Finally, a peasant army shouting *Visca la terra*, swept down on Barcelona, drove out the Castilians and massacred the viceroy on 7 June. The disturbance would not have gone so far without the support of the townspeople, or without peasant anger coinciding with the frustrations of the whole social body. Suspicion of Madrid, an attitude of reserve towards the war effort and its centralising consequences, the prestige lost through defeat and the memory of the principality's contractual constitution had, over a number of years, undermined fidelity to the king of Spain. The unanimity of all of Catalonia's social orders, as well as rapid support from French regiments, transformed a peasant revolt into a major political secession. Its seriousness struck contemporaries who compared it to the crisis of Dutch independence. 'All that is lacking is the preachers for them to abandon their faith as well as their obedience.'

The easy reconquest in 1652 and the placatory government of the viceroy Don Juan José, who was careful to respect Catalan privileges, succeeded in making men forget the 1640 revolt and the interlude of French domination. During these travails, Aragon remained loyal to the crown. As for the disturbances in Seville and its region between 1647 and 1652, they were nothing more than disorders connected to the high price of grain, and confined to the towns of lower Andalusia.

The most extensive Spanish popular uprising of early modern times again occurred in Catalonia in 1688–89. It brought together more communes than that of 1640, but its total failure, which contrasts with the explosive conditions of 1640, has consigned it to oblivion. At its roots, we again find the provocations of billetting that had been imposed in country districts, which had also had to endure the devastation caused by plagues of locusts each year since 1684. As in 1640, it all began with isolated riots against the soldiery. The convergence of the insurgent communes on 8 April 1688 led to Barcelona being surrounded by 18,000 well-armed and well-supplied peasants. Promises by the townspeople of an alleviation of military expenses made them disperse, but the villages remained under arms throughout the summer. Spain's entry into war in April 1689 and the Estates' consent, which was regarded as scandalous, to a *donativo*, revived the peasant assemblies. 'That under pain of death, all men over fourteen years come to Barcelona where the army of the land is based; the decrees are signed in the name of the land.' On 27 November 1689, 8,000 peasants camped under the walls of the capital, and summonses were carried as far as the upland valleys of the provinces of Lerida and Urgell. As in the previous year, the townspeople kept their gates locked. A few repressive raids mounted from the coastal fortresses triumphed over peasant resistance.

·The War of Spanish Succession breathed life back into peasant irredentism. An uncertain legitimacy and the burden of military contributions for a conflict being fought on Spanish soil rekindled their anger. Most of the areas of established centrifugal traditions recognised the Austrian claimant, the Archduke Charles who was proclaimed Charles III, while Castile on the other hand, remained fully loyal to the Bourbon, Philip V. In October 1705, Charles took Barcelona, in December Valencia, and in June 1706, he was acclaimed at Saragossa. Nearly everywhere, his victories were preceded by riots in which hostility to the Castilians and the French went together. The latter were not only hereditary enemies, emigrants who were despised in Spain where they competed for work, but also champions of a very authoritarian centralism. The imposition in August 1705 of a *donativo* without consulting the Cortes brought Aragonese animosity towards the Bourbon cause to the boil. When besieging Philip V's fortresses, the Habsburg party received the support of hundreds of peasants who, led by their parish priests, came to provide assistance.

In the kingdom of Valencia, support from the peasantry came in response to a rumour which first circulated when the Imperialists landed in August 1705, proclaiming that taxes were to be discontinued. But here, irredentism and antifiscalism were complicated by an agrarian situation similar to that of the second serfdom. The Valencian tenant–farmers were Spanish colonists who had been settled on lands left vacant with the expulsion of the Moriscos in 1609. They had never either understood or accepted that the fields they had cultivated for two or three generations did not in any way belong to them, or that seigneurial dues should be heavier there than elsewhere. They thought that old title-deeds guaranteed their property-rights, and that seigneurial rights were concessionary in nature. In July 1693, a thousand peasants revived, in the tradition of the 1520s, the title of 'Army of the Fraternities' (*Eixercit dels Agermanats*). They marched northwards for a few days in the direction of the royal domains, where they wished to publish their petition to the king. So in 1705, the Archduke's regiments saw large numbers of peasants come to join them, encouraged by a leader who had survived the 1693 revolt. "The excited peasants of the entire coastal region came to Denia, where the general granted them letters of freedom from their lords. This sweetened pill was prized by those whose loyalty was uncertain; many even came from other parts of the province in order to enjoy the favour promised by the proclamation of exemption from taxation.' To give greater credence to this renaissance of liberty in the peripheral provinces, the Archduke summoned the three orders of the Cortes of Valencia in December 1706.

Marshal Berwick's victory at Almansa on 25 April 1707 sealed the fate of irredentist hopes. The Franco-Castilian cause triumphed. Significantly, on the express advice of Louis XIV, the *fueros* of the kingdoms of Valencia and Aragon were abolished on 29 June 1707. No other laws would have force there except those of Castile, which were henceforth extended to the two kingdoms.

The revolt of Naples

It is tempting to impute the instability of the Iberian kingdoms, which were for a long time no more than a juxtaposition of personal unions, to geographical determinism. In the Mediterranean region, Spain was the only instance of a monarchy moving towards centralisation, one which, moreover, was founded more on American expansion than on the resources of the peninsula. In fact, the traditional pastoral economy continued to survive in its southern areas. The very antiquity of cattle-farming and its concomitant nomadic practices could not but create, in the long term, appropriate institutions and social relations. A permament state of arms, detachment from authorities possessing fixed territorial jurisdiction and seats, and a clash of interests with the settled communities from which most of the government's officials originated – all of this prevented the establishment of strong centralised states. Abdication of its prerogatives by the state and a traditional state of insecurity were somehow linked to a pastoral society.

The kingdom of Naples may, better than any other region, serve to illustrate this situation. The great city's revolt of 1647 was in origin and explicit aims centrifugal and anti-fiscal, but it would never have spread to all the southern provinces, had not the peasantry's position worsened during this period in a manner similar to that of the second serfdom in eastern Europe. The sacrifice of regalian powers to local lords was a consequence, not merely of the evolution over the centuries of the Mediterranean pastoral world, but also of a specific political history which must be reviewed here. Alfonso the Magnanimous, king of Aragon, and then of Naples (1436–58), transferred the seat of his court to Naples. Having placed in his councils and fortresses the few Catalans who had followed him, he left the rest of government to the native nobility. In 1442, he even granted full jurisdiction, both high and low (*merum et mixtum imperium*) to the barons on their estates, an abdication of sovereignty that was to last 300 years. The barons' authority was already sufficiently strong by the early sixteenth century for them to dominate events and to turn cyclical price-rises to their advantage. They had the means to alter share-cropping leases in their favour, by shortening their duration, by consolidating the farms and by entrusting the management of them to seigneurial agents.

In the early seventeenth century, the demands of war obliged the kings of Spain to raise the contributions they required of the kingdom of Naples. However, the Madrid government preferred to respect the 'constitutions' of its various dominions. In the disputes, often of a fiscal nature, which might oppose viceroys and local representatives,

Madrid often decided to impose compromise on its viceroys. It became necessary to invent other sources of revenue, so recourse was had to an unending auction of government posts and magistracies. Local royal jurisdictions were systematically sold. The towns, whose treasuries were in deficit because of calamities (food-shortages, epidemics) and expenses imposed on them from above (costs of tax-collection, military supplies), thus found themselves being subjected to a new, seigneurial fiscality. Municipal institutions were emptied of any substance and reduced to the role of fief-administration. Suddenly middle-sized towns with a rich history and inhabited by old noble families or a privileged bourgeoisie, found themselves subject to the lordship of a purchaser, and lost their direct link with the crown. Thus, in 1647, Lanciano and Chieti, having been recently sold, demanded in vain their return to the royal domain.

Fiscal revenues were themselves subject to alienation. The practice of abandoning a source of revenue (*arrendamento*) was far more serious than mere tax-farming by lease (*affitto*). The decree of abandonment was itself alienable and thus subject to speculation, transmissible by inheritance and, consequently, difficult to recover. It was estimated that, as a result of these various diversions, only one-fifth of the central taxes benefited the crown.

The stagnation of ground rents visible at the end of the sixteenth century became more pronounced by 1630. To obtain cash, the barons entrusted the management and collection of their dues to *fermiers* recruited from among the merchants of the neighbouring towns. In order to sustain revenues despite adverse economic trends, they confined themselves to increasing their demands of the tenant–farmers. Some Italian historians have spoken of this as 'refeudalisation'. At the same time, the rate of turnover of baronial families rose sharply. According to a survey of 1636, 1,200 fiefs out of 2,700 (44·4 per cent) had changed hands. The purchasers were Genoese who were, so to speak, the bankers of the Spanish Mediterranean. Nowhere else were tenants so completely separated from the owners of fiefs – newcomers whom they had never seen, and foreigners.

In the midst of the disasters of the 1640s, the Spanish fisc wished to tap the revenues of the major privileged cities through taxes on items of consumption. In France, the Fronde had similar early beginnings. It was Sicily which set the example – the guilds and lower classes of Palermo rose in revolt on 19 May 1647 with cries of 'Down with the gabelle, long live the king, death to the evil government' (*Fuera gabelle. Viva il re e muora il mal governo*). Agrigente, Taormina, Catania and a few smaller towns followed them in June. In Naples, there were only urban and anti-fiscal riots. On 7 July, the market-day crowd led by the fisherman, Masaniello, prevented the enforcement of taxes on fruit and vegetables. During the following three days, eighteen town palaces were burned down; the targets were exclusively financiers involved in the tax farms. The rioters shouted, 'Long live the king of Spain.' The viceroy, the duke of Arcos, resolved throughout the summer to avoid clashes, to temporise with the different orders, corporations and pressure groups within the immense city of about 300,000 inhabitants. It was the defeat of a Spanish fleet in October and the retreat by garrisons of the fortresses into their citadels, which transformed riot into secession. On 23 October 1647, the republic of Naples was proclaimed under the protection of the king of France. In December, the duke of Guise landed, was declared 'duke of the republic' and invested with powers modelled on those of the Dutch stadtholder.

From the summer, but especially after the break with Spain in October, the revolt spread to the kingdom's twelve provinces. In each city or town, it was based on the municipal organs of the *popolari*, the urban notables hostile to seigneurial hegemony. It assumed some of the features of a social war, and of an insurrection of townspeople and rural tenants against the fiscal tyranny of the barons. The conflicts were especially fierce in the Basilicata and the Upper Abruzzi. They were not to last long. By late October, the barons loyal to Spain had assembled a 3,000-strong army. The reconquest of the provinces did not take long, owing to the striking military superiority of the royal troops, as for example at Bitonto where 150 cavalry belonging to the barons defeated 2,500 men supporting the *popolari*.

Naples opened its gates to Spanish reinforcements on

5 April 1648. A general pardon, which excluded only the major leaders, was published on 11 April. The significance of this year of disturbance is far from unambiguous, and its social divisions were far from simple. Firstly, hostility to the Spaniards was neither universal nor irreversible, and from January 1648, the lower-class beggars (*lazzari*) demanded their return. In Calabria and Campania, the major towns remained firm in their loyalty to Spain. On the other hand, a large number of nobles had taken sides with the *popolari* and given leadership to the regiments established by the republic of Naples. Noble support for it was especially strong in the Lower Abruzzi. The province, bordering on the Papal states, had always provided sanctuary, and enabled men to arm and plot. It was the most feudalised province of the kingdom (10·8 per cent of all its fiefs), and the most affected by the concentration of estates (over forty per cent of the fiefs were held by six families). The families of the nobility, often the product of papal nepotism, were from the early sixteenth century traditionally attached to the French cause. Several times during the 1630s, they had anticipated the revolt; their resistance in the Abruzzi carried on until the summer of 1648.

The Neapolitan 'revolution' was not without positive results. Count Oñate, the new viceroy, and his various successors devoted themselves as far as was possible to restoring regalian privileges. Oñate conducted an inquiry into the alienation of crown revenues. He freed himself from dependence on the goodwill of the grain-exporting barons of Puglia, by supplying Naples with grain purchased in Flanders. He reduced the powers of the baronial military units and of their hired bandits through strengthening the detachments of *sbires* stationed by royal commission in the provinces. 'The count boasted that he had not only returned the kingdom to the king, but also of restoring the rigour of justice, which had languished because of the nobles' excessive power; because he had brought the people the tranquillity of peace, the object of so many desires, and had left no other disparity between the nobles and the lower classes than that of birth'. It is true that the fall of seigneurial revenues continued more steeply. The year of the revolt was a turning point, either because the collection of these rents was impossible thereafter, or because they were reduced on the intervention of the viceroys. For the next 150 years, neither Neapolitan particularism nor social tensions would breed rebellion in the southern kingdom. As proof of this, we may note that the great change of sovereignty there after the Franco–Spanish defeat, occurred without a blow being struck or provoking the least disorder in the provinces.

Other Italian annals of the seventeenth century furnish examples of uprisings of popular origin, which strove to defend local positions against invasion by a centralising fiscal machine. The 'Fermo war' of 1648 was an insurrection by the inhabitants of this governorship in the papal states against the export of grain which the Roman authorities in charge of provisions, the *Annona*, unilaterally imposed on them. The 'salt war' in Piedmont from 1680 to 1684 was a stubborn defence by the citizens of Mondovi and by its jursidiction against the introduction of the *gabelle*, which operated in the lands of the house of Savoy.

In the German lands, the splintering of sovereign states and, as a corollary, the relative lack of administrative traditions, restricted the growth of states, thus making occasions for resistance to them uncommon. By depopulating the country-side, the terrible destruction of the Thirty Years' War sapped the vitality of the rural communities for a long time to come. However, in its early phase or on the margins of the conflict zones, it did produce peasant reactions of self-defence – chasing isolated soldiers or resisting pillagers. From August 1620 to May 1625, Upper Austria was ceded by Emperor Ferdinand II to his ally and creditor, duke Maximilian of Bavaria, as a pledge of payment for his war debts. The duke's governor, count Heberstorff, resided at Linz. The inhabitants were exasperated by the Bavarian desire to exploit to the utmost a temporary pledge, and by the imposition of foreign garrisons; the protestants, who were quite numerous among the nobility, were irritated by the arrival of large numbers of catholic clergy, who were often Italian. The assembled peasants desired to present their complaints to the emperor, their legitimate sovereign, while the anxieties of the protestant nobles who felt threatened with expropriation, transformed the movement into a genuine armed revolt, led by a peasant notable, Stefan Fadinger. The rebels were defeated in 1626.

The Swiss peasants' war

The Swiss Peasants' War was also a sequel to war. The cantons had benefited from events in Europe, supplying armies with provisions, while remaining protected against their incursions. After the treaty of Westpahalia, the inhabitants of the valleys experienced real economic difficulties. Their urban creditors began demanding the settlement of debts incurred when the sales trends gave no grounds for fear. At the same time, the peasants only received as payment for their produce the copper coinage which the towns refused to touch. Small copper coins (*Handmünzen*) for minor transactions were often minted in order to stimulate trade. Of little value in a barter economy, this measure periodically caused violent and limited instances of inflation among the lower classes. Local accumulations of vellon, the consequence of speculation, led to devaluations which selectively hit the monetary culs-de-sac of the countryside. This is what happened in December 1652 in the canton of Lucerne. The Sabotiers' war of 1658 in the Sologne had similar roots.

Around Christmas 1652, a 'secret diet of the peasants' brought together notables from Entlibuch, a valley subject to Lucerne. They criticised the arbitrariness of the townspeople (monetary ordinances) and their fiscal increases (on salt); they demanded that the territories subject to the cantons should have the right to form political associations, to hold *Landesgemeinden*, that is general assemblies of all the heads of families, in accordance with the democratic practice of the original cantons. They wished to shake off the seigneurial yoke of the cities, to free themselves from their *baillis* and their cohort of taxes and fines, to create cantons, or at least to govern with equal liberty their various rural areas and valleys. Their leaders were a rich villager, Hans Emmenegger, nicknamed 'the fair standard' or 'the jewel of the peasants', and an organist-schoolmaster, who undertook to draft their grievances. On 26 February, ten rural bailiwicks formed a genuine *Landesgemeinde* in the church at Walhausen. They created a league (*Bundschuh*), the solemnity of which was guaranteed by the presence of their priests, their standards and their Tells, personages who were symbolically clothed in the ancient costume of the fifteenth-century Confederates.

In the following spring, the letter of alliance drafted at Walhausen, having been circulated to other areas, extended the peasant league without distinction of canton or even as to whether its adherents were catholic or evangelical. Bailiwicks subject to Berne and even to Soleure and Basle joined. This enlarged peasant league selected as its leader another wealthy, educated valley notable, Nicholas Leuenberger, while Emmenegger took the title of colonel-general. A peasant army of 16,000 men besieged Berne on 21 May. By negotiating with the peasants while requesting reinforcements from the old mountain cantons, the Bernese deflected the threat. In that month of May 1653, the high point of their movement, the peasants were said to number up to 80,000 adherents. On 31 May, the cantons' army, numbering 2,000 troops, drove the peasants from the town of Mellingen on the Reuss. Indecisive engagements followed, culminating in the rout of the principal peasant units at Herzogenbuchsee on 8 June. Throughout June and July, courts martial and the tribunals of each of the cantons involved, put several dozen peasant leaders to death.

But here too, the peasants' revolt was not wholly futile: the *baillis* were changed, taxes lowered and debts reduced. However, the countryside secured no representation; political power remained the monopoly of the townspeople. The changes which occurred in early modern Europe arose from the initiative, and were for the benefit, of towns.

The War of Spanish Succession provided new occasions for self-defence by country districts. The elector Max Emmanuel of Bavaria's support of the French, and his invasion of the Tyrol in 1703, sparked off spontaneous resistance by the mountain people. On the other hand, the Imperial armies invaded Bavaria in 1705, forcing him into exile. With their sovereign absent and their country occupied by enemy troops, the mountain people of the Bavarian Oberland took up arms in November 1705. This overwhelmingly peasant revolt sought to defend their lands and to restore their legitimate ruler. Moreover, these upland rebels acquired a social awareness from their solitary struggle. They denounced the submission to the enemy of the notables, the nobles and magistrates whom they contemptuously called *Paruckenhanseln*. They demanded the creation of a political association for the countryside; the peasant deputies would have formed a fourth order in the assemblies of estates, behind those of the prelates, the nobles and the towns. Their cause was supported by nearly 30,000 men. Overcome by Austrian regiments on 8th January 1706, their defeat turned to massacre, the horrific memory of which survives in the sinister word *Mordweihnacht* (literally, Murder-Christmas).

The centuries-long conflict with the Ottoman empire, apart from clashes between powers and religions, also highlighted differences in styles of government. The development of western fiscal systems contrasted with the sultan's distant tutelage – with sovereignty limited to questions of war, and war itself conceived merely as an annual succession of enormous and short-lived incursions by horsemen. Here, the uncertain character of sovereignty and the fluctuations of frontiers provided scope for irredentism and models of military liberties, as well as means of escape from the clutches of authority, either by temporary refuge or by the choice of emigration or exile.

Far from always being an object of horror and repulsion, or a detested overlordship, the Turkish régime could appear rather as a sanctuary, and a land of tolerance and freedom. In fact, once the bloody shock of conquest was over, the long Ottoman peace began, indifferent to the ethnic and religious identity of the subject peoples. Distant and rudimentary, the Turkish state allowed the defeated Christians to keep to their customs, being satisfied with tributes recognising its overlordship and, from time to time, with military recruits and supplies for the army. Inefficiency and corruption were themselves guarantees of tranquility and autonomy. The nobilities, repositories of local independence, were wiped out by the Turks, so that the peasant communities were left to themselves and even emancipated from potential seigneurial obligations. On the other hand, the christian Greek nobility were protected in the Venetian territories, and their agrarian demands led to peasant disturbances in Crete in 1567–73 and the Ionian islands in 1638. The mildness of the Turkish regime, frozen in a relative administrative backwardness, a simple agglomeration of submissions and fidelities, emerged quite clearly in comparison with the ever more demanding fiscal systems of the christian rulers. In the Peloponnesus and the islands, the Venetian dominions experienced heavier taxation and more rigorous commercial tolls. We have the frequently-cited evidence of Stephan Gerlach, chaplain of the imperial embassy in Constantinople, who wrote in his diary for 1575: 'The Venetians treated their Cypriot subjects, as do the Genoese those of Chios, worse than slaves . . . when the Turks arrived, these poor people were delivered of their yoke and are equal in freedom; as for their masters who had tormented them, they were taken prisoner and sold in Turkey.'[6] In 1645, when the Turks landed in Crete, the inhabitants joined them and assisted them in the capture of Canea, and then in 1648 as they began the interminable siege of Candia. In 1715, when the grand vizir Damad Ali reconquered the Peloponnesus from the Venetians, the peasants likewise assisted the invaders who succeeded in expelling all the Italian garrisons in a campaign lasting one hundred days.

In the Banat, the Romanian shepherd population retained, under Ottoman domination, their village chiefs (*Knez*) and their priests, under the vague authority of the pasha of Temesvar. The imperial reconquest, begun in 1688 and sealed by treaty in 1716, meant from the beginning an increase in taxation, compulsory labour on the roads, billetting, subjection of the clergy to taxation and, above all, expropriation of the sheep runs for the benefit of immigrant settlers. The strengthening of the frontier was in fact entrusted to colonists from western Germany and even from northern Italy. Over some twenty years, 30,000 grain-growing, catholic, German-speaking colonists settled there. This peasant élite, which comprised 10% of the population, produced grain, rice and silk, or worked the mines; it contrasted with the traditional patterns of the Romanian transhumant shepherds and foresters. When war resumed in 1736–39, aggression in the form of taxes and confiscations, and differences of language, religion and custom, brought the Romanians onto the side of the Turkish invaders. Their peasant leaders declared: 'For three years, the flags bearing the red cross devoured the produce of our fields and left them to starve, so that we had to eat the bark of trees in the forests, while the flags without crosses assembled the villages, distributed food, and asked for no armed support apart from that of the paid mercenary'. The insurrection of the Banat shepherds ended with the massacre of 300 rebels gathered at the fair of Caransebes in 1739.

The progressive decline in Ottoman power may, in the final analysis, be reduced to an enduring inability to create, as the western states were to do, institutions capable of dominating the provinces and which are the foundation, at the centre, of the co-ordinating power of the finance state.

7 Peasant wars II: the eighteenth century

The fall of the seigneurial systems

During the sixteenth and seventeenth centuries, the peasantries of eastern Europe were, in fact and in law, cut off from, and even abandoned by the sovereign state. Serfs could be wholly and exclusively subject to their lord, subservient to his fiscal demands, judged by his tribunals, attached to his estate and reduced to being no more than disposable elements in his patrimony. This subjection, however, was not from time immemorial, having gradually become heavier in recent history. The oldest villagers preserved the memory of better conditions, or, at the very least, had heard it recounted. Nowhere had hope been lost of a return to ancient customs, to charters of liberty that had not been forgotten. Because these alleged laws had frequently been no more than tacit affairs, they had not been formally abrogated, so that reference to them was always possible. Lastly, men knew there was a higher law than that of the lord, and that the ruler or the emperor, however distant they might be, would necessarily come to recognise the wrongs done to the peasantry. In spite of disappointments, loss of court cases, refusals of justice and repeated acts of repression, no serf believed the bonds of servitude were unbreakable; they knew that one day they would see the end of it, and that this would come from the judgement of a just king. Such irrepressible expectations survived every tribulation.

Besides, this awareness of the political aspects of their fate was not so mythical. It is true that economic fluctuations, of whatever kind, always proved advantageous to the nobilities, simply because they held the reins of power. Thus from 1680 to 1750, the Baltic grain-trade suffered a lasting decline due to the stabilising of the relations between population and production in western and southern Europe. On the other hand, Hungary's agricultural profits rose after 1730 because of supplies needed by the armies which would again criss-cross central and eastern Europe for thirty years. Although moving in opposite directions, these trends produced identical results. Peasant work-days were increased, and the acreage of seigneurial estates grew either to compensate for falling revenues or to increase production under the stimulus of profit.

Each stage in the evolution of the peasants' condition and each degree of their slowly achieved 'second emancipation' during the eighteenth and nineteenth centuries may be connected to an ideological development and to a constellation of political events. Suddenly, an all too common fact was seen to be scandalous; some customary piece of excess was identified, described and denounced by a ruler or a minister imbued with new principles of humanitarianism and physiocratic effectiveness. The seigneurial structures to be found in most of eastern Europe, whose economy they would long continue to dominate, found themselves henceforth without any justification other than the fact of their existence, inertia and accumulated interests. Serfdom now seemed an anomalous and absurd scandal to most politicians; all the chanceries of enlightened Europe promoted agrarian reform.

On the lookout for change and sensitive to reports which confirmed their passionate expectations, the peasantries reacted in their turn, adding the echo of their chaotic disturbances to the crises of conscience among legislators. In a dialogue of events, in which rulers' legislation and popular impatience followed each other, were in vague harmony or else collided in bloody confrontations, a connecting link was provided by the rural elites. Indeed, serfdom notwithstanding, a comfortably-off peasant class either succeeded in surviving on the margins or else began to make its appearance. This was composed of free smallholders, village merchants or serf tenants who had enough land in order to afford several plough teams, servants and livestock. Such people were able to follow opinion in the towns, and attempt to engineer changes to their advantage. To generations of the 'enlightened', they were a model of the ideal peasant – property-owners, free and enterprising, concerned with production and progress. In the absence of a western-style bourgeoisie capable of being a more effective social bridge, this peasant elite produced, on the one hand, the leaders of rebellion and, on the other, the basis for the idealised image of the physiocratic sheepfold.

Common customs had likewise survived. Despite the dispossession of village jurisdictions which were transferred to seigneurial judges, and despite the fading of customary laws which were replaced by Roman law or by the written jurisprudence of early modern states, whole sectors of rural daily life were still governed by oral usage, ancient tradition and the unanimous consent of the inhabitants. The Bohemian lords learned to live with the continuation of a village chief (*Dorfrichter*) who served as intermediary. The authority of the oldest and leading inhabitants was a customary forum of wisdom. Every village had its church and tavern, its religious feasts and pilgrimages, its dances and youth rituals. The most universal custom of all was that of free grazing on empty lands. It was more than a mere concession; it corresponded to certain roles and, in the Danubian principalities, for example, they referred to a popular right, known as the *jus valachicum*. Grazing there was even sanctioned by the law codes, by that of Moldavia in 1646, and of Wallachia in 1652; such sanction would only disappear with the Roumanian civil code of 1849. In short, nearly everywhere – in Danubian, Czech, German, Polish and Russian lands – traditions consisting of usages and rites, and collections of rules and counsel guaranteed, in spite of the burdens of serfdom, strong village solidarity. When the time came, resistance and hope would build on these community traditions which had been preserved, transformed and endlessly revivified.

Seigneurial institutions and their socio-economic consequences varied considerably from one state to another; even within a single legal system, the situation was not the same from one estate to the next. Hungarian tenants had retained the right to abandon their holdings which was denied in other states. The serfs of the Danubian estates were relatively protected by comparison with the abject fate of the peasants in the northern and eastern kingdoms. The areas of greatest deprivation of liberty and of the heaviest demands for labour services were the centre of Muscovy, certain Polish–Lithuanian estates, parts of the Baltic coastland, the Danish islands, Brandenburg, Pomerania and Livonia.

'The age of Pugatchev'

The vast Pugatchev revolt bequeathed such a fearsome memory that a single word – the *Pugatchevshchina* – served to both signify and damn the episode. It was the last great Cossack revolt, following those of Bolotnikov (1606), Razin (1670), Bulavin (1707), and others. If western ideas did indeed reach St Petersburg, the enserfment of the labour force was no more than an academic issue there. The terms of economic and philanthropic debate were totally forgotten on encountering the harsh simplicity overwhelmingly evident by the time one reached the first stop on the road to Moscow. Scruples and remorse, successive but partial reforms, and peasant expectations – all were just beginning. The *Pugatchevshchina* belongs clearly to this age of initial hesitations. Of course, rumours of change had a hand in the origins of the insurrection. However, serfdom was little undermined by it. At this point, Russian experience was out of step by a century with the rest of Europe.

Once again, the core and the leadership of the revolt was Cossack. Hostilities with Turkey, which had resumed in 1768, again placed the southern Cossacks on a continuous war footing. They came at a time when, for several years, government had been trying to control their lands. A province was established around Orenburg in 1744, thus bringing imperial administration well to the south of the Urals. Cossack freedoms were subjected to scrutiny and, after 1760, their military units increasingly incorporated into the regular regiments. :

The extraordinary geographical spread of the revolt was connected to the peasantry's condition. Serfdom had only worsened over the centuries, and this progression left no room for resignation. The blessed day of its abolition might be at hand, and people stubbornly believed it. Meanwhile, flight and revolt were the only remedies. It has been calculated that, during the 1730s, five per cent of the registered serfs had fled. There were cases of whole villages, with their wagons and flocks, leaving; sheer distance and the bad roads often protected them from pursuit. As for the revolts – sporadic, isolated, desperate – they doubled in frequency during the 1750s.

Murders of estate managers, burnings of seigneurial title-deeds and of the *pomiestchikis'* manors occasionally required the dispatch of troops, as in the province of Penza in 1765.

The reign of Catherine the Great produced both misfortune and hope, and so played a role of *provocateur*. The free peasants of the north and the relatively protected serfs of the crown's estates could be granted purely and simply to private owners. Between 1740 and 1801, 1.3 million people were so handed over, reaching its peak in Catherine's reign. After 1765, grants of land and their inhabitants were extended to the regions east of the Volga and the hitherto free steppes. Besides, the rapid industrialisation of the Urals, which developed the iron and coal mines, created the category of factory serfs. New races and areas were introduced to serfdom by the Urals metallurgy industry. In the provinces of Muscovy and the Middle Volga alone, there were fifty-three localised servile revolts in 1762 and 1769.

So much for the misfortunes. Hope, for its part, lay in the accession of young rulers. The *ukase* of Peter III who, in 1762, dispensed the nobility from state service, seemed to herald a similar deliverance for the peasants. The creation, in 1767, of a commission to examine the conditions of the peasantry, confirmed such expectations; the collection of territorial petitions of grievance put it beyond doubt. The ideas expressed and circulated then throughout the countryside produced some bitter fruit. As a perspicacious observer noted later, 'they sowed contagion in the hearts of the lower classes, and installed in uneducated and uncouth souls a spirit of rebellion and corruption, whence the fundamental evil came.'

Lastly, the notion of a saviour-tsar, hidden and promised, sustained the irrepressible confidence of the peasants. Since the charisma of the tsar made it impossible to imagine a sovereign who would be contemptuous of peasant grievances, the throne must necessarily be occupied by a usurper and the true monarch be concealed. The tragic and obscure disappearance of Peter III in 1762 gave new life to the myth of the risen king. From 1763 to 1772, there were no less than seven alleged Peter IIIs who had escaped death, who attracted supporters and proclaimed the arrival of true justice. The eighth was a Don Cossack, Emilian Pugatchev. He spent his youth fighting in

Germany and Turkey. A wandering deserter, he reached the Iaïk Cossackdom, which had been shaken between February and June 1772 by a wave of insubordination. It was there, in the autumn of 1773, that he achieved recognition as the returning tsar Peter III.

Having convinced several hundred Cossacks that he would see their fishing and pasture rights restored to them, Pugatchev embarked on the siege of Orenburg. In October, he had 2,500 men and some artillery. To the immigrants, he promised 'faith and the law', i.e. respect for their religions and their customs. The Bashkirs, whose revolts had been crushed in horrifying fashion between 1735 and 1740, rallied to him. Disturbances spread to the Urals and western Siberia. In the spring of 1774, he set about winning over the serfs of the Urals foundries; the whole region followed them. Only a third of the factory serfs remained aloof, preferring to defend their villages against the ravages of the Bashkirs. The first clashes with the imperial regiments sent against him occurred in May, and nearly every time, small detachments of regular troops pushed back the incomparably more numerous insurgents. Despite these reverses, new allies joined him and the advance continued. The city of Kazan was captured in a surprise raid, and in July the rebels reached Kurmysh, the most westward base on the road to Moscow. On 18 July, Peter III made an appeal to the serfs of the very densely populated Middle Volga. Promising them 'freedom and liberty as perpetual Cossacks', he ordered the hanging of the *pomiesctchiki* (landowners), 'enemies of the empire and of the peasants.'

Instead of continuing westwards, Pugatchev wished to win over the army of the Don Cossacks, so he returned southwards, down the Volga, chased by the regular troops of the able colonel Mikhelson. The rebel army oscillated around 20,000 men, and was constantly reinforced; the immigrant nomads only accompanied him through their own grazing lands, while the peasants returned home as the harvest-time approached. Everywhere he passed, town-gates were opened, and the local clergy and merchants came to meet him, bearing bread and salt, and kissed his hands. This journey lasted five months, attracting six different races.

Against the alleged Peter III's expectations, the Don

Cossacks did not budge. On the other hand, the imperial regiments were strengthened by the conclusion of peace with Turkey (Treaty of Kutchuk Kainardji, 10th July 1774). On 25th August, in the final massed battle, Peter III lost 2,000 dead and 6,000 prisoners. Obliged to flee, he was captured in September and decapitated in Moscow on 10th January 1775.

Irredentism continued in Bashkir territory until November. Contemporary calculations were made of the number of victims. The victims of the rebels came to 2,846, of whom fifty-five per cent were nobles, but the proportion of peasants and merchants was doubtless greater, because it was less identifiable. In clashes with the government regiments, the rebels lost 10,000 men. As for the hangings and punishments that followed the revolt's collapse, estimates vary from several thousand to 20,000. However, such horrific totals are evidence of a measured repression, very different from the exterminations of 1671.

Until his capture, Pugatchev clung tenaciously to his identity as tsar, eliciting acts of acknowledgement, and prescribing ceremonies of hommage and fidelity with all the trappings of majesty. His ideal was that of maintaining the sovereignty of the tsar in an empire in which there would be no other hierarchies or laws apart from the ranks of military command and the customs of the Cossacks (manifestos of 17th September 1773 and 31st July 1774). Leadership in his army belonged almost exclusively to the original core of 4,000 Iaïk Cossacks. Peter III rebuilt around himself imperial institutions – a secret council resembling the senate, a war college, and governors of provinces and fortresses. He imposed an oath of fidelity, the Old Believers' sign of the cross made with two fingers, and the Cossack practice of shaving the head. Successive appeals to the immigrants and then to the serfs were part of a pragmatism which, for the purpose of immediate effectiveness, brought him into tune with the expectations of all the excluded in Russian society. The uprising affected one-fifth of the empire, or provinces with a population of over four million inhabitants who were virtually won over to its cause.

Pugatchev's defeat was military and political. The government machine and its military instrument left no hope of success to the undisciplined rebels in the important engagements. Beyond the crisis, centralism triumphed. In place of sixteen poorly controlled provinces, the empire was divided into fifty governorships that were better supervised by imperial officials. Cossack privileges were dented; the *Sech*, or stronghold of the Dnieper Cossack brotherhood, was abolished in August 1775, and the privileges of the Iaïk suppressed the same year; the Volga Cossacks were deported further east in 1776 and, finally, serfdom entered their lands, even including the Don Cossacks in 1796.

The reign of Catherine represents the final degree of peasant degradation. A long term movement in the opposite direction began to take shape. The proportion of serfs in the rural population was to decline from then on, owing to emancipations, redemptions, flight and the growth of a free peasantry. At the final abolition in 1861, serfs numbered only forty-six per cent of the peasantry. Between 1772 and 1861, 1,800 instances of peasant violence have been counted, but none of them posed a real danger to the stability of the empire. Serfdom was abolished because the ruling class had convinced themseves it was scandalous and harmful. The literary reputation of the *Pugatchevshchina*, illustrated by Pushkin's *The Captain's Daughter* (1836), was a benchmark in this slow turnaround of the views of nobles and administrators.

Revolts in the Danubian states

The seigneurial system in these lands became discredited in the minds of the authorities during the eighteenth century, and peasant rebellions were clearly a response to government hesitations.

It was in Bohemia that popular resistance was most frequent and vigorous. Serfdom was, in fact, introduced later there; the terrible devastation of the Thirty Years' War prepared the way for its completion. Around 1650, labour shortages (minus fifty-five per cent), led to a ban on free movement and raised labour services to 150 days a year. The children of serfs were obliged to serve for two or three whole years on the lords' farm. Banalities were added to manors in respect of salt, beer, and herring. The dependence of the subject (*Untertan*) and his obligations towards the seigneurial domain (*Obrigkeit*) can be summarised by three fundamental forms of personal servitude: a ban on avoiding labour services (*Robot*), on emigrating and on marrying outside his village. It is reckoned that Bohemia contained nearly 1,000 seigneurial estates; each one formed an administrative unit, one of agrarian autarky, a kind of agrarian state where the lord was wholly master of everything. The Estates of Bohemia, Moravia and Silesia which composed the kingdom of Bohemia, each pledged to return fugitive peasants.

Among the labour services, the long-distance carting of wood or stone were the least tolerated. In a context of European war, the arrival of French emissaries succeeded in organising a peasant uprising. In the spring of 1680, in northern Bohemia, village assemblies compiled their grievances, and demanded the return to ancient uses. Having forcibly dispersed them, the emperor Leopold I published a degree regulating labour services (*Robotpatent*), the sovercign power's first intervention in order to limit the ordeal of the peasantry. This document, published on 28th June 1680, limited labour services to three days a week but, at the same time, forbade tenants to invoke the oldest customs or even to seek direct recourse to the monarch. Besides, fixing a ceiling for labour services was an ambiguous measure which could harm those tenants who had hitherto found themselves below this requirement.

In 1741, war again set Bohemia alight, with an occupying Franco-Bavarian army using it as stakes in the war of Austrian Succession. Numerous peasants, Czech or German, rallied to invaders in their invincible hope of an end to labour services. For her part, the legitimate sovereign, Maria Teresa, promised emancipation in May 1742 to the peasants enlisting in her armies while, on 13th July, the marshal of Belle-Isle, on behalf of the Bavarian pretender, made a more generous promise of liberty to every peasant who would rebel against Austria. A peasant army even began recruiting in the areas controlled by the French.

Once secure in her authority, Maria Teresa took a few steps towards satisfying popular expectations. Legislation obliged seigneurial courts to pass on peasant grievances to the crown, thereby restoring, at least on paper, the long-interrupted connection between the monarch and the lowest of his subjects.

Timidly and slowly, but irreversibly, government decisions had changed course. Peasant resistance became more frequent and audacious. The least tolerated parts of serfdom were the bonds of personal servitude and physical punishment. It has been calculated that, over twenty years, isolated revolts affected about one-third of all Czech villages, stopping abruptly, fumbling or giving in, only to recur in the same places a few years later. Their heralds were the prosperous peasants who tailored their demands to the risks involved and who did not venture beyond the realms of compromise or of commitments they wished to extract from their lords. Physical repression inspired genuine terror, and the impotence of the imperial courts was only too apparent. As the saying went, 'God is in heaven, and the emperor in Vienna.'

One of these isolated revolts occurred in one of the most remote regions of Upper Silesia, Teschen, an area without trade or towns, and inhabited by mostly Polish peasants who were subject to more burdensome labour services than those of the more advanced and urbanised districts of Lower Silesia or Bohemia. The beginnings of reforms on the crown estates, and the introduction of leases and money rents in place of labour services provided examples of change. The conspiracy embraced 137 villages in 1767, and the empress sent one of her councillors to investigate the real condition of the peasantry; the event was the source of a further reform decree which reiterated the limits on demands for services. These documents applied to Silesia and Hungary. Clearly, relations between lords and subjects were moving outside the sphere of private law; emancipation and the development of peasant landownership were the objectives from now on.

Successive interventions by government gave more credence than ever to news of the end of labour services. The upheavals of the Seven Years' War were followed by the accession of a young emperor, Joseph II, crowned in 1765 at the age of twenty-four and, like his mother, enamoured of humane ideas. Imperial commissioners investigated the scandal of peasants who had died under the lash on the estates of prince Mansfeld near Prague in 1768. A serious epidemic in 1771 led to a general census, in which peasant misery amazed the inspectors from Vienna. A rumour then spread that military conscription terminated labour services; it was said that the emperor had drafted a decree of abolition in letters of gold, but that the accursed estate managers refused to publish it. An instruction dated April 1774 requested all seigneurs and communities of tenants to agree within six months on new statutes to be submitted to the authorities. The Diets protested at this, and agreements were reached in only three Circles.

During 1774, the village *bailiffs* laid their plans, sending out emissaries and collecting arms. On an agreed day, the alarm would sound and horns would summon the villagers to gather and march on Prague. They would enter the city on 16th May, day of the great pilgrimage of St John Nepomuk, and its governor would grant them the abolition of labour services. Disturbances broke out openly in January 1775, castles around the Riesengebirge were ransacked and burned, and estate managers forced to sign exemptions from services. One unit was led by the clever and handsome Matthew Chvojka, a prosperous peasant who had studied with the Jesuits; he was said to resemble Joseph II and was called 'the peasants' emperor'. Another band, comprising 15,000 men, reached the gates of Prague, where the grand burgrave of Bohemia, prince Furstenberg, a great lord and *philosophe*, tried to parley with them prior to dispersing them without much difficulty. A general pardon was issued by April. On 13th August 1775, the emperor signed the decree on labour services that had been so long awaited, and it was solemnly published in all the Bohemian Circles; other decrees were applied to Moldavia and Carinthia.

This latest ruling divided into eleven categories those liable for labour services, the burden of which rose in relation to the rate of the government land tax; the poorest tenants owed only thirteen days a year, while the biggest farmers of the eleventh class had to provide two plough-teams three days a week. Outright suppression was still a long way off. On the lands confiscated after the expulsion of the Jesuits, the tenants were allowed to buy out their labour services, something which was extended little by little to all crown domains. Above all, Joseph II suppressed all forms of personal servitude in November

1781, and introduced royal justices of the peace into country areas in 1785.

Among the Danubian countries, a tougher fate was reserved for the peasants of Transylvania. Labour services there were twice as heavy as in Hungary; even the sultan's vassal states of Moldavia and Wallachia, had abolished personal servitude in 1749. During a journey there in 1783, Joseph II discovered the abject state of the rural population, where all the bonds of personal servitude survived. The emperor decreed that the frontiersmen should enjoy all the military privileges granted to the districts bordering the Turks. News of this led the peasants to rush to enroll in the military registers. The reluctance shown by the landowners led to an insurrection which, starting in the comitat of Hunyad (Hunedoara), spread to the entire country. Its leader, Horia, had been part of a delegation to the court at Vienna; he appealed to the emperor's protection and promises: 'they were not rebels, had only taken up arms to free themselves from the nobles' exactions, and wished to acknowledge no other master than his majesty.' The three peasant units which threatened the towns were broken up after a few weeks and their leaders executed at Alba Julia in February 1785.

The decree of 1789, the last achievement of Joseph II's fruitful reign, attempted to reform the fiscal system. Seventy per cent of the harvest should rest with the producer, the remainder being divided among obligations to lords and the state; the decree proclaimed the imminent abolition of labour services, the promulgation of which in October 1789 sparked off great enthusiasm. Rejoicing villages organised carnival-type burials of 'king Robot'. 'What ecstasy among these villagers when it was announced that no one would ever again order them, with their wagons and animals or on foot, to perform labour services. No one who has not experienced the burden of such services can believe it.' The big farmers sold off the plough teams that they kept only out of obligation. However, the application of the decree during 1790 was to be full of disappointment, as it was conditional on buying out the services; failure to do so meant their continuation as before. Refusals increased and acts of violence against estate managers were reported everywhere; secret assemblies planned for revolt. The emperor's death in June and the resumption of war with Turkey halted it. In September 1798, Francis II reiterated the decree of abolition with redemption. Most of the labour services remained throughout the Danubian kingdoms until 1848.

Interaction between the reforming designs of rulers and the impatience of the peasantry provided the popular violence which in the Danubian states accompanied the breakdown of the seigneurial system, with its rhythm and character. Such outbursts stood out on the map of a more general attitude of resignation. Elsewhere, the different stages of the establishment of servitude and, later, of its decomposition during the eighteenth and nineteenth centuries reveal only decisions from above, with no evidence in them of outbursts of the frustration or expectations of the peasantry. Thus, here and there the traditional triggers of revolt – the models of provocation represented by personal or local privileges, the counterweight or aggression of the towns, the cultural intermediaries who broke down rural isolation, and so on – were absent. The troubled history of Poland provides no instances of peasant revolts, apart from the brief Silesian revolts of 1767 and 1811. There was no tradition of monarchical power, and the Polish crown was incapable of fostering the idea of recourse to a supreme judge. For long the holders of real power, the Polish nobility succeeded very early on in securing legal sanction for obligatory labour services, which appeared in the acts of the Diets of 1519 and 1529. The sharpest rise in the amount of work owed by those subject to them occurred between 1580 and 1620. In the eighteenth century, the burden was already two centuries old, and the rural communities only quibbled when the use-rights which had survived despite the seigneurial yoke, seemed to be under attack. The only disturbances encountered in the annals of the Polish countryside involved concerted refusals of labour services, the smashing of enclosure fences, and acts of aggression against those guarding fields.

The fate of the Scandinavian peasantries shows considerable differences. While the Norwegian and Finnish rural communities remained firmly autonomous over the centuries, and the Swedish traditions of liberty were scarcely undermined by the power of the nobility, the bonds of servitude were, on the contrary, extreme in Denmark. Although secure in their prerogatives and prospering from abundant domain and customs revenues, the kings of Sweden had retained an assembly of Estates (*Riksdag*) which was consulted on financial and administrative questions. After the nobility, the Lutheran clergy and the towns, a fourth estate represented the peasants of the crown lands. Although seigneurial peasants were not part of it, the peasant estate often played a peculiar political role, especially in the crises of the seventeenth and eighteenth centuries. Under Gustavus Adolphus and queen Christina, alienations of royal domain to noble families which had distinguished themselves in the German wars doubled the size of noble estates. The free peasants came to fear falling into 'Livonian slavery', under the conditions of servitude of Baltic or Pomeranian villagers. The 1650 Diet protested sharply against the extension of noble power: 'Is Christina queen of the Swedish lands, or queen of the tolls and the unjust taxes?' This political crisis, which might have given rise to a civil war, as happened elsewhere at this point, aborted. The nobility agreed to limit labour services to eighteen days a year. The expansion of noble estates was halted and even reversed during the reign of Charles XI, who implemented a policy of 'reductions' i.e. of reuniting the royal domains.

Other tensions surfaced under the government dominated by the aristocratic 'Hats' after 1719. The peasants' spokesmen inveighed against hunting bans and competition from manufacturers in the use of forests belonging to the village communities. The accession of the 'Caps' to power in 1765, and later the necessities of war against Russia after 1789 temporarily restored to the countryside its voice in national affairs.

In Denmark, the *Rigsraad* was composed of nobles only, as the clergy were excluded in 1536. The king's rights were limited by the elective nature of the crown and the grant of election charters. With no law of *dérogeance*, some 250 noble families monopolised the grain-producing lands, the rich pasture-lands and the commercialisation of their produce. Grants of royal estates and of jurisdiction multiplied under Frederick II (1536–88). Later, under Christian V (1670–99), as Baltic trade was declining, the nobility secured the attachment of tenants to glebe lands; lords could themselves sentence fugitive tenants to work in the foundries (1682). Recruitment of the militia was left to the lord's authority; freedom of movement was suppressed for men aged between eighteen and thirty-six (*Stavnsband* of 1773). As elsewhere in Europe, the movement of ideas brought the rules of servitude into question. In August 1786, a rural commission was created with the task of completely reforming the condition of the peasantry; it was to sit for twenty years. By 1788, fixed residence was abolished. Labour services were restricted and commuted into money payments by ordinance between 1791 and 1799. These measures were first applied in Jutland, then in the duchies in 1804 and, lastly, in the islands where conditions had always been harshest.

If the institutions of personal servitude were generally swept away by the tide of 'enlightened' reforms, the economic aspects of the seigneurial system endured well into the nineteenth century. It was such prolonged survivals which caused agrarian disturbances in regions where the peasantry had been passive for three centuries, as in the Polish provinces or the Baltic countries such as in Estonia and Lettonia in 1805 and 1822.

The abolition of 'feudalism' in western states

In general, the west did not experience the 'second serfdom'. Limitations on individual freedom and restrictions on the condition of persons had been more or less swept away by the emancipation of the towns, the importance assumed by the middle classes, and the momentum of state development. The varieties of legal servitude which survived here and there were seen as unseemly anachronisms. It was often the case, as in England and many of the French provinces relatively unaffected by the seigneurial system, that the aristocracy, which continued for the most part to live off ground rents, were, in law, no more than owners of land, even if, in other respects, they profited from the prestige of their family name and the magistracies they held. Elsewhere, which amounted to the majority of states and provinces, the seigneurial system lived on in its guise as economic extraction, as well as in that of political and social tutelage over those subject to it. Therefore, it was with the political institutions and economic performance of lordship that western governments in the age of the 'Enlightenment' were confronted.

The example of Savoy, which has been exhaustively studied, illuminates the ambiguities of the reforms, and the distance between rulers' notions and popular expectations. With enthusiasm and disappointment succeeding each other, the Savoy case precedes that of France, and foreshadows its behaviour patterns. By an edict of 19th December 1771, the Turin government initiated a reform policy that was still exceptional, proclaiming the abolition of the seigneurial system in the duchy of Savoy. The countryside was swept with rejoicing, maypoles were erected in honour of Charles Emmanuel II, thanksgiving masses were sung, and bonfires were lit in which straw models holding seigneurial registers were burned. When it came to applying the edict, the obligation to buy out the dues brought a change of tune. The indemnities granted to the lords amounted to sizeable sums, corresponding to the dues which generally represented seven to ten per cent of annual yields. In 1792, only two-thirds of the communities had reached agreement with their lord over the cost of buying him out and the period set for payment. Such transfers benefited the merchants and lawyers (*feudistes*) who handled them; as transferees, they made considerable gains by consolidating at cheap rates the leases of holdings which they could then raise the value of vis-à-vis the tenants. The latter quickly realised that the end of dues also meant the end of charitable works, local solidarities and community customs connected to the seigneurial system. Moreover, the political and honorific aspects of lordship, such as patronage of local jurisdictions, the exclusive right to hunt, and ceremonial privileges, were retained. From these disappointments and contradictions arose a host of court cases and instances of violence, for example against the purchasers of forests hitherto in collective use, against the middle classes who benefited from the redemptions of dues – 'these accursed wigs will not govern us' – and against the symbols of a noble power – destructions of coats of arms and church seats – that they believed had been totally abolished. Owing to the tensions and bitterness that built up in this way, the events of the French revolution evinced a particularly strong response in Savoy.[1]

In France, the feudal régime had practically disappeared from public law for about three centuries, but locally, onerous forms of servitude survived in private law. The scandal of their continuing existence prescribed in eighteenth-century usage the vague term 'feudal' for the body of obligations lying on the land. It was a word which lumped together all seigneurial rights, which were uniformly rejected as odious survivals of laws that obtained during the 'barbarian ages'. The eradication of civil war and insecurity under Louis XIV, and the simultaneous urbanisation of the nobility robbed lordship of any justification. Dues no longer had a counterpart in the defence of the countryside, in services of recommendation or in vertical social solidarity, but had become a kind of pure economic parasitism. The periodic revision of the seigneurial registers reached, during the eighteenth century, juridical and archival perfection, which was reflected in the revaluation of seigneurial rents that has been described as a 'feudal reaction'. Revisions of the registers, reinstatements of defunct rights, encroachments on empty lands, enclosures and reductions of use-rights turned the 'feudal' rent into an aggressive novelty. In this way, peasant fixation with the past united with the ideology of progress in a common condemnation of noble privilege. When the revolt came, it would unite the forces of restoration and of anticipation.

Rights devoid of any economic effect were often the most detested because their visible character was regarded as humiliating and insulting. Among them were the right to occupy seats before the altar at mass, to decorate church walls with hatchbands containing a coat of arms, to preside over festivals and to receive on set days the hommage of the young people. Indignant denunciations of them, and their mythological fortune, testify to the strength of bitterness against them. Riots attacked the material symbols of lordship, leading to burnings of church seats, and destructions of turrets, dovecotes and weather-vanes. 'Not content to tyrannise the honest farmers, the former lords seemed to want their own dwellings to exercise a kind of aristocratic domination over the cottages of these unfortunates.' The vandalisation of monuments was ordained by the revolutionary assemblies. This was no more than a response to the spontaneous thrust of popular violence.

The privileges of hunting and bearing arms were more resented than any others, as were those of keeping hunting dogs and, especially, pigeons. The noble monopoly of the hunt, erected into an aristocratic pastime, was not a reality until after Colbert's ordinances. Before then, the general carriage of arms, the requirements of defence against wild animals and the quest for additional provisions made every peasant master of the game to be found in his locality. This dispossession, the insolent character of the aristocratic hunt and the damage done by their farmyard fowl were frequent complaints in the *cahiers* of 1789. 'Try to imagine. . . .' Tocqueville wrote incisively in 1856, 'the reserves of hatred and envy stored in the hearts' of the peasantry.

The value of seigneurial extraction differed considerably from province to province, and within the same province. Through detailed studies, historians of the Revolution have tried to measure the burden of the various fiscal demands on the yield of the land. Estimating them is not essential for our present purposes, since the refusals of rebels always follow more from their psychological image of what is extracted than from its arithmetical total. Moreover, this calculus is not easy in an economy in which the relationship between the monetary sector and that of simple barter is not well known, and in which the very notion of a peasant budget must have often been anachronistic. In the upper Auvergne, an area of a numerous and resident lower nobility, it varied from six to nineteen per cent. While beyond dispute in the short-term, the burden of seigneurial rights and the effect of their suppression may have been far more important in the long term. The events of the Revolution freed the small producers from a badly tolerated tutelage, whatever its real weight on them; by propelling them into the political arena, they also gave them a socio-economic opportunity which was to be illustrated throughout the nineteenth century.

The destruction of seigneurial rights in France was, in law, the work of the revolutionary assemblies, but this formal process had been launched, and was to be constantly accelerated, by the spur of peasant agitation. The decisions of deputies who belonged to the *robe* or the merchant bourgeoisie always fell short of peasant expectations. In its early years, the political revolution of the middle classes was thus preceded and accompanied by a peasant revolution. At times, the latter corresponded to the incitement of news from the capital, but its claims were distinct from the programmes of the assemblies, obstinately pursuing their objective of a complete emancipation of the land. Several waves of rural disturbances are discernable throughout the provinces between 1789 and 1793, without any connection between them apart from distorted echoes of events in Paris.

The hopes raised in the spring of 1789 by the convocation of the Estates General led, in July, to the scenes of panic known as the Great Fear. After these days of panic had ended, anti-seigneurial riots formed a sequel to them in Dauphine, Vivarais, Mâconnais, Franche-Comté and so on. During the night of 4th August, the assembly abolished seigneurial rights and the tithe, but the enthusiasm of the legislators soon contrasted with the disappointment of the peasants who believed in a total, immediate abolition without distinctions, conditions, redemptions or delays.

During the winter of 1789, serious disturbances swept through Upper Brittany and the western foothills of the Massif Central, Limousin, Upper Auvergne, Périgord and Quercy. Redemption of rights having been stipulated in the law of 15th March 1790, disturbances often resumed in the same places in the winter of 1790 and the summer of 1791. Between February and April 1792, and then between July and October, they continued in Languedoc, Lower Limousin and Auvergne; they became politicised, and their agrarian motifs were transmuted into a hunt for 'suspects' that corresponded to the beginnings of war abroad. The agrarian laws of June and August 1792, by laying the burden of proof of title on the lord, effectively abolished redemption and satisfied the expectations of the peasant producers. Final sanction came with the Convention's decree of 17th July 1793. It abolished 'feudal rights' completely, irrevocably and without indemnity, and even ordered the destruction of titles to them.

The forms assumed by these sporadic riots reflect their

agrarian basis. The assembled peasants wished to extract from their lord or one of his agents a signed renunciation of the rights. They set about overturning the symbolic stones, and waging 'war on the châteaux', burning noble houses and their cartularies. This destruction of seigneurial archives in a bonfire was a repetition of the traditional actions of popular revolts that attacked the mysterious and hostile documents which, they believed, were the foundation stone of their oppression. In this too, the legislators of the Convention would merely follow insurrectionary *praxis*. The number of participants, a few hundred only, and the relative isolation of each uprising, do not enable us to speak of a peasant war. Such actions only went wrong when the national guards arrived from the towns and set about dispersing them. If never very serious, these riots were, on the other hand, very numerous, and their geographical features are not without significance. The regions most affected were the periphery of the Massif Central, Upper Brittany and the Dauphiné. In examining the smallest of them, we observe geographical constants and veritable traditions of insurrection – for example, the Mirambeau districts of southern Saintonge and Gourdon in Quercy. The same villages and towns provided detachments for the seventeenth century revolts against the royal fisc, and would do so in 1848 against that of the republic. They took up arms in 1789–92 against a seigneurial fisc that was equally regarded as evil and illegitimate.

It was only because of the pressure of peasant agitation that the abolition of seigneurial rights in France was so complete and rapid. Having become a legal obligation, abolition was to be exported by the revolutionary armies. At that point, it was not a consequence of popular anger, but of decrees by governing assemblies. As early as the winter of 1792, the assembly set up in Brussels suppressed most of the dues. The new Franch advance after Fleurus (June 1794) and the union of Belgium to France in October 1795 made the abolition complete in the former Austrian Netherlands and the principality of Liège. In the United Provinces, the Batavian Republic, established in 1795, prudently waited until the drafting of its constitution in 1798 before publishing a qualified suppression. Everywhere, the French armies carried with them the principles of the Revolution. The fact that they were imposed from above, and the advance or retreat of the armies, affected the success of these measures. Occasionally, uprisings preceded or accompanied such emancipation by decree, rather like the uncertainty and impatience of the first years of the Revolution. This was true in the Valais country, where the suppression of the 'tithes, dues and feudal rights' with indemnities for their holders, had been proclaimed in 1798. From February to May 1802, peasant bands surrounded about twenty towns and castles in order to destroy seigneurial titles. Called *Bourla papey* in Swiss provincial dialect, these rustics successfully entered Lausanne in arms on 8th May, and burned archives at Morges, Grandson, Yverdon and so on. Final abolition in the canton of Vaud was not proclaimed until May 1804.

Even when the fortunes of war caused legislation to vary, the seigneurial fiscs could never regain their previous effectiveness. The slow disintegration of 'feudalism' occasionally followed a stop-go rhythm. In sum, the shock administered by the French revolution played the role of accelerator in the history of a long development on which 'enlightened' Europe had embarked around the 1770s.

The agrarian communities' struggle for survival

Anti-seigneurialism disappeared in France in 1793, but in the same year the greatest peasant war in its history broke out. The coincidence is instructive; emancipation from noble fiscality was only one of the many stakes in agrarian conflicts. State control, aggression in the form of innovation, and the growth of landownership by townspeople – all developments that rural communities had long combated – more than ever reappeared in the front rank of the frustrations experienced by the rural population.

Peasant resistance to the revolution

If historians dealing with peasant struggles exclude the Vendée wars from their field of study, it is perhaps because they remain bound to a wholly political conception of history, or are concerned to follow an ideological line which is incompatible with their being so included, or simply that they conform to the thought patterns that dominate contemporary intellectual circles. However, the great uprising of the western provinces that began in March 1793 was overwhelmingly a peasant affair. Its immediate cause was the refusal of conscription; it was also passionately royalist and catholic. It is not a question of reducing the role of political fidelity or religious faith if we attempt to offer an agrarian interpretation of these factors, or to explain why, at that juncture, they were open to a particular development in the countryside.

The military recruitment decided by the Convention decreed the mobilisation of young men on an unheard of scale. Never before had the state assumed the power to summon youth as a whole. This sudden increase in the state's prerogatives involved the departure of young men who, for the most part, had never left their parish or even thought of doing so. It was thought that the absence of the best workers would be cruelly felt in farmwork. The royalist cause espoused by the Vendéens was the very opposite of this demand; it also identified itself with objectives that were more fundamental and instinctive, such as those of legitimacy and continuity, and of a supreme, paternal protector. The country people, attuned to the benefits of continuity and to the arguments of tradition, were better placed than anyone to experience such needs. Finally, the Revolution's measures concerning religious practice and its persecution of the non-juring clergy offended more strongly the people of the *bocage*, with its isolated farmsteads. The priest serving his parish was not merely a consoler and a teacher, but also a cultural intermediary, a source of information, an emissary and a counsellor. His social functions were broader than in regions of concentrated habitat where the influence of the clergy might, on the contrary, appear oppressive to some people.

More straightforwardly, agrarian factors were joined to this collection of frustrations. The establishment of communes as administrative entities was accompanied by the suppression of a large number of parishes which were held to be too small for such an honour. These places of habitation lost their church and position as a community. The former parish was visited by a kind of dethronement which deprived it of worship and abolished its institutional conviviality. In the four departments at the centre of the insurrection, the suppressed parishes formed twenty-two per cent of the total. The property of the parish chests (*fabriques*) was to be consolidated; such transfers were akin to spoliation. The sale of church property was also viewed as another misuse of the community's patrimony. As for the dismantling of church bells in order to recover their metal content, it was a symbolic insult to the body of the community, because the bell, a kind of collective voice, personified the parish. As an inspector sent to the Sables d'Olonne district in November 1790 noted, 'to cross the country areas over the attachment to their church-bells, is to sow rebellion there.'

Put schematically, there were five Vendée wars between 1793 and 1833. Their scale is not fully realised, but left to heroic legend or else systematically undervalued, and even ignored altogether in public instruction. Starting as marches on towns or as resistance to urban power, the Vendée wars were the bloodiest illustration of the irreducible opposition between town and country. The repression mounted by the revolutionary authorities deliberately took the form of terrorist extermination. If the suspicious and envious hostility of the peasantry towards townspeople is a commonplace, the crushing of the rebellious provinces was the result of an opposing fury – the middle classes' hatred of the peasantry – which espoused and worsened the totalitarian logic of the revolutionary ideology. Estimates of the numbers of dead for the Vendéan wars are not reliable, and rise as high as 600,000.[2]

The same demands (young conscripts and war contributions) made in similar circumstances (eviction of traditional authorities, persecution of the clergy) and according to the same methods of military emergency (requisition and pillage), were exported to conquered foreign territories, producing similar defensive reactions among foreign peasantries. As early as 1793, the occupation of Belgium provoked peasant resistance to military contributions paid for in *assignats*. Advancing through the Catalan Pyrenees between 1793 and 1795, the French troops believed they had the support of the population, to whom the suppression of tithes and seigneurial rights was announced. In reality, they encountered guerilla war fought by the mountain people for whom the invasion signified above all destruction and the confiscation of their crops.

The introduction of conscription in the 'united départments', namely the Walloon and Flemish provinces, was established by a decree of 5th September 1798. The first gatherings of conscripts around 15th October were a signal for revolt by the Luxembourg peasants. The village units were easily routed on 30th October by army columns sent from the towns. This passing incident, in which several hundred peasants died, was christened the *Klepelkrich* (*Klöppelkrieg*, or war of the cudgels). At the same time, the peasants of Limburg, which had become the département of the Lower Meuse, also rose in revolt (*Boerenkrijg*), and succeeded in seizing the towns of Diest and Hasselt on 4th December. They proclaimed their fidelity to the emperor and the church, attacking those townspeople, called *Franzgezinden*, who had bought church property. General Jardon's troops retook Hasselt and massacred the fleeing 'brigands'.

The establishment of French garrisons in Switzerland, even in the Alpine fastnesses of the oldest cantons (*Waldstätten*), clashed with uprisings by the mountain people led by their notables. The movement started in Uri on 26th April 1799, gaining the support of all the original cantons, followed by the Grisons, Tessin and even the Valais. The assembled peasants were dressed in shepherds' overalls (*Hirtenhemden*), hence the name of *Hirtenhemdlikrieg* given to it. General Soult overcame the revolt relatively quickly, and the *Landmann* of Schwyg, Aloys Reding, surrendered in May. Guerilla war continued in the valleys, ending in massacres and burnings of villages (Nidwald, September 1799).

It was in Tuscany and the kingdom of Naples that the popular counter-revolutionary uprisings had the greatest success. Southern Italy, as we saw earlier, had been the scene of a centuries-long abdication by the sovereign power; the provinces were left to the barons, to administration by their agents, to their justice and their fiscal systems. Only thirty per cent of the population of the kingdom of Naples depended directly on the king, and this proportion was reduced to twelve per cent in the most feudalised provinces, the Basilicata, Molise and the Lower Abruzzi. The property-owning élites were seduced by the new ideas of the second half of the eighteenth century. From this sprung temptations to improve agriculture by enclosure of fields, the division of common lands, the suppression of use-rights, and the demand for re-valued leases. Such changes did not lighten the peasants' burden, while depriving it of the power of familiar habit. In this tale of dereliction, the Bourbon dynasty was the only personification of a national power specific to the old southern kingdom. The church was the only institution present every-where, down to the lowest parishes; it was so marginally implicated in the seigneurial system as not to be compromised by anti-fiscal resentment (only six per cent of the feudal popu-lation depended on church fiefs).

In 1799, General Championnet took Naples and, with the support of the 'enlightened' groups there, proclaimed the Par-thenopean Republic on 24th January. The more or less general adherence of the notables ensured the simple rallying of all the provinces, while Ferdinand IV took refuge in Sicily. The republican interlude was brief. The Austro-Russian offensive in the north forced the bulk of the French troops to retreat, while there was harassment from the English along the coasts. Landing on 8th February at Catona, near Reggio Calabria, Cardinal Ruffo was to lead an extraordinary peasant march of reconquest which, in five months, victoriously brought him as far as Campania. On the first day, he had with him only 300 men from his brother's estate. They wore white crosses on their hats and shouted, 'Long live religion, long live the king, death to the Jacobins.' His army rose to 40,000 men, with endless new arrivals. 'It remains a miracle of providence, since it is never the same people, but only those from the neighbour-hood of a town that we wish to besiege. They could well, if discontented, not come or abandon us, but, thank God, they have never failed us.' As Ruffo approached, the peasants set about 'royalising' the local strongholds, that is to drive out the republican garrisons, kill the middle-class Jacobins and pillage their property.

The royalists' march was clearly a revolt by the poor. Cardinal Ruffo took it on himself to reduce customs duties, to suppress the purchase monopoly of raw silk for the royal manufactures, and especially to reduce seigneurial rights and to effect re-distributions and sales from the confiscations made against the numerous and wealthy republican property-owners. A cynical adage went: 'whoever had bread and wine was held for a Jacobin.' Championnet confirmed this by saying: 'in general, everyone who owns something is on our side.' Count Ettore Carafa (1767–99), heir to the great fief of Andria, near Bari, was an example of such adherence by property-owners. Won over to French ideas, he led the military detachments engaged in repression in his own province. The people of Andria remained hostile to the republic personified by their lord. On 23rd February 1799, the town had to be taken house by house, and General Broussier abandoned it to the 'will of the soldiers.'

The revolt of the southern peasantry recurred in the same manner, and with the same social and cultural divisions, during the second French invasion of 1806. Concentrated especially in Calabria, the resistance of the legitimist groups was not broken until 1811. Like the French *chouanneries*, these movements have suffered a travesty at the hands of historians. The rare legitimist chroniclers strove to erase the ferocity of peasant guerilla war; the later unitary nationalist writers denounced them as the result of clerical conspiracy; lastly, contemporary Marxists see them merely as a blind form of class war and of colonial resistance.

The seigneurial regime did not survive these shocks. Stricken from 1799 onwards, it was suppressed with provision for redemption by Zurlo, the royal minister, in 1806, and in 1815 there was no question of restoring it. Counter-revolutionary movements were in no way identical with social restoration. Neapolitan irredentism and peasant legitimism were long-term affairs, not accidents of politics. Such movements were carriers of an utopia of the land, one was peripheral, communal and opposed to bourgeois centralisation. They built upon peasant community structures which were in large part unchanged for decades or centuries. Their proliferation when confronted with the colossal upheaval that was French revolutionary imperialism, corresponded to the dying moments of these structures. They were still capable of violent explosion, before more insidious forms of aggression, dispossession and the population exodus, drained them of their energy.

The agony of old community traditions

We saw how, in spite of serfdom, invasion and catastrophe, village communities succeeded in preserving a structure, the autonomy of which was discreet and tacit, customs which governed the behaviour of villagers towards each other, and intangible usages in agricultural activities and in the relations of man and his environment. The capacity for survival and revival of such community elements was related to a relative immobility of economic techniques and remoteness from the processes of urbanisation and commercialisation. Yet it should not be thought that such traditions could only operate in poverty-stricken pockets: the richest vineyards still had to have their grape-picking timetables and the richest grain areas the constraints of field-rotation. Nor ought we to idealise the village republic, free of inequality and tension. Communities had their methods of resolving their habitual conflicts; the system enabled a group of inhabitants whose numbers varied very little to co-exist and continue together. Regular emigration by young people to armies or trades was, for many traditional societies, the means of limiting the population to the area's traditional capacity. In addition to the oldest families sharing most of the tenancies between them, there was a body of labourers who were mobilised for the major tasks of the year. These people possessed little or no land and, apart from seasonal employment, they could not survive without their small parasitic pastoral activities. Thus, they would have a goat or a pig that grazed along the roadside or foraged in the woods during the autumn, or else a few head of sheep that mixed with the village flock which roamed the fields or the local moors. The fallow land also provided profits from hunting, fishing, picking, wood-gathering (dead-wood and brush-wood) in the forests, and collecting rushes and turf in the marshes.

Customs and usages were anything but anarchic. People knew who had a right to them, when and how. They had the means of excluding intruders and undesirables. Newcomers were subjected to the payment of entry fees. Pioneer communities, as in northern Russia, ritually welcomed newcomers to the labour force. Elsewhere, those who disturbed this order were the object of collective revenge in a cruel rite of rejection. The social space of a village was conditioned by its agrarian landscape and kind of habitat. It might or might not correspond to institutional divisions. It was a unit of behaviour, or worship (the parish), an area for intermarriage and familiarity; it comprised established conventions of mutual help in farmwork and of solidarity in misfortune that even included recourse to arms. Depending on the environment, the community might be more or less self-supporting, but it generally found room for distinctions of rank and craft. It could integrate farmers, tree-fellers and artisans, as well as the few familiar outsiders like seasonal jobbers or the usual peddlers.

Precarious and immemorial, these forms of equilibrium found themselves being undermined at the end of the early modern period; it happened more or less early depending on their degree of integration into the market economy. New ideas of technical progress, of improvements in yields, of more intensive farming, and of the most effective utilisation possible of the resources of the environment implied the overthrow of ancient agrarian structures and of use-rights. Custom now appeared as an obscurantist straightjacket. The owner must have absolute disposition over his domain, and its size be commensurate with his farm machinery. In this venture, he must not depend on anyone, on any tutelage or parasitic tradition. Agrarian individualism and the plenitude of property rights pre-supposed, among other things, the demise of the village community.

We shall follow this development through the state's interventions and the communities' violent reactions over forests, grazing-rights and common lands. The waterways and forest ordinance of 1670 already sketched out this trend by prescribing the enclosure of royal forests and the restriction of neighbouring inhabitants' usages. Effective limitation of hunting rights also began with Colbert's ordinances. In England, it was a whig government, significantly, which made crimes of estoving and poaching. The Black Act of 1723 was the result of minor disturbances in the forest counties of the south. In one instant, this set of measures created fifty new criminal offences. French revolutionary legislation fitted into this long-term trend. The law of 27th March 1791 stipulated that no use-right could be included in the sale of church property. This considerable volume of land thus escaped from the immemorial encroachment of neighbours. There followed a marked rise in forest offences; over a thousand were quoted in *Germinal* of the Year Four for the forest of Haguenau. The Forest Code of 1827 finally dispossessed the villages bordering on the forests. The mountain-folk around Foix did not bow to this, and began a long struggle against the forest guards known as the war of the *Demoiselles*; similar incidents were still occuring in the late nineteenth century. The year 1848, when legitimacy was in doubt, gave the forest-people of Alsace or the valleys of the Pyrenees the illusion of recovering their prerogatives. In fact, the legislation which guaranteed intensive forestry was not the sole obstacle; rural overpopulation also rendered the old usages unworkable. At this time, such opposition existed throughout Europe. The Prussian codes of 1821 stiffened the penalties for the theft of wood. Competition between manufacturers and the poor foresters of the Rhineland was debated at length in 1841 at the Düsseldorf diet; around Koblenz and Trier, thefts of wood were twenty to thirty times more frequent than ordinary forms of theft. Commenting on these discussions, the journalist Karl Marx wrote: 'They have succeeded in making a monopoly for the rich out of a customary right of the poor.'

The question of whether to preserve or divide common lands, to keep open fields or to enclose them in plots, fuelled many polemics in France and England all through the eighteenth century. The right to enclose seemed linked to progress in the liberation of property from every form of seigneurial or communal servitude. Some were more sensitive to the anxieties of the small-holders and the recriminations of labourers who were reduced to emigrating to the towns, because of a lack of opportunities for additional husbandry. Several edicts issued between 1769 and 1781 permitted the division of communal lands in certain provinces, and here, too, the Revolution speeded up the movement. The Rural Code published by the Constitutional Assembly on 2nd September 1791 declared that the right to enclose emanated from the right to own property, which was itself 'natural and imprescriptible'. To the revolutionary legislators, communal servitudes were identified as side-effects of 'feudalism'. In principle, use-rights were condemned and the division of commons decreed. However, those in office soon discovered the numerical importance of the agrarian proletariat. Local protests increased, and then disputes over the equal distribution of the commons or the pure and simple auction of them prevented any radicalisation of procedures and extended tolerance for old practices. The more or less slow disappearance of community servitudes and the erosion of communal lands henceforth opened the door to bitter disputes within villages. The sale of church property widened differences in wealth there. Such conflicts were insoluble within the old community framework, and indeed postulated its collapse.

Stock-raising areas had their own peculiar changes. Transhumance, its ancient nomadic practices, and the size of its area of commonage, had ceased to expand in certain Mediterranean countries since the second half of the seventeenth century. Pasture lands gave ground before the still hesitant advance of a more sedentary and extensive agriculture. Enclosures spread from the plains into the valleys; the settlers pushed the pastoralists ever higher into the uplands; the former enjoyed the blessing of the authorities, and often enjoyed fiscal privileges while the stock-farmers, on the other hand, felt more than anyone else the burden of the salt tax in respect of their sheep, cheeses and salted products. The moderating, pacifying role of the village assemblies and of the estates of the valleys declined in effectiveness, either because it was usurped by government organs, or because the monopoly over the assemblies held by wealthy farming families robbed them of their standing. Raids by shepherds who harassed the graingrowers' villages express both their vengeance and their slow decline (e.g., Sardinia and Corsica in the eighteenth and nineteenth centuries).

There is another example of a custom destined to fall into disuse. Around farm-houses, there was often a little plot for hemps and linen which the woman of the house cultivated and wove, and from which she made household fabrics. During the summer, the damp areas were used for retting, which made the surroundings stink. The arrival of cheaper industrial fabrics would sooner or later lead to the disappearance of these domestic techniques. Before that, 'sanitary policing' decrees attempted to regulate the practice. Riots followed in which the villagers defended their pestilential retting-pits.

All of the contradictions between ancient customs and new laws would be resolved in the long term by the force of circumstances and rural emigration. In the meantime, the small-holders clung fiercely to their miserable plots. Each time a political crisis offered them hope, or a year of scarcity crippled them a little more, they resumed their angry, disorderly demonstrations in defence of their ancient position and their survival. Their enemies and victims were forest officials, rural policemen, the local moneylenders, the purchasers of village lands or the bourgeois who came to hunt across their fields.

Periods in which food was expensive always produced disturbances among the urban lower classes. Their riots acquired a new, rural dimension in the late eighteenth century. The rising curve of food prices led owners and tenants to pay their servants and wage labourers in money, rather than house, feed and pay them in kind as previously. The hired work-force of the great plains of northern France or of the English counties was no longer sheltered against price fluctuations, and henceforth played their part, like the urban masses, in the acts of violence of times of high prices. In England, these demonstrators demanded the application of the Elizabethan poor-laws on poor relief. In France they demanded that the town authorities fix bread prices by decree. Because of war, economic trends were again for a time favourable to wage earners. After 1815, rural violence resumed its course. The most serious outburst took the form of agrarian luddism – burnings of farms and destructions of harvesting-machines which deprived agricultural labourers of work. There were riots in 1830 known by the name of 'Captain Swing', because the burnings were preceded by a threatening letter dispatched to the owners. In Ireland, a different system of land use produced a different type of violence. In place of disturbances by wage-earners defending their right to remain on the land, we encounter resistance by small-holders to dispossession, resembling the anger of the French peasantry. From the 1760s, the rioters were known as Whiteboys (i.e. 'pets', an old name given to the seventeenth century conspirators by inversion of its meaning). Their action was to deliberately murder landowners wishing to adapt to market conditions, and who had to evict tenants hindering their efforts at expansion. Specific decrees condemned Whiteboyism from 1787 onwards, and periodic resurgences of their terrorism later surfaced in the central and southern counties of Munster and Connaught. A rural police force, the Irish Constabulary, was organised against them. It was the disaster of the 1847 Famine which got the better of their resistance. In 1846, sixty-one per cent of the farms in Tipperary were under six hectares; this proportion had fallen to forty-four per cent fifteen years later.

Almost everywhere in the history of rural Europe, we find a decisive turning-point around 1847 or 1848. Agrarian catastrophe had ruined the small-holders and started trends of desertion and emigration from the countryside. Political crises swept away the final legal vestiges of the 'second serfdom' in central Europe, as well as reviving the illusions of the western peasantries. Breakdowns in political legitimacy and power vacuums engendered a sort of contagion and acts of violence. It is only with hindsight that the odds appear hopeless. In the summer of 1848, the peasant marchers who chased off the tax-collectors, occupied the forests and the commons were in no doubt of their success. In the long term, this last outburst by the village communities takes on the appearance of a final act. Thereafter began the desertion of villages, accelerated by conscription and the railways.

Conclusion

Our itinerary through the ideas and the practice of revolt in earlier societies cannot reveal historical laws; nor can it formulate either a mechanism of subversion, or a model of balanced government. It does, however, suggest recurrences in the aspirations of rebels, and permanent features in the manner in which they rebelled. It is these expectations and behaviour patterns which make up the long-term structures of political violence. We have also seen along the way coincidences of time and place, in which we can see traces of circumstantial factors -- the role of economic events, the effect of changes within society, and the imprint of institutions, whether temporary or enduring.

At the source of every surge in insurrection, it should be possible to unveil a few essential myths which appear as the proverbial cat with nine lives, and which escape from the confines of timelessness, disguising themselves according to historical circumstances. Eschatological hope thus feeds forever reviving expectations of God's reign on earth. Such millenarianism tinged a good number of the religious and social outbursts of the sixteenth century to a greater or lesser extent. When applied to the entire universe, anthropomorphic ways of thinking sustained the idea of a golden age, of a return of happiness, whose restoration men wished to hasten. Every nation's history contained one such legendary point in time, which could serve a subversive purpose. The quest for a reassuring, immanent justice, and the need for continuity of government generated myths of the deceived or the hidden king. Such fundamental loyalism and reference to an underlying law that was good and generally personified by the king, were perhaps the strongest and most constant features of early modern disturbances.

Enduring myths and despairing, passionate appeals enjoyed greater currency at certain historical moments, when social tensions or changes then underway were more nakedly visible, and when the most divergent hopes and demands suddenly came into the open. During the English civil war or the Fronde in France, bitterness that had hitherto been concealed or kept silent, or that had gone unperceived by people themselves, suddenly emerged. Moments of revelation like this were always times when there was a power vacuum or an uncertain legitimacy. Socio-political vertigo of this kind is, of course, not specific to the early modern period; the nineteenth and twentieth centuries also provide clear instances of it.

In lived experience and the heat of action, myths are obliterated by human passions, and by ideas which are conscious and immediate. Hence, an insurrection's legitimacy might be grounded in the misappropriation of power by a tyrant, be he a usurper or a conqueror, or in the perversion of power because of a breach of the alleged original contract binding sovereign and subjects. Their right to reject him then sought refuge in the most visible civil alternatives of the day – the city-stage, whether it was the city-fatherland or the village community, and the noble state as the nation personified exclusively in the families of the nobility.

Finally, the model of political equality dominated the close of the early modern era. The idea of progress moved from the realm of science to that of human affairs. The objectives of subversion no longer implied either a substitution or a re-formation of government, but aimed to innovate. The appearance of this belief in a progressive evolution of history coincided with a renewal of the doctrine of the social contract. Because of the founding contract, there was no longer any doubt as to the people's sovereignty. Difficulties in identifying who the people were, in delegating its power to its representatives, and the hopeless confusion between the people and the state, would appear in due course; the problems of our own time illustrate these ambiguities or contradictions. The new sociability which took shape in the 1760s contained all the possible developments of regimes claiming to be democratic. We are therefore not being misled by the violent spasms of political events, if we see the beginnings of a new period of history in the late eighteenth century.

In outlining these few, but vast ideological trends, we might be tempted to believe in some orderly development, but it would account rather badly for the luxuriance of historical events. Political violence is not to be reduced to a pursuit of universalising goals. We must work our way inside human groups if we are to seek and discover more historically personified forces and the locations of violence in society. The possible connections between violence and social hierarchy and mobility, and agreement or opposition between elites and masses, are never clear. It is by no means easy to identify a movement of insurrection with a social group. In this period, the frustrations arising from barriers to mobility, decline or a refusal of status were experienced in isolation, and were not rationalised in political terms. If we can perceive such motives in the careers of individual leaders, we cannot simply posit such causation of whole movements; monistic social explanations of major crises have failed to withstand critical attack. We cannot say, for example, that the English Revolution was led by the gentry, or that the Neapolitan Revolution pitted the pro-Spanish nobility against the rest of the city and kingdom. On inspection, we soon realise that these groups, so clearly distinguished by historians, were in reality divided into two or three factions – for, against, or indifferent. In addition, many complex movements like the Dutch Revolt or the Fronde evade all social labelling. Finally, the appearances of social conflict are often the result of either the attractiveness of Marxist vulgarisation, which colours all our arguments, or quite simply, the convenience of categorisation and language.

Most of the time, rebels took traditional figures, such as the lord, the parish priest or the mayor, for their leaders. This might be because the revolt was itself an answer to their appeal, and that a notable had taken the initiative in it, or because the crowd forcibly placed a notable at their head as a symbolic personification of their common purpose or for his familiarity with military matters.

In cases which approximate most closely to models of struggles between social groups, for example when the issue at stake was power within a city or a just distribution of the tax burden, the revolt was led by artisans. Most forms of urban violence demonstrate this fundamental role of artisans and shopkeepers, who dominated the sociability of their place of habitation and the feelings of their neighbourhood. They were not lost in the mass of servants, day-labourers and porters who flocked to the scenes of pillage after a riot. The master craftsmen represent the core of insurrections, not their marginal aspects; from the outset, it was they who were leaders of movements in which involvement by marginal groups was merely tolerated or, more than that, feared and rejected. Thus, participation by women and children signalled a more basic issue when the very survival of the community was at stake, as in the bread riots.

Above all, study of the revolts enables us to distinguish the men of action from the opinion formers. If the traditional leaders were numerous in the revolts, the shaping of opinion, on the other hand, belonged to specific, literate groups, above all to legal practitioners. In the course of events, when the ferment of ideas was greater than mere violence – it was then that the men of law appeared at the forefront. When a challenge to government took the form of ideological competition, as in the Reformation or the French Pre-Revolution, the discreet influence of cultural mediators such as barristers, doctors, schoolmasters and ordinary men of law, came into the open.

Very few revolts were successful in seizing the totality of power; in truth, they did not even conceive of doing so. Their object, a very direct one, was confined to demanding daily bread and survival, a refusal of taxes or the defence of a particular liberty. An analysis of behaviour during these minor disturbances reveals some of the functions of political violence, that is, the satisfactions that were more or less consciously expected from it. Revolt was a festive interruption of everyday life, an exercise of justice and a purifying act that brought renewal. Commonplace, indeed scarcely avoidable, revolt surprised nobody. Attempts were made to ignite it among enemies, while at home prudent remedies against it were sought through moderating the fiscal demands made of the most dangerous groups, such as the nobility, the towns and the frontier provinces. Societies of orders and their primitive state structures tolerated these outbursts of anger among their subjects passably well. Revolt in them was a sort of community right, a crude form of popular justice that was custom-based and conservative, and a reaction against aggression from above, whether as expansion in government, innovations by élites or the demands of property owners.

The history of past political violence cannot be regarded as a collection of exceptional facts, nor confused with, say, the revolutions of the nineteenth century which burst in on the ordinary functioning of institutions and produced upheavals in government. Collective recourse to force was too frequent, and was legitimated by the self-defence of inhabitants who were constantly armed, by the traditions of guerilla war, the endemic warfare of certain frontiers, the privileged status of particular individuals or provinces, and so on. Political violence was thus a possible court of appeal, an extreme but still legitimate resort that was doubtless far removed from any idea or possibility of subversion. This justification and ordinariness of revolt would last as long as the state was incapable of pacifying social relations and of confiscating the use of violence exclusively for itself.

However, the course of history was altered by a number of major crises, whose common secret of success was their organisation of revolutionary parties which gathered recruits around a religious persuasion, such as Calvinism in the Dutch war of independence or Puritanism in the English Revolution. The radicalisation of their campaign, their secessions and political subversion were the result of the enduring character of the hostilities, accompanied by power vacuums and the ideological profusion they generated. If all we conclude is that the movements of political violence which were most likely to succeed were those based on passions of a religious or patriotic kind, then we are merely repeating the oldest lessons of traditional historiography. Every generation has its pattern of emotions. For a particular time or place, religion or patriotism were the principal code, the obvious frame of reference, and the language in which all the forces and values of the time expressed themselves.

The peasant wars deserve a particular place in the history of the early modern period. More than any other type of revolt, they could respond to the fluctuations of economic cycles, since the condition of the various peasantries, their aspirations and their fears were to some extent connected to the marketing of the produce of the land.

Firstly, we see a bunching of rural insurrections in the early sixteenth century, in the early stages of the 'second serfdom'. The absence of strong monarchical traditions, the sparseness of the population and the rise in food prices explain this slow tying down of the peasantries of central and eastern Europe during the sixteenth and seventeenth centuries.

Another wave of revolts, located roughly in the first half of the seventeenth century and coinciding with the Thirty Years' War, corresponds to the western peasantries' rejection of the state's fiscal expansion. France, Spain and Austria preferred to base rises in their income on direct contributions from the countryside rather than on consumption taxes which would have hit the towns, which enjoyed privileges everywhere. France was especially the theatre of many of these popular, anti-state revolts; indeed, for a long time its budget was based on the peasant *taille* alone. Astonished contemporaries kept saying that 'the king of France had sheep with golden fleece.'[1]

Finally, the last decades of the eighteenth century witnessed a multiplication of insurrections among the eastern European peasantries who believed that the suppression of their servitudes and services was nigh. In the west, the seigneurial rights, which were rejected in the tumults of the Pre-Revolution, were completely suppressed by the decrees of the revolutionary assemblies. In the French experience between 1788 and 1792, urban ideologies and rural demands seemed to briefly meet. In fact, the intensive agriculture desired by the urban middle class carried with it the death sentence of the old rural communities. The political and economic innovations of the Revolution would soon sweep away as absurd survivals village autarchy, local solidarities and community usages and servitudes.

The disappearance of agrarian communities was the last stage of a long, structural antagonism. The parasitic character of the townspeople who drained agricultural goods and fixed their prices, introduced their own fashions and ideas, imposed their mastery and, finally, purchased lands, evolved throughout the early modern era. Such forms of dependence and rivalry were already apparent to sixteenth-century authors. Etienne Pasquier wrote around 1560: 'How annoyed the farmer who tills his family acres must be when the loss of the harvest falls on his shoulders, but how much more so when he tills another man's land and when, through the calamity of a single bad year, he falls into the clutches of a heartless master who has nothing else to blare into his ears than an accursed rise in grain prices, which leaves him without any hope of an alternative for the future. I shall not enter into details like the pillaging of the *gendarmerie*, or the collection of *tailles* and subsidies . . . things which one does not readily encounter in towns. So we say that the farmer draws behind his cart all the evils of his time.'[2] François de La Noue wrote around 1580: 'What do large cities do except attract to themselves all the profits they can, make a great show of their privileges, and unload every burden and misery onto the poor people of the countryside? It is a wonder what they survive on, being in addition pressed by the subtle hand of the financiers and by the usury which the bourgeois practice on the poor peasants.'[3]

The recurrence of the word misery in these writings on peasant misfortune should not mislead us. It is necessary to dispel the over-simple image of an obligatory coupling of misery and revolt. It is never the destitute who take up arms, but rather the well-off, the minor notables who fear for their future. Even peasant revolts do not necessarily break out at the most crushing moments or in the places where status conditions are at their worst. Such outbreaks result from the convergence of a feeling of injustice (legal or fiscal) and a source of provocation (the threat or the hope of a change). The provinces that were richest in privileges gave the signal for revolt; peasant élites and traditional leaders placed themselves at the head of them. *The trigger of revolt is not destitution, but injustice – and not objective injustice, but the conviction of it.* Political violence arises as a result of opinion, not of an objective situation. For example, inequality in itself does not lead to indignation, as it is regarded as more or less inevitable, and even natural, but changes in the social hierarchy, the efforts of the rich to usurp status or of the parvenu to obtain exemption from common contributions, are viewed as intolerable. Political violence is above all a cultural fact. Of course, like every global social fact, it depends on a multitude of factors and it inevitably reflects the long rhythms of economic cycles. However, in its historical setting, in the short-term perspective of its early phases, its outbursts, its developments and even its influence on men's destinies, such violence is an accumulation of opinions and behaviour, of conventions and particular aspects. It would be one-sided to tie it to the movements of economics, politics, society or religion, all of which influence it, but do not suffice to define it.

Not all discontent or frustration leads to violence. A catalogue of all the tensions present in a society would not correspond to that of its revolts and revolutions. Some tensions are transmuted into rancour, some are resolved in compromises, and some are subsumed into litigation. The extension of state-made law, and the acceptance by society of judicial appeals served to blunt resentments and to sap even collective forms of aggression. A quarrel which produces violence in one time and place evinces only irritation and chicanery in another, while in that same time and place, competing forms of extraction were either accepted or rejected, not in terms of their burden-someness, but of their status in public opinion. The fiscal systems of lords, church tithes and states were not opposed at the same time, nor by the same rebels. It is as if recourse to violence passed through thresholds which vary, depending on factors like opinion and culture. It is the autonomy of collective violence that we have tried to illustrate in this book.

Notes

Chapter one

1. *The Philosophy of History* (Dover edition: New York, 1956), p. 417.
2. *The Communist Manifesto*, in David McLellan (ed.), *Karl Marx: Selected Writings* (Oxford, 1977), p. 236.
3. *The Reason of State*, trans. by P. J. and D. P. Waley (London, 1956), p. 45.
4. *Considérations politiques sur les coups d'état* (Paris, 1639) p. 149.
5. *Ibid.* p. 174.
6. Pierre Chaunu, *Le Temps des réformes* (Paris, 1975).
7. Florimond de Raemond, *Histoire de la naissance, progrez et décadence de l'héresie de ce siècle* (Arras, 1611), book 2, Ch. 18, 'comment chacun vouloit estre l'auteur d'une religion'.
8. *Considérations politiques sur les coups d'état*, pp. 152–4.
9. *Of Crimes and Punishments*, in James Anson Farrer, *Crimes and Punishments* (London, 1880), p. 220.
10. *Schriften und Briefe*, ed. G. Franz (Gütersloh, 1968), p. 455.
11. Michael Eyzinger, *Pentaplus regnorum mundi* (Antwerp, 1579), p. 14.
12. W. E. Mühlmann, *Messianismes révolutionnaires* (Paris, 1968), p. 299.
13. *Mémoires* (Paris 1652), 'Livre des observations meslées de la justice et qu'elle appartient au roy', pp. 69–72.
14. *Le Prince chrétien* (Arras, 1610), p. 318.

Chapter two

1. *Chronologie novenaire*, ed. J. A. C. Buchon [*Choix de chroniques et mémoires sur l'histoire de France*] (Paris, 1836), p. 373.
2. *Discourses on Livy*, ed. Max Lerner [Modern Library edition] (New York, 1950), pp. 254–5.

Chapter three

1. *Reason of State*, pp. 86–7.
2. Paul Bois, *Paysans de l'ouest* (Paris, 1960).
3. S. C. Gigon, *La Révolte de la gabelle en Guyenne* (Paris, 1906), p. 46.
4. *Musée Neuchâtelois* 50 (1913), pp. 196–7.
5. Robert Mandrou, 'Les Français hors de France aux xvi et xvii siècles. 1. A Génève: le premier refuge protestant', *Annales: Economies, Sociétés, Civilisations* (1959), pp. 662–6.
6. *Commentaires*, ed. Paul Courteault [*La Pléiade* edition] (Paris, 1964), p. 471.

7. *The Complete Works of Michel de Montaigne*, translated by Donald M. Frame (London, n.d.), p. 591. *Maître* is the title still used in French by notaries and barristers.

8. Robert Mandrou, *De la culture populaire aux xvii et xviii siècles* (Paris, 1964), pp. 124–5.

9. Quoted in Peter Laslett, *The World We Have Lost* (London, 1965), pp. 187–8.

10. See Gabriele Turi, '*Viva Maria*'. *La reazione alle riforme leopoldine* (Florence, 1969), p. 344.

Chapter four

1. 'The organisation of revolutionary parties in France and the Netherlands during the sixteenth century', *Journal of Modern History* 27 (1955), pp. 335–51.

2. Elie Barnavi, *Le Parti de dieu. Etude sociale et politique des chefs de la ligue parisienne* (Louvain, 1980).

3. *Les Estats, esquels il est discouru du prince, du noble et du tiers estat* (Lyon, 1596), pp. 255–7.

4. *Sur le commerce des bleds*, ed. Fausto Nicolini (Rome, 1959), p. 212.

5. David Herlihy and Christiane Klapisch-Zuber, *Tuscans and their Families. A Study of the Florentine Catasto of 1427* (London–New Haven, 1985).

6. René Pillorget, *Les Mouvements insurrectionels de Provence entre 1596 et 1715* (Paris, 1975), esp. pp. 427ff.

7. Fleurance de Rivault, *Les Estats*, pp. 385–6.

8. G. J. de Cosnac, *Souvenirs du règne de Louis XIV*, 8 vols. (Paris, 1866–82), vol. 5, p. 394.

9. Jeronimo de Conestaggio, *De l'union du royaume de Portugal à la couronne de Castille*, French translation by T. Nardin (Besançon, 1586), pp. 265–6.

10. Rivault, *Les Estats*, pp. 382–3.

11. *Reason of State*, pp. 73–4.

Chapter five

1. On the threat of mutiny and desertion owing to non-payment of wages by the Swiss regiments in France during the Fronde, see Yves-Marie Bercé, 'Le Rôle des Suisses pendant la Fronde', in *Cinq siècles de relations franco-suisses. Hommage à L.–E. Roulet* (Neuchâtel, 1984), pp. 73–86.

2. Palma Cayet, *Chronologie Novenaire*, p. 109.

3. *La Petite guerre*, ch. 1, pp. 1–2.

4. Quoted in Denis Davidoff, *Essai sur la guerre des partisans* (Paris, 1841), p. 29.

5. Heinrich Dietrich von Bülow, *Esprit du système de guerre moderne* (Paris, 1801), p. 224.

6. Henri de Jomini, *The Art of War*, translated by G. H. Mendell and W. P. Craighill (Philadelphia, 1862; reprinted Westport, Conn., 1971), p. 31.

7. Yves Durand, 'La contrebande du sel au xviii siècle aux frontières de Bretagne, du Maine et de l'Anjou', *Histoire Sociale* (1974), pp. 227–69.

8. Philippe J. Hesse, 'Géographie coutumière et révoltes paysannes en 1789', *Annales Historiques de la Révolution Française* 51 (1979), pp. 280–306.

9. Alan Everitt, *The Community of Kent and the Great Rebellion, 1640–1660* (London, 1966).

10. Francesco Capecelatro, *Degli annali della città di Napoli, 1631–1650* (Naples, 1849), p. 189.

11. Eric Hobsbawm, *Bandits* (London, 1969), p. 16.

12. Quoted in Hélène Tuzet, *La Sicile au xviii siècle, vue par les voyageurs étrangers* (Strasbourg, 1955), pp. 208–15.

Chapter six

1. Paolo Giovio, *Histoires sur les choses faites et avenues en son temps* (Lyon, 1552), Book 13, p. 84.

2. *Ibid.*, pp. 90–1.

3. *The Revolution of 1525* (Baltimore–London, 1981).

4. Majolino Bisaccioni, *Historia delle guerre civili di questi ultimi tempi* (Bologna, 1653), p. 525.

5. See Robert O. Crummey, *The Old Believers and the World of Antichrist* (Madison, Wisconsin, 1970).

6. Quoted in L. S. Stavrianos, 'Antecedents of the Balkans revolutions of the nineteenth century', *Journal of Modern History* 29 (1957), p. 338.

Chapter seven

1. See Jean Nicolas, 'La Fin du régime seigneurial en Savoie', in *L'Abolition de la féodalité*, vol. 1, pp. 27–108; *idem, La Savoie au xviii siècle: noblesse et bourgeoisie* (Paris, 1978).

2. The maximum figure of 600,000 is derived from a letter written by General Hoche, 12th February 1796. Official republican historiography has always refused to consider the true scale of the massacres. A recent demographic study has evaluated the population decline in 773 communes spread through four *départements* at fifteen per cent, or 117,000 people. Bearing in mind that the Western counter-revolutionary uprisings extended to six other *départements*, this figure needs to be raised by the same proportion. See Reynald Seycher, *Le Génocide franco-français. La Vendée-Vengé* (Paris, 1986).

Conclusion

1. P. Merula, *Cosmographia Galliae* (Amsterdam, 1636), p. 168.

2. *Lettres familières*, ed. Dorothy Thickett (Geneva, 1974), p. 38.

3. *Discours politiques et militaries*, ed. F. E. Sutcliffe (Geneva, 1967), p. 30.

Select bibliography

The works listed below do not embrace all the sources of this essay, but merely provide an inevitably arbitrary guide to reading. The size of the subject and the need to select limit the choice to comparative works, or ones which are useful for bibliographical purposes. Because the study of a controversial subject requires reference to numerous articles, I pay my intellectual debts and refer readers to the most commonly used of them: *Archivio storico per le provincie napoletane*; *Annales: Economies, Sociétés, Civilisations*; *English Historical Review*; *Journal of Modern History*; *Past and Present*; *Revue d'Histoire Moderne et Contemporaine*; *Social History*.
Note. Unless otherwise indicated, all works in French are published in Paris, and all works in English in London. ET = English translation.

L'Abolition de la 'féodalité' dans le monde occidental, 2 vols., 1971.
Anatra, Bruno; Puddu, Raffaele; Serri, G., *Problemi di storia della Sardegna spagnola*, Cagliari, 1975.
Aston, Trevor (ed.), *Crisis in Europe 1560–1660*, 1965.
Avrich, Paul, *Russian Rebels 1600–1800*, New York, 1972.
Bak, Janos (ed.), *The German Peasant War of 1525*, 1976 (republished from *Journal of Peasant Studies*, 1975).
Beloff, Max, *Public Order and Popular Disturbances 1660–1714*, Oxford, 1938.
Bérenger, Jean, 'La Révolte paysanne de Basse-Autriche, 1597', *Revue d'Histoire Economique et Sociale*, 53, 1975, 465–92.
Bisaccioni, Majolino, *Historia delle guerre civili*, Venice, 1665.
Blickle, Peter, *Die Revolution von 1525*, Munich 1975. (ET: *The Revolution of 1525*, Baltimore and London, 1981.)
Blum, Jerome, 'The internal structure and polity of the European village community', *Journal of Modern History*, 43, 1971, 541–76.
——, 'The rise of serfdom in Eastern Europe', *American Historical Review*, 62, 1956, 807–36.
Bobinska, Celia, 'Les Mouvements paysans en Pologne aux XVIII–XIX siècles', *Acta Poloniae Historica*, 22, 1970, 136–57.
Bülow, Heinrich Dietrich von, *Esprit du système de guerre moderne*, Paris, 1801.
Burke, Peter, *Venice and Amsterdam, A Study of Seventeenth-Century Elites*, 1974.
Busquet, J., *Le Droit de la vendetta*, 1920.
Caracciolo, Francesco, *Il Regno di Napoli nei secoli 16 e 17*, Rome, 1966.
Castellan, Yvonne, *La Culture serbe au seuil de l'indépendance*, 1967.
Clasen, Claus-Peter, *Anabaptism. A Social History, 1525–1618*, 1972.

Davies, C. S. L., 'Les Révoltes populaires en Angleterre, 1500–1700', *Annales: Economies, Sociétés, Civilisations*, 1969, 24–60.
Davis, Natalie Z., 'The rites of violence: religious riots in sixteenth-century France'. in *Past and Present*, 59, 1973, 51–91 (reprinted in Davis, *Society and Culture in Early Modern France*, Stanford, 1975).
Desroche, Henri, *Dieux d'hommes*, 1969.
———, *Sociologie de l'éspérance*, 1973.
Dominguez Ortiz, Antonio, *Alteraciones andaluzas*, Madrid, 1973.
Eeckaute, Denise, 'Les Brigands en Russie du XVII au XIX siècle', *Revue d'Histoire Moderne et Contemporaine*, 12, 1965, 165–202.
Elliott, J. H., *The Revolt of the Catalans 1598–1640*, Cambridge, 1963.
———, 'Revolution and continuity in early modern Europe', *Past and Present*, 42, 1969, 33–56.
Ellul, Jacques, *Autopsie de la révolution*, 1969.
Fletcher, Anthony, *Tudor Rebellions*, 1968.
Foisil, Madeleine, *La Révolte des Nu-pieds et les révoltes normandes de 1639*, 1970.
Forster, Robert and Greene, Jack P. (eds.), *Pre-Conditions of Revolution in Early Modern Europe*, Baltimore, 1970.
Fourquin, Guy, *Les Soulèments populaires au moyen âge*. 1972. (ET: *The Anatomy of Popular Rebellion in the Middle Ages*, Amsterdam, 1978.)
Furet, François, *Penser la révolution française*, 1978. (ET: *Interpreting the French Revolution*, Cambridge, 1981.)
Geyl, Pieter, *The Revolt of the Netherlands 1559–1609*, 1966.
Giovio, Paulo, *Histoires sur les choses faites et avenues en son temps*, Lyon, 1552.
Godechot, Jacques, 'Caractères généraux des soulèvements contre-révolutionnaires en Europe à la fin du XVIII siècle', in *Homenaje a Jaime Vicens Vives*. Barcelona, 1967, vol. 2, 169–82.
———, *La Contre-Révolution*, 1969. (ET: *The Counter Revolution*, 1972.)
Goulart, Simon, *Thrésor d'histoires admirables et mémorables*, 2 vols., Cologne, 1610.
Grandmaison, Captain, *La Petite guerre*, 1756.
Grüll, Georg, *Bauer, Herr und Landesfürst*, Linz, 1953.
Heers, Jacques, *Le Clan familial au moyen age*, 1974.
Hérésies et sociétés dans l'Europe pré-industrielle, XI–XVIII siècles, 1968.
Hobsbawm, E. J., *Bandits*, Manchester, 1959.
——— and Rudé, George, *Captain Swing*, London, 1969.
Johnson, Chalmers, *Déséquilibre social et révolution*, 1972. Original English title: *Revolution and the Social System*, Stanford, 1963.
Kamen, Henry, *The War of Spanish Succession 1700–1715*, 1969.
Kamen, Henry, 'A forgotten insurrection of the seventeenth century: the Catalan peasant rising of 1688', *Journal of Modern History*, 49, 1977, 210–30.
Koenigsberger, H. G., *Estates and Revolutions*, Ithaca, New York, 1971.
Koenigsberger, H. G., 'The organisation of revolutionary parties in France and the Netherlands during the sixteenth century', *Journal of Modern History*, 27, 1955, 335–51.

Bibliography

Köpeczi, Bela (ed.), *Paysannerie française, paysannerie hongroise, xvi–xx siècles*, Budapest, 1973.
Landsberger, Henry A. (ed.), *Rural Protest: Peasant Movements and Social Change*, 1974.
Le Roy Ladurie, Emmanuel, *Le Carnaval de Romans, 1579–1580*, 1979. (ET: *Carnival. A People's Uprising in Romans 1579–1580*, 1980.)
Ligou, Daniel, 'Forêts, garrigues et maquis dans la guerre des Camisards', *Cahiers d'Etudes Comtoises*, 1967, 129–40.
Lutaud, Olivier, *Winstanley, Socialisme et christianisme sous Cromwell*, 1976.
Macek, Josef, *Jean Hus et les traditions hussites, XV–XVI siècles*, 1973.
Martines, Lauro (ed.), *Violence and Civil Disorder in Italian Cities, 1200–1500*, Berkeley, 1972.
Mathieu, Vittorio, *Phénoménologie de l'esprit révolutionnaire*, 1974.
McNeill, William H., *Europe's Steppe Frontier, 1500–1800*, Chicago, 1964.
Mesnard, Pierre, *L'Essor de la philosophie politique au xvi siècle*, 1935.
Jean Meyer *et al.*, 'Les Révoltes paysannes de 1675', *Annales de Bretagne*, 82, 1975, 405–75.
Momblanch, F., *La Segunda Germania del reino de Valencia*, Alicante, 1957.
Moote, A. Lloyd, 'The pre-conditions of revolution in early modern Europe: did they really exist?', *Canadian Journal of History*, 7, 1972, 207–34.
Morrill, John S., 'Mutiny and discontent in English provincial armies, 1645–1647', *Past and Present*, 56, 1972, 49–74.
Mousnier, Roland, *Fureurs paysannes. Les paysans dans les révoltes du xvii siècle*, 1967. (ET: *Peasant Uprisings of the Seventeenth Century*, 1971.)
Nicolas, Jean, 'Ephemerides du refus. Pour une enquête sur les émotions populaires au XVIII siècle: le cas de Savoie', *Annales Historiques de la Révolution Française*, 45, 1973, 593–607; 46, 1974, 111–153.
Nordmann, Claude, *Charles XII et l'Ukraine de Mazepa*, 1958.
Parker, Geoffrey, *The Army of Flanders and the Spanish Road 1567–1659*, Cambridge, 1972.
Pascal, Pierre, *La Révolte de Pougatchev*, 1971.
Pascu, Stefan *et al.*, 'Les Mouvements paysans dans le centre et le sud-est de l'Europe du XV au XX siècle', in *XII International Congress of the Historical Sciences (Vienna, 1965), Reports*, vol. 4, 211–35.
Paysans d'Alsace, Strasbourg, 1959.
Pérez, Joseph, *La Révolution des Communidades de Castille*, Bordeaux, 1970.
Pillorget, René, 'Le Massacre d'une ambassade de la résidence d'Alger, 14 mars 1620', *Revue d'Histoire Diplomatique*, 1974, 44–58.
——, *Les Mouvements insurrectionnels en Provence, 1596–1715*, 1975.
Post, John D., *The Last Great Subsistence Crisis in the Western World (1816)*, Baltimore, 1977.
Press, Volker, 'Der Bauernkrieg als Problem der deutschen Geschichte', *Nassauische Annalen*, 86, 1975, 158–77.
Richet, Denis, 'Aspects socioculturels des conflits religieux à Paris dans la

seconde moitié du XVI siècle', *Annales: Economies, Sociétés, Civilisations*, 1977, 764–89.

Rodriguez, Laura, 'The Spanish riots of 1766', *Past and Present*, 59, 1973, 117–46.

Roots, Ivan, *The Great Rebellion*, 1966.

Rothenberg, Gunther, *The Austrian Military Border in Croatia, 1522–1881*, 2 vols., Chicago, 1960–6.

Rudé, George, *The Crowd in History, 1730–1848*, 1964.

Rudé, George, *Paris and London in the Eighteenth Century. Studies in Popular Protest*, 1969.

Séguy, Jean, *Les Assemblées anabaptistes-mennonites de France*, 1977.

Snyder, David and Tilly, Charles, 'Hardship and collective violence in France, 1830 to 1960', *American Sociological Review*, 37, 1972, 520–32.

Soboul, Albert, *Problèmes paysans de la révolution, 1789–1848*, 1976.

Stavrianos, L. S., 'Antecedents to the Balkan revolutions of the nineteenth century', *Journal of Modern History*, 29, 1957, 335–48.

——, *The Balkans since 1453*, New York, 1958.

Stone, Lawrence, *The Causes of the English Revolution, 1529–1642*, 1972.

Tilly, Charles, 'The chaos of the living city', in T. N. Clarke (ed.), *Comparative Community Politics*, New York, 1974, 203–27.

Tilly, Louise, 'The food riot as a form of political conflict in France', *Journal of Interdisciplinary History*, 2, 1971–2, 23–57.

Turi, Gabriele, *Viva Maria. La reazione alle riforme leopoldine, 1790–99*, Florence, 1969.

Villari, Rosario, *La Rivolta anispagnola a Napoli. Le origine, 1585–1647*, Bari, 1967.

Weinstein, Donald, *Savonarola and Florence. Prophecy and Patriotism in the Renaissance*, Princeton, 1971.

Williams, George H., *The Radical Reformation*, Philadelphia, 1962.

Wollbrett, Alphonse *et al.*, *La Guerre des paysans, 1525*, Saverne, 1975.

Zagorin, Perez, 'Prologomena to the comparative history of revolution in early modern Europe', *Comparative Studies in Society and History*, 18, 1976, 151–74.

Bibliographical supplement

Like the original bibliography, the list of works that follows does not aim to be exhaustive; it is designed to make the present work more useful to English-language readers. It is mostly confined to works that appeared since the original French edition, and includes some in languages other than English; a number of them contain extensive bibliographical references (translator)

Aston, T. H. and Philpin, C. H. E. (eds.), *The Brenner Debate. Agrarian Class Structure and Economic Development in Pre-Industrial Europe*, Cambridge, 1985.

Bak, Janos and Benecke, Gerhard (eds.), *Religion and Rural Revolt*, Manchester, 1984.

Barnavi, Elie, *Le Parti de Dieu. Etude sociale et politique des chefs de la ligue parisienne 1585–1594*, Louvain, 1980.

——, 'Mouvements révolutionnaires dans l'Europe moderne: un modèle', *Revue Historique*, 271, 1985, 47–61.

Beames, Michael, *Peasants and Power. The Whiteboy Movements and their Control in Pre-Famine Ireland*, Hassocks, Sussex, 1983.

Behrens, C. B. A., *Society, Government and the Enlightenment. The Experiences of France and Prussia*, 1985.

Blickle, Peter, *Deutsche Untertanen. Ein Widerspruch*. Munich 1981.

——, 'Paysan et état dans le saint empire germanique', *Francia*, 8, 1980, 191–211.

——, 'Peasant revolts in the German empire in the late Middle Ages', *Social History*, 4, 1979, 223–39.

——, *et al., Aufuhr und Empörung? Studien zum bäuerlichen Widerstand im Alten Reich*, Munich, 1980.

——, Rublack, Hans-Christoph; Schulze, Winfried. *Religion, Politics and Social Protest. Three Studies on Early Modern Germany*, 1984.

Blum, Jerome, *The End of the Old Order in Rural Europe*, Princeton, 1978.

—— (ed.), *Our Forgotten Past*, 1982.

Bonney, Richard, *Political Change in France under Richelieu and Mazarin 1624–1661*, Oxford, 1978.

Brady, Thomas A., Jr., *Turning Swiss. Cities and Empire 1450–1550*, Cambridge, 1985.

Brewer, John and Styles, John (eds.), *An Ungovernable People. The English and their Law in the Seventeenth and Eighteenth Centuries*, 1980.

Burke, Peter, *Popular Culture in Early Modern Europe*, 1978.

Bush, M. L., *Noble Privilege (The European Nobility*, Vol. I), Manchester, 1983.

Caracciolo, Francesco, *Sud, debiti e gabelle. Gravamini, potere e società nel Mezzogiorno in età moderna*, Naples, 1983.

Clark, Peter (ed.), *The European Crisis of the 1590s*, 1985.

Coveney, Peter (ed.), *France in Crisis 1620–1675*, 1977.

Descimon, Robert, *Qui étaient les seize? Mythes et réalités de la ligue parisienne (1585–1594)*, 1983.

Goubert, Pierre, *La Vie quotidienne des paysans français au xvii siècle*, Paris, 1982.

Hale, J. R., *War and Society in Renaissance Europe 1450–1618*, 1985.

Hunt, Lynn A., *Politics, Culture and Class in the French Revolution*, Berkeley, Calif., 1984.

Kamen, Henry, *European Society 1500–1700*, 1984.

——, *Spain in the Later Seventeenth Century*, 1980.

Kaplan, Steven L. *The Famine Plot Persuasion in Eighteenth Century France* (Transactions of the American Philosophical Society, vol. 72, 1982).

Keep, J. L. H., 'Emancipation by the axe? Peasant revolts in Russian thought and literature', *Cahiers du Monde Russe et Soviétique*, 23, 1982, 45–61.

Kelley, Donald R., *The Beginnings of Ideology. Consciousness and Society in the French Reformation*, Cambridge, 1981.

Muchembled, Robert, *Popular Culture and Elite Culture in Early Modern France*, Baton Rouge, La., 1985.

Mullett, Michael, *Radical Religious Movements in Early Modern Europe*, 1980.

Nicolas, Jean (ed.), *Mouvements populaires et conscience sociale, XVI–XIX siècles*, Paris, 1985.

Pocock, John (ed.), *Three British Revolutions, 1641, 1688, 1776*, Princeton, 1980.

Reay, Barry and McGregor, J. F. (eds.), *Radical Religion in the English Revolution*, Oxford, 1984.

Rebel, Hermann, *Peasant Classes. The Bureaucratization of Property and Family Relations under Early Habsburg Absolutism*, Princeton, 1983.

Recueils de la Société Jean Bodin, XLIII: Les Communautés rurales, vols. 4–5, 1984–86.

Renaissance and Modern Studies, vol. 26, 1982, special number on 'The "Crisis" of Early Modern Europe'.

Sabean, David W., *The Power in the Blood: Popular Culture and Village Discourse in Early Modern Germany*, Cambridge, 1984.

Schulze, Winfried, *Bäuerliche Widerstand und feudale Herrschaft in der frühen Neuzeit*, Stuttgart, 1980.

Schulze, Winfried (ed.), *Aufstände, Revolten, Prozesse*, Stuttgart, 1983.

Schulze, Winfried, *Europäische Bauernrevolten der frühen Neuzeit*, Frankfurt, 1982.

Scott, Tom, 'Peasant revolts in early modern Germany', *Historical Journal*, 28, 1985, 455–68.

Scribner, Bob and Benecke, G. (eds.), *The German Peasant War of 1525 – New Viewpoints*, 1979.

Sharp, Bennett, *In Contempt of All Authority. Rural Artisans and Riot in the West of England, 1580–1660*, Berkeley, Calif., 1980.

Skocpol, Theda, *States and Social Revolutions*, Cambridge, 1979.

Slack, Paul A. (ed.), *Rebellion, Popular Protest and the Social Order in Early Modern England*, Cambridge, 1984.

Sutherland, D. M. G., *Revolution and Counter Revolution* (Fontana History of Modern France, I), 1985.

Thompson, E. P., *Whigs and Hunters*, 1975.

Tilly, Charles, 'Food supply and public order in modern Europe', in Tilly (ed.), *The Formation of National States in Western Europe*, Princeton, 1975, 380–455.

——, 'War and peasant rebellion in seventeenth-century France', in Tilly, *As Sociology Meets History*, New York 1981, Ch. 5.

Underdown, David, *Revel, Riot and Rebellion 1600–1660*, Oxford, 1985.

Watts, Sheldon J., *A Social History of Western Europe 1450–1720. Tensions and Solidarities among Rural People*, 1984.

Williams, Penry, *The Tudor Régime*, Oxford, 1979.

Wrightson, Keith, *English Society 1580–1680*, 1982.

Zagorin, Perez, *Rebels and Rulers. 1500–1650*, 2 vols., Cambridge, 1982.

Index

Index

Index